Islam
A CONCISE INTRODUCTION

Islam

A CONCISE INTRODUCTION

D S Roberts

1817

HARPER & ROW, PUBLISHERS, San Francisco
Cambridge, Hagerstown, New York, Philadelphia
London, Mexico City, São Paulo, Sydney

FIRST U.S. EDITION 1982

Library of Congress Cataloging in Publication Data

Roberts, D. S.
  Islam, a concise introduction.

  Bibliography: p. 192.
  1. Islam.   I. Title.
BP161.2.R57   1981   297   81-47845
ISBN 0-06-066880-6   AACR2

---

82 83 84 85 86 10 9 8 7 6 5 4 3 2 1

Contents

Introduction   1

1. The Prophet Mohammed: His Life and Times   5
Arabia in the Seventh Century *5*, Mohammed's Life *9*, The
Prophet's Successors *29*

2. The Message   35
The Five Pillars of Islam *36*, The Koran *39*, *Hadith* and *Sunna*
41, *Jihad* *42*, Sacred Places *43*, Sacred Days *43*, Sin *44*, Death
44, Resurrection *45*, The Hour *45*, Judgement *45*, Paradise and
Hell *46*, *Kalam* (Theology) *47*, Muslim Sects *50*

3. Islamic Law   54
The *Sharia* *54*, The Basic Features *55*, The Concepts of Islamic
Law *56*, The Schools of Law *58*, Procedures *60*, Punishment *62*,
Property *66*, Ownership *67*, Contracts and Obligations *68*,
Marriage *70*, Divorce *70*, Legitimacy *71*, Inheritance *71*, Law
Reform *72*

4. Society and Politics   77
Islamic Principles: Theory *77*, Islamic Principles: Practice *80*

5. Social Behaviour and Customs   101
Traditional Hospitality and Courtesy *101*, Ritual Ablution,
Bathing, Shaving *102*, Food and Taboos *103*, Drink and Alcohol
105, Greetings *106*, Mosques *107*, The Prophet's Tomb *109*,
Dress *109*, Charms *109*, Names *110*, Entertainments *111*, Sport
113, Animals *113*, Deportment *114*, Vices and Virtues *115*

6. Family and Domestic Life   116
Family Structure *116*, Fathers *117*, Mothers *118*, Children *118*,
Collective Responsibilities *123*, Respect for Elders *124*,
Neighbours *125*, Houses and Homes *125*, Death and Burial *127*

7. The Status of Women   130

The Status Defined *130*, Property Rights *132*, Marriage *133*, Prostitution *137*, Unlawful Intercourse *137*, Divorce *139*, Seclusion of Women *140*, Sex *143*, Employment and Public Life *145*, Women Saints *147*, Swiss Civil Code in Turkey *147*

8. Commerce and Trade   149

The Traditional Role of Commerce *149*, The Example of the Prophet *151*, Associations and Combinations *152*, Customs in Business *153*, Making Contracts *156*, Usury *157*, Debt *159*, Insurance *159*, Decision Making *160*

Conclusion: The Oil Factor   162

Appendix 1: The Islamic Calendar   169

Appendix 2: Modern Islamic States   170

Appendix 3: Mohammed's Wives   176

*Appendix 4: Chronological Table of Events
in the Muslim and Non-Muslim World*   182

Bibliography   192

Author's Acknowledgements

I am grateful to my daughter Hannah Roberts for the help and criticism she has given in the writing of this book, and the suggestions she made for its organization and form.

My thanks are also due to the following for permission to refer to source material: Abacus (Sphere Books Ltd) — *The Arabs* by Thomas Kiernan (Abacus, 1978) for material in the chapter on Society and Politics; Oxford University Press — *An Introduction to Islamic Law* by Joseph Schacht (OUP, 1964) for material in the chapter on Islamic Law, and *The Koran Interpreted* by A J Arberry (OUP, 1964) for all quotations from the Koran except those contained within other quoted texts.

Introduction

To the ordinary Western mind the world of Islam seems incomprehensible. Its attitudes appear bigoted and uncompromising, and its actions harsh and arbitrary. Nor is this only a modern judgement. As far back as the Middle Ages the propaganda of the Christian church presented the Muslims as savages, and throughout Europe men flocked to the banners of the Crusades to restore the Holy Land to Christendom. Yet even then the propaganda sometimes proved self-defeating, for on making contact with the enemy the Crusaders found them to be, as often as not, quite gentish knights. Indeed, for some the discovery was so startling that they began to question their own cause. In the 14 centuries that Islam has been with us, both it and its founder, Mohammed, have been subject to all manner of denigration and abuse, and although scholars from East and West alike have laboured to modify this unsavoury image, they have met with little success.

After languishing in a historical backwater for hundreds of years, Islam is now once more on the rise and its image in Europe and the West is little changed. This is not because works on Islam are not published in the West. There are voluminous works in every European language examining Islam and its ways in the minutest detail. But for the most part these are scholarly and academic works, or works actually promoting or interpreting the faith. There are also a few recently published books analyzing, from various points of view, the current political situation in the Middle East. What is conspicuously missing, however, is a popular work setting out clearly the beliefs, attitudes and customs of Islam in a way that is readily understandable to the Western reader but is not viewed through a veil of Christian values.

The author's purpose in writing this book has been to avoid the two common mistakes of seeing Islam either as uncompromising and uncivilized at worst or as mysterious and inexplicable at best. It does not seek to justify the Muslim faith nor gloss over the harsher aspects of the Islamic code; nor does it attack or pass moral judgements on the religion and its faithful. In a word, the intention is not to examine Islam through a telescope made in Christendom but to try to see Islam as it sees itself.

It is impossible to understand the most elementary things about Islamic life without knowing something of its religion; but, although the main features and basic beliefs of the faith are described, this is not a book primarily about religion. Islam, it is true, is a way of life based upon the will of God, which is known through its holy book, the Koran, and the sayings and actions of its prophet, Mohammed. But many of its characteristics have been inherited from the traditions of the society into which Mohammed was born, and this combination, together with the different interpretations put upon its teachings in different places and at different times, makes up 20th century Islam.

The first difficulty in attempting to gain some insight into the Muslim mind and setting it down on paper is one of presentation. It is more likely than not that the average Western reader is the product of an educational system which has set the qualities of clarity, order, logic and sequence high in the list of educational virtues. Traditional Islam, however, does not pursue enlightenment in this way. Every aspect of life is seen as part of an indivisible whole, literally inseparable from all other aspects. Sequence is not important. On the contrary, the more man attempts to order existence the more likely he is to stumble into error. For a Muslim, life as it was created by God is complete by definition. The task of man is not to rearrange or order it, or even to understand it, but to obey the laws laid down for him.

How, then, does man know what those laws are? For Muslims the answer is simple: they are laid down in the holy Koran. Yet for the Westerner this often obscures the question still further. The qualities of the Koran are discussed in greater detail later, but it is fair to say that, however good the translation, no recognizable 'structure' would be apparent to the average Western reader. It is a work which can be read from the beginning or from the end or from any point in the middle with no difference to the Message contained within it. In a fundamental sense the Koran has no beginning and no end. Because of this, and although modern Muslim scholars adopt perfectly recognizable forms in their work, there is, underlying all Islamic culture, an element that, notwithstanding the repeated calls that the Koran itself makes to logic, ultimately undermines communication with outsiders.

This point needs emphasis because, in an attempt to achieve a comprehensible balance and form for this book, the chapters and headings have been divided into distinct subject areas. The only reason for choosing these chapter and section headings, however, was to provide familiar points of reference for the Western reader. To a conservative Muslim it would seem strange to attempt to separate law from religion, and bizarre to separate the status of women from either.

In a system seeking to control all aspects of a believer's life it is sometimes difficult to distinguish between what is fundamental law and what is merely tribal or social custom, allowed or even encouraged by Islam, but not actually required by its law. As a result there are many important issues where theory and practice are confused. And even when the law is clear the outcome is often not. For example, the Koran is uncompromising in its declaration that the penalty for theft is amputation, as it is that a man has an absolute right to take up to four wives if he treats them equally. But this clear-cut authority is not uniformly accepted throughout Islam. Few countries allow amputation; and, even in countries where it is not statutory, monogamy is becoming increasingly common.

Another temptation to be avoided is the association of everything Islamic with Arabia and vice versa. Arabia has a special place in the fabric of Islam because it has its roots there — the language of the Koran is Arabic and Mohammed himself was an Arab. Yet the Arabs represent no more than a third of all Muslims, and, furthermore, not every Arab is a Muslim.

The range of the subject has made it difficult to know not only where to stop but also, often, where to begin. There is common agreement that the Koran is the supreme authority in directing the life of a believer. If a clear precedent cannot be found there, the next level of authority is the *Sunna*: the sayings and actions of the Prophet Mohammed. Human interpretation is heavily involved at this stage, as the various schools of law adopt their positions. If we add to these considerations the tribal and social customs of both pre-and post-Islamic times, and allow for the regional variations which are to be found in Islam from Spain to China, there is clearly considerable scope for oversimplification in any book of manageable length.

The object of this book, then, has been to set out the main features of Islam against the general background of relevant world events and ideas and to sketch in what Muslim society is actually like — the sort of thing a Westerner can expect to find in an Islamic country, or the attitudes he or she will encounter if dealing with Muslims at home. For, despite the differences readily observable between Muslims, it would be a mistake for an outsider to see such disagreements as anything more than family quarrels. In the heat of the moment it is often easy to miss the underlying hard core of human unity. It is this unity which underpins the faith of every Muslim, and if you find yourself discussing Islam with a Muslim anywhere in the world, you are likely to be asked 'Why do you have all these questions? Become a Muslim and you will have answers.'

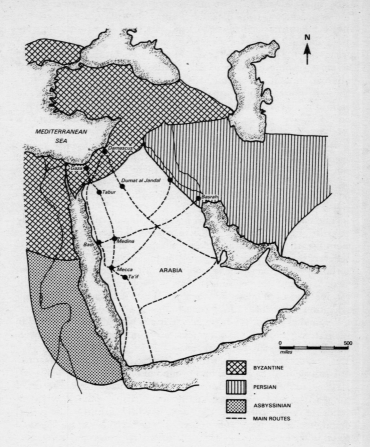

N

MEDITERRANEAN
SEA

Damascus

Gaza

Dumat al Jandal

Tabur

Basrah

Badr

Medina

ARABIA

Mecca
Ta'if

0   500
miles

BYZANTINE

PERSIAN

ASBYSSINIAN

MAIN ROUTES

Arabia and Western Asia c AD 630

Chapter 1

The Prophet Mohammed:
His Life and Times

Arabia in the Seventh Century

The prophet of Islam was Mohammed ibn (son of) Abd-allah. He was born in the town of Mecca in Arabia about AD 570. The exact year of his birth is not known and the details of his early life remain obscure. His father died before he was born and he became the ward of his grandfather, Abd-al Muttalib, but it is believed that he spent most of his early years with his mother, who belonged to another clan. It was the custom among Meccan families to send their children away for a year or two from the town to the hard but healthy life of the desert, and the infant Mohammed was sent to a Bedu[1] tribe to be wet-nursed by one of their women. When Mohammed was six his mother died and he came directly under the care of his grandfather until he too died two years later. He then passed into the care of his uncle, Abu Talib, the new head of the clan Hashim.

From this obscure and unpromising beginning grew the man who was to found a new religion, unite under its banner the previously hostile tribes of the Arabian peninsula, and lay the foundation for an immense empire which, 100 years after his death, stretched from Spain to the Punjab. To be both an orphan and poor in seventh century Mecca were crushing handicaps for even the most gifted and able man. Mecca was a commercial town, an oasis, mid-way between the Indian ocean and the Mediterranean. It controlled the caravan routes between Yemen, India and Abyssinia, and the markets of the North. Thus the popular idea that Islam sprang from the nomadic way of life in the desert needs revision; the first homes of Islam — Mecca (the place of Mohammed's birth) and Medina (the place in which he sought refuge from persecution) — were both towns.

Arabian Society before Mohammed

In pre-Islamic Arabia communities took the form of a number of

1. Bedu or Bedouin: desert nomads, living off herds of camels, goats and sheep.

groups or tribes who were held together by loyalty to a leader or by descent from a common ancestor. The family units that made up the tribes were equal in status to each other. The head of each family had power to select the tribal chief or *sheikh*[1], who could theoretically be anybody, but in practice normally came from certain families. Such families held positions of great importance within the community at the time of Mohammed, and the major factor in a man's authority was his birth. Moreover, the test of superiority was family purity, and no family tainted with ancestors of servile or negro origin was eligible for high office. Society was stratified into a self-perpetuating class system in which careers, opportunities and social position depended very largely on the circumstances of birth. Slavery was commonplace and persisted throughout the centuries almost to the present day. Before Mohammed's time slaves were either prisoners of war, or taken in raids in hostile territory, or the offspring of slaves. In those days it was still possible for Arabs to enslave their fellow countrymen by capture, or to sell themselves for a gambling debt.

Outside the towns the way of life was dictated by the land and what it would support. Apart from a few oases and trading centres the peninsula was desert, and the way of life nomadic and pastoral. Desert life was harsh and uncompromising, and was often accompanied by grinding poverty. There was a strong temptation to lay hands on the possessions of others who were apparently more fortunate. This took the form of raids (*razia*) in which there were strict rules laid down by tradition. Where possible, goods were seized without loss of life. Manslaughter carried severe penalties according to the tradition of the desert. The free Arabs were bound by no written law, and no authority existed to enforce statutes. Therefore, the only protection for any man's life was the certainty, established by custom, that it would be dearly bought. Blood must be paid for by blood, a life by a life. the tribe protected its own under all circumstances, and undying shame attached to the man whom tradition designated as the avenger if he allowed a murderer to live. Retribution or vendetta (*tha'r*) was one of the pillars of Bedu society, and this made Mohammed's survival possible during the early days of his Prophethood (see page 13).

Tribal society was not rigidly structured. Leadership was not inherited but was conferred upon the man most able to command prestige and respect. Although selected by popular will, the leader could use only his moral authority to command obedience. He had no power to lay duties or inflict penalties on others, and he led through

1. In modern usage the title *sheikh* might still signify the leader of a tribe, or might be used by those claiming descent from the first two caliphs or from Abbas, the Prophet's uncle. More common, however, is its use as a courtesy title, designating respect.

sensing and directing the climate of opinion. A member of a tribe had a singularly independent position and offered his services voluntarily. He conformed to the minimum rules concerning the rights of property, and observed traditional practices concerning marriage, in return for which he could claim allegiance and protection. Otherwise he was free to do as he wished (including, in the last analysis, withdrawing from the tribe) without invoking any penalties.

The fortunes of the nomadic tribes varied with the circumstances of plunder, trade, war or drought. In the towns commercial stability, such as it was, made the fortune of tribe or family somewhat less vulnerable. In terms of culture the Arabs admired men of eloquence and persuasion, who could argue their point of view well in the tribal council. Wise men were highly esteemed, but poets were valued still more. They were both respected and feared because they were believed to be possessed by spirits, and their work was considered to be of supernatural origin. The poet sang of love, grief, joy and sorrow, but also played an important part in public affairs. Contests were held at which each contestant boasted of his own tribe and satirized those of his rivals.

The Bedu had religious beliefs but these were not necessarily central to their social life. They believed that the land was peopled by spirits, the *jinn*, who were often invisible but could appear in animal form. Offerings were made to them, and cairns of stones were erected on their graves. Certain trees and stones housed spirits and divinities. The number and names of divinities varied from tribe to tribe, but there were some common denominators. One was Allah, creator of the universe and keeper of sworn oaths. In addition there were three goddesses who were the daughters of Allah, and other gods were worshipped in various places. Certain places became sacred, within which no creature could be killed. These became places of asylum where the pursued could take refuge. Some sanctuaries were the object of pilgrimage (*hajj*), and rituals were performed within them. Notable among these rituals was the ceremonial procession around the sacred object. Prohibitions, such as abstention from sexual relations, had to be observed during these rites. Boys were ceremonially circumcised. Superstition prevailed and magic was practised. As Maxime Rodinson[1] has pointed out, these tribes were evolving their own concept of morality in the formation of which religion played no part. What was important was courage, endurance, loyalty to the group and social obligations, generosity and hospitality. A man strove to conform to these ideals out of a sense of honour (*ird*).

But the unwritten rules followed by the Arabs were often broken.

1. *Islam and Capitalism*, Allen Lane, 1974.

The savage excesses which appeared on certain occasions prompted some devastating comments from their more civilized neighbours. A Syrian soldier, Ammianus Marcellinus, said in the fourth century: 'I would not wish to have them either as friends or as enemies'.

By contrast, the settled and relatively civilized people of southern Arabia lived a life of comparative wealth and luxury in organized states of some complexity. These southern states employed the wandering Bedu as mercenaries in their auxiliary forces, each state favouring its own tribe. It is possible that they acknowledged some distant kinship, and some northern tribes claimed later to have come originally from the cultivated regions of the South. After the triumph of Islam under Saracen leadership, the southern Arabians were rapidly assimilated, and the inhabitants of the peninsula as a whole embarked on the conquest of the world. But the memories of their superior civilization did not fade at once for the Yemenis in the Muslim ranks; they stuck together and set themselves apart from the northern Arabs, and knowledge of their old tongue and writing persisted in some places for several centuries.

Mecca and the Caravan Trade

Little is known about the commercial life of Mecca during Mohammed's early life. It is clear, however, that it was a prosperous commercial centre, whose power and influence was growing. Although tribal structure and authority still dominated society, the settled way of life and commercial organization demanded by the caravan trade to some extent modified the grip of traditional values. The demands of trade made Mohammed and others aware of new worlds outside their own experience, and brought them into contact with new ideas about the way the affairs of men should be ordered. The influence of the clan in the towns was waning, but it remained the only structure available to organize affairs; no other semblance of regional or local authority emerged. Commercial interests needed to be defended and the clans were not slow to form the so-called League of the Virtuous, an alliance to keep out foreign interests and to preserve the Meccans' monopoly of the caravan trade. Although there were tribal conflicts within Mecca, the town had by legend the reputation for self-control when its best interests were threatened.

Once the Bedu tribe had settled, they formed themselves into trading companies to finance caravans. The transportation of valuable goods gave rise to large profits, and the commercial structure dictated its own forms of organization, not only in Mecca but in the whole of western Arabia. The town of Ta'if, south of Mecca, did a prosperous trade in fruit, vegetables and wines. In the string of hill towns near

Medina, Jewish settlements created a flourishing agricultural life. The mercantile economy encouraged the use of money rather than barter for trade. In this process the Bedu often borrowed from the rich, got into debt, and were either sold into slavery or reduced to a dependent status. Success became vested in personal achievement, and no longer in the well-being of the whole tribe. The bond of kinship became weaker and gave way to others based on common commercial interests. As people became aware that new values were beginning to replace those of tribal tradition, they became more susceptible to the idea of a religion based upon individual salvation rather than group survival. Judaism and Christianity were known, if not properly understood, but these were foreign faiths associated with powers that were fighting for the control of the Arab peninsula. What was required was a man who could provide a focus and an inspiration, and into that situation Mohammed was born.

Mohammed's Life

Origin and Background

The Koran makes frequent reference to the rights of orphans, and this is no doubt some reflection of the difficulties Mohammed experienced in his early years. Traditionally the clan was responsible for the welfare of its weaker members, but the old ways were changing under the commercial pressures generated by the caravan trade in Mecca. Although he was clothed and fed, not much attention was given to Mohammed's education or interests. He had to be satisfied with the trade of camel driver, and make what he could from the experience of travelling to Syria with his uncle, Abu Talib.

Almost nothing is known about Mohammed's youth, although numerous stories and legends were supplied by subsequent generations, who were keen to present the early life of the Prophet in an idealized way. The oldest collections of historical narratives date from 120 years after the Prophet's death. These stories are fragmentary and contradictory, and Muslim scholarship has been content to repeat these contradictory traditions, one after the other, quoting the source for each and adding 'but God knows best'. Yet many facts can be established, as there is wide agreement about the main features of the Prophet's life.

Of major importance in Mohammed's life was his marriage to Khadija in about AD 595. Although few details of this period are recorded, the young man clearly took full advantage of his new situation and quickly established himself in the commercial life of Mecca. As his business flourished he lived in reasonable prosperity for the next

15 years, and consolidated his reputation for straightforward and trustworthy dealing. He was able to betroth his daughters to quite prosperous men, who were all in some way related to either himself or Khadija.

His marriage to Khadija relieved him of the daily pressure of earning a living, and provided leisure to contemplate other matters. Great changes were taking place, but they were not changes he liked. The upheavals in the north represented the death throes of two enormous empires, the Persian and the Byzantine. Nearer home, the dislocation caused by the pursuit of commerce was accompanied by a decline in moral standards and an abandonment of traditional values.

In seventh century Arabia, as elsewhere, religion fulfilled much more than spiritual needs. It also embraced and defined social and political relationships. By all accounts the pagan Arabs were not particularly interested in religion, but some, including Khadija's uncle, had adopted the Christian faith, and there were established Jewish communities throughout Arabia. The extent to which Mohammed was familiar with either religion is not certain, but he would certainly have come into contact with their ideas when travelling in pursuit of his trade.

The Call

At the age of about 40 Mohammed was used to retiring to a rocky hillside near Mecca and spending time there alone in meditation and seclusion. He sometimes spent several nights in a cave, and on one of these occasions began to have extraordinary experiences. He had vivid dreams and visions, and in one of these a mighty being appeared high on the horizon and began descending towards him until he was 'only two bow lengths away'.

The voice spoke a command in Arabic which was to change the world:

> Recite: In the Name of Thy Lord who created,
> created Man of a blood-clot.
>
> (Koran 96:1)

The effect on Mohammed was traumatic: 'I was standing but I fell to my knees and dragged myself along while the upper part of my chest was trembling. I went to Khadija until the terror had left me.'

This and subsequent experiences convinced Mohammed that he was formulating ideas and expressions that were not his own. He perceived these words and ideas as recitations by God — Koran (Arabic *Qur'an*) literally means recitation. Slowly Mohammed became aware that he was the Messenger of God. The realization was so stunning that he was wracked by self doubt. He, a modest merchant of humble origin in the obscurity of Arabia, had to convince the people of Mecca, who had known him from a boy, that he had been chosen as the Messenger of God. He was so overwhelmed by the burden that for some time he kept these events secret, confiding only in his wife, Khadija. On occasions the measure of the task seemed so great that he was tempted to take his own life. Stories are told of how on such occasions inspiration would always return to him, and he would be reminded of the importance of the task he had to complete.

It is important to understand that for Mohammed, and for all Muslims, the revelations which began so dramatically and continued over a period of 20 years, came from a source outside the Prophet. He was merely the human mouthpiece through which the messages were conveyed, and this was quickly recognized by his followers. In his own lifetime he became known, even to his wives, as the Messenger of Allah. Neither Mohammed nor any of his followers ever claimed that he had any direct relationship with God. It is perhaps the fundamental principle of Islam that God is alone and unique. Even in making His will known to Mohammed, he used an intermediary in the form of the angel Gabriel. It therefore follows that nothing must be associated with God, and there are many references in the Koran condemning 'associaters'. Mohammed was clear that he could distinguish between his own thoughts and opinions, and the revelations that came from outside his own experience. The revelations are therefore literally the speech of God. It is probable that most of these were written down during the Prophet's lifetime, either by him or under his direction, but in any case the Koran in its present form was finalized about 20 years after his death, in AD 650.

The organization of the Koran reflects the fragmentary nature of the revelations and the fact that they came over a long period. There is no recognizable time sequence, and each *sura*, or chapter, deals with a variety of subjects and incidents, even though it is given a single name by which it is generally recognized. This is an important matter when trying to understand the Muslim mind. What is important about the Koran, and therefore important to a Muslim, is meaning and not sequence. Clearly, the Message, if it was to be comprehensible, had to be related to the conditions and beliefs prevailing at the time in Arabia. From the first revelation in about AD 610 it took Mohammed some three years to understand the nature of his future work: and it is a historical fact that in about 613 Mohammed began preaching in the streets of Mecca and publicly claimed the title of Prophet.

The Message

When Mohammed stood up for the first time in public there was nothing revolutionary in his message: at least not at first sight. In his first revelations he did not attempt to deny either the existence or power of other divinities. The monotheism of the Jews and Christians was not unknown, and Mohammed was after all relating his message to the same God. No disquiet was caused by the thought of mankind being judged since this was not a new or unfamiliar idea. Criticism of the rich and their declining moral values was accepted in moderation. The idea of almsgiving had a pedigree which stretched back to the old tribal ideal of putting generosity foremost among virtues, although it had subsequently rather fallen out of favour. Making sacrifices to pacify the divinity was common practice. So in the beginning Mohammed's method was to win men over to his ideas by persuasion, and he was not challenging established authority outright by presenting a radically new way of life. What was unique was the way in which those ideas were made available to him in order to be passed on. The individual was to be judged without reference to class, position or tribe, and some basic Judao-Christian ideals became acceptable because they were presented in Arabic through the personality of an Arab Messenger. At the beginning, then, Mohammed posed no great threat to the Meccan establishment, and the new movement seemed indistinguishable from others that were thriving in western Arabia at the time.

The first Muslim was the Prophet's wife, Khadija, and the second was either his freed slave, Zayd, or his teenage cousin, Ali. Apart from these, converts numbered about 40, who for the most part were either very young, uninfluential or slaves. But what they lacked in influence they made up for in independence of mind.

Opposition from the Meccan Ruling Class

No doubt the class consciousness of the Meccan ruling council played a part in postponing recognition of the threat that Mohammed posed. If God was to make His will known and point the community in a new direction, surely He would make it known through them and not through a minor citizen preaching in the streets. The conflict came into the open only after Mohammed attacked the pagan cult of goddesses, *jinn* and spirits that had served the Arabs from time immemorial. This had deep religious significance, for it condemned the ancestors of all the worthy Meccans to damnation and hell fire. It also had political significance. The pagan Arabs had shown that they were not afraid of the ideas of a monotheistic religion as such. There were thriving Jewish and Christian communities living among them, and no-one became anxious if a few Arabs were converted. But these religions were foreign imports; Mohammed was preaching to the Arabs in their own language and offering them their own religion and ideology. The leading citizens of Mecca were not slow to see the implications of this. They themselves believed in God as the Creator, but they did not concede his uniqueness. If the new movement gathered strength and Arabs came to believe that God was giving them a new creed by which to live their lives and reorganize their society, then political as well as religious power would be taken from the ruling council and priests of the old system, and passed into the hands of God's Messenger and his followers. The Meccan ruling class had to defend not only an ideology but also commercial and economic interests, and when they realized the true nature of Mohammed's mission they reacted violently against him.

For the most part there were strict limits to the persecution that Mohammed and the early Muslims had to endure, because of the system of kinship and the protection offered by the clan to all its members, even the most wayward. All members of a clan could rely absolutely on physical protection unless it was specifically withdrawn by the leader. If a member were harmed for any reason, the clan was honour bound to avenge the injury and seek retribution, whether or not they thought the victim deserved his treatment. Only slaves could not rely on this protection, and there are accounts of physical torture being used to make them renounce their faith. But if violence was generally ruled out, all other forms of pressure were not. The full weight of social pressure was brought to bear: the new Muslims were abused, castigated and ostracized, and merchants were boycotted. The conservative Quraysh tribe brought every pressure to bear on Mohammed's clan, the Hashim, in order to get them to withdraw their protection from him. No-one was to do business, or form marriage ties, with any members of the clan of al-Muttalib. The boycott lasted for about two years, although it was not always strictly enforced.

In the meantime the revelations continued and the new doctrine took shape. The little community in Mecca continued to gather converts, and in time totalled about 100. The Meccans were unable to suppress it, but at least it was being comfortably contained and, except for unforeseen events, might have remained a small and insignificant cult like many others. But in 619 Khadija and Mohammed's uncle Abu Talib both died within a few days of one another. The death of his wife must have been a great blow to Mohammed, but the death of Abu Talib had very serious consequences. He was succeeded as head of the Hashim clan by his brother Abu Lahab, who at first agreed to extend his protection to the Muslims because he was moved by Mohammed's

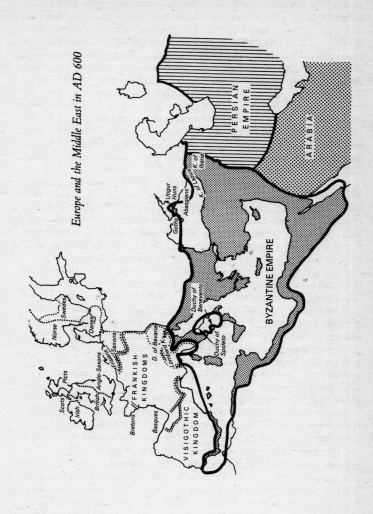

Europe and the Middle East in AD 600

misfortune and grief. But the Prophet's enemies persuaded him otherwise. They suggested to him that, according to his nephew, both his grandfather and the newly departed Abu Talib were suffering the pains of hell as unbelievers who had rejected Mohammed's message. When Abu Lahab confronted Mohammed with this suggestion the Prophet could only confirm it, whereupon his uncle, angry at the lack of family feeling, withdrew his protection on the spot.

Hijra: Emigration to Medina

From then on the situation rapidly worsened. The insults and provocations increased, and Mohammed and his people were pilloried and physically attacked. The community seemed to be losing ground. There were no more spectacular conversions, and it is quite likely that the pressure caused some new defections. A new base had to be found for Mohammed's operations. He considered the possibilities open to him, first looking at Ta'if, a green hillside town where many Qurayshites had property. He spoke to all the prominent people there, but could persuade no-one to take in the Muslims, and he returned to Mecca a dejected man. After some hesitation, he cast further afield and saw possibilities in the city of Yathrib as his new base. Yathrib, or Medina as it became known, was strictly speaking not a city at all but a collection of oases with clusters of houses and fortified huts among plantations of palms and fruit trees. Relationships between the various groups there were at a very low ebb, although at that time there was an uneasy truce. The Arabs had inherited from their nomadic past a tradition of blood feuds which were continually erupting in wholesale slaughter, and it was clear to all sides that the war would be revived in Yathrib before long. This was a desperate situation for an agricultural community which depended upon relatively settled ways to secure its harvests. Eventually, good sense suggested to some that it was intolerable for the whole community to be drawn into wars because individuals had spilled blood which had to be avenged regardless of consequences.

People from Medina made frequent visits to Mecca, especially to take part in the holy rituals nearby. Mohammed spoke with some of these and at last found common ground. He already had connections with Medina; his father was buried there, and he had relatives living there whom he had visited as a child. Meetings and negotiations took place over a period of two years. Gradually Mohammed won over converts from Medina, and he sent one of his ablest followers to the city to recite the Koran and teach the people the doctrine. Eventually an agreement was made at a decisive meeting at Aqaba at which 75 Medinans, among them two women, were present. The Medinans were promised that God, through Mohammed, would arbitrate in any future disputes and put an end to the internal tribal conflicts. In exchange the Medinans pledged protection.

This movement of Mohammed and his followers from Mecca to Medina was known as the *Hijra*, and it secured the future of the Islamic movement. It is sometimes rendered as 'flight', but 'emigration' is a better translation, suggesting as it does the travelling of Muslims in small groups over a period and ending with the departure of Mohammed himself. The significance of the new era was such that, later, the Islamic calendar was designated from that date, and the Christian year AD 622 became the Muslim year AH 1. So it came about that this tiny group found sanctuary in an obscure Arabian town on the very edge of the civilized world. The conditions were right for a new community to take root and to develop its own laws and customs based on the new religion.

Acceptance: the Followers

In Medina Mohammed let God decide where he should build his house and seat of operations by settling on the spot where his camel stopped. Once settled, he set about his work as arbitrator in disputes, thus establishing a new principle. He had become the leader of most of the Arabs in Medina by letting the will of God be known not only in spiritual matters but also in the things that affected men's day to day lives. For the most part his decisions were accepted and the only opposition that irritated him came from some pagan poets, who satirized the Medinans for accepting the decisions of a stranger.

The Prophet also had to face up to the potentially dangerous problem of the Jewish communities in Medina. At first he expected to gain their support, as the message he brought was substantially similar to that received long before by the Jews at Sinai. He was impressed by the antiquity of Jewish scriptures and the reliance on them of other religions, and he seems to have thought it possible to form a united front with these confirmed monotheists against the pagan forces surrounding them both. Before moving to Medina he had become acquainted with Israelite customs, and certain instructions to his followers suggest a willingness to cooperate wherever possible. These included facing Jerusalem to pray, organizing large prayer meetings on Fridays, (the day on which the Jews prepared for their festival of the Sabbath), observing the fast on the Day of Atonement, setting aside a time for prayer in the middle of the day as the Jews did, and even adopting Jewish modes of dress and hairstyles. An additional revelation gave the faithful permission to eat the food of the People of the Book (ie Jews and Christians) and to marry their women. He did not consider imposing the Jewish dietary laws in full, since he took the Christian view that these were God's punishment of the Jews' sins. But he did introduce a more limited prohibition: on the eating of pork or blood, or any animals that had died a natural death, had their necks wrung, or had been sacrificed to idols. Nor did Mohammed observe the custom of resting on the seventh day, for the very simple reason that God did not need a rest.

But on the whole the Jews did not respond to the call of Islam. They may have mistrusted Mohammed's long-term political motives, but it is more likely that they were unwilling to endorse the revelations claimed by the Prophet. From their point of view the Koran distorted the Old Testament stories, and they could probably see no reason to adjust their religious or social position in any way. This was a situation that Mohammed would have to face at some time, but first there were more urgent problems pressing for his attention.

Attack on Meccan Trade

The first of these problems was simply a matter of subsistence. None of the emigrant Muslims had the means to buy land in the oasis, and without lands or flocks survival was becoming a desperate mater. In these circumstances the traditional Arab solution was that of the raiding party, and a suitable target was the Quraysh caravans from Mecca that had to pass within 60 miles of Medina. The Quraysh were obvious targets because they had forced the Muslims to flee in the first place, and attacking them rather than other tribes would avoid making unnecessary enemies. This was not such a violent solution as it might seem, since raiding was carried out by strictly observed methods designed to avoid bloodshed. The general principle was to send out a raiding party of such overwhelming numbers that the victim could run with complete justification and without losing face. The raiders would then help themselves to the booty left behind. The next stage was generally that the dispossessed would amass a party of even greater numbers and would set off in pursuit of their property. This kind of private war was an accepted custom and could be initiated by any chief who was so minded. If he were wise he would weigh the circumstances before setting out and be prepared to take the consequences if anything went wrong, such as someone getting killed, which would initiate a vicious circle of vendettas.

Under Mohammed's direction the Muslim raids on the Meccan caravans began in earnest, and in year 2 of the *Hijra* (AD 624) the inevitable happened and a caravan guard was killed. From then on what had been a religious and ideological struggle between the Meccans and the Muslims developed into an armed conflict that was to be fought to the finish.

The Battle of Badr

Two months later Mohammed learned of a large rich caravan leaving from Mecca which was said to be worth 50,000 *dinars*. He had no difficulty in raising a party of 300 men, of whom only 90 were Meccan emigrants. They set an ambush at the well of Badr on the road to Syria and laid in wait. The leader of the caravan, Abu Sufyan, either anticipated or discovered the danger and sent word to the merchants of Mecca to come out and protect their property. As they were nearly all involved, they quickly raised a force of over 900 which must have been almost every able-bodied man in the town. Abu Sufyan diverted his caravan around Badr, whilst the Meccan army marched to engage and put down the Muslims once and for all. At this point the Muslims captured a young Meccan water carrier who told them of the relief expedition bearing down upon them. If Mohammed needed any excuse to retire without dishonour, the overwhelming superiority of the enemy provided one. But he decided to stand and fight, even though his original objective was now out of reach. At Badr he filled in all the wells except one and took up his position in front of it. The two sides began hurling traditional insults and throwing down challenges and the battle began with single combat of champions from either side.

After a while a pitched battle developed and the Meccans were startled by the fury of the Muslim onslaught. Mohammed had promised his followers certain entry to Paradise for all those who fell in battle, and this had its effect on the Muslim army. The Muslims also had a unified command, while the Meccans fought as individual tribes and made little use of their overwhelming strength or of their cavalry. Many Meccans were inhibited by tribal custom from killing men who were related to them, and shortly before midday panic swept their ranks and they fled. They lost over 50 dead, including two of their leaders, and another 70 or so were taken prisoner. On the Muslim side about 15 were killed.

The spoils were substantially less than those carried by the caravan, but were still considerable. 150 camels and horses and large quantities of arms and armour were seized, as well as some merchandise. Quarrels broke out as to how this should be divided. The Prophet settled the matter by ordering the spoils to be collected together and then distributed equally. Traditional custom laid down that the leader of a victorious side should have one quarter of the booty, but Mohammed as a general rule took one fifth, as prescribed:

Know that whatever booty you take, the
fifth of it is God's, and the Messenger's,
and near kinsman's, and the orphan's,
and the needy, and the traveller.

(Koran 8:41)

The Battle of Badr is a landmark and had far reaching consequences. It sanctioned a concern for material existence and the use of
force as a means of survival, and both were built into the foundations
of Islam. The practical gains of victory were considerable, since the
ransom paid for the prisoners was heavy, but the gain in prestige and
influence was of greater importance. The Muslims had defeated a
powerful city in open fight and had demonstrated that they had not
only the Message but also the power to back it up. It confirmed and
reinforced Mohammed's position in Medina; those who wavered
rallied to his side, and the Bedu tribes came offering friendship. Above
all, the effect upon Mohammed himself was remarkable. After all the
doubt and despair of the early years, here at last was a sign that God's
hand had intervened. Mohammed had not intended to do battle, but
God had not only decided on confrontation but had also made the
Muslims victorious.

The victory was interpreted by the Muslims as a sign that the city of
Mecca would fall and that all Mohammed's opposition from Christians, Jews and pagans was in the wrong. Mohammed henceforth saw
his task as overcoming all opposition.

Certain pagan elements were dealt with first, and the targets were
the two poets who had irritated him most: Asma bint Marwan and
Abu Afak. When it became known that the Prophet wanted them
silenced, his followers responded by assassination.

Even before Badr Mohammed had doubts about an alliance with the
Jews. Their unresponsive attitude caused him some irritation. Before
the battle he was content simply to loosen his ties by decreeing that
Jerusalem was no longer to be the direction of prayer, but it was
noticeable that not a single Jew had volunteered support for the expedition, and afterwards the Prophet decided to make the break. The
Jewish fast soon ceased to be observed, and the fast during the month
of Ramadan was substituted.

Mohammed had shown the uncompromising side of his character
for the first time when dealing with the pagan opposition, and this was
underlined shortly afterwards when he turned against the Jews. Clearly at some point the Prophet realized that the Jews must be treated as
opposition rather than as potential allies. Some sources say that the
matter came to a head after some Jewish tribes made formal alliances
with the Meccans against the Muslims, while others take the view that
the mere presence of such an intractable religious and cultural body at

the heart of Mohammed's operations was in itself a threat to his political stability.

In any event, the incident which brought matters to a head started casually enough. A Bedu girl who was married to a Muslim was selling some vegetables in the market when some young Jews began teasing her. They tried to life her veil, and one of them hitched her skirt in such a way that when she stood up it came off. A young Muslim bystander came to her aid, and in defence of the girl's honour killed one of the Jews. The Jews retaliated in kind and the quarrel was on.

The Jewish clan, the Qaynuqa, withdrew inside their fort. this may have been done to limit the conflict, as they had reason to believe that some of their Arab allies would intercede for them and that the matter would be settled with indemnities on either side. But Mohammed would have none of it and sent his army to blockade the fort.

After 15 days the fort surrendered, and Mohammed's first reaction was to condemn all its occupants to death. But at this point one of the Arab leaders, Ibn Ubayy, made a strong intervention, threatening to review his allegiance if the sentence was carried out. Ibn Ubayy was a powerful ally, and Mohammed relented on condition that the Jews left Medina within three days, leaving their goods for the victor. Ibn Ubayy and others renewed efforts for a more merciful decision, but Mohammed was adamant. The Jews departed to join their kinsmen in the North, leaving behind their considerable wealth.

The Battle of Uhud

In the meantime the Quraysh were stirring themselves for further action. The news of the disaster at Badr had been greeted in Mecca first with disbelief, then with sorrow, and finally with a fierce determination for revenge. This determination was reinforced when Mohammed sent 100 men to attack another of the Meccan caravans bound for Mesopotamia, taking goods valued at 100,000 *dirhams*. The Quraysh prepared their retaliation carefully. Negotiations were begun with all the neighbouring tribes and an alliance was sealed which raised an army of 3000 men, many of them armoured, and a cavalry force of 200.

It took the army 10 days to reach Medina, whose inhabitants had plenty of time to withdraw into their fortified dwellings. At first the Medinans agreed that their strategy should be to stay where they were and fight off the attack. But some of the young men, eager for excitement, urged that they should go out and meet the Meccans head on. Mohammed was persuaded, perhaps believing that, as at Badr, numbers were not important, and his army prepared to leave its stronghold. But then his young followers approached him saying that they had changed their minds and that it might be better to stay where they were. By this time Mohammed had put on his armour, and he announced that, having gone thus far, he was not going to take it off until after the battle. About 1000 Medinans were assembled without cavalry. They marched out to face the Meccans, but on the outskirts of the oasis Ibn Ubayy turned back, taking about a third of the army with him. The next day, undaunted, Mohammed and his 700 followers took the field against the Meccan army.

This time the Meccans were much better organized. They used their cavalry to great effect, drove wedges through the Muslim ranks, and overwhelmed and cut down the isolated groups. The Prophet himself was obliged to fight, surrounded by his faithful bodyguard. At one stage he was knocked down and the rumour spread that he had been killed, causing further consternation and confusion among the Muslims. In fact he was only wounded, and had to be carried off to safety. The Muslims were comprehensively defeated, and the pagans celebrated their victory in the barbarous manner of the times. Their women mutilated the dead by making necklaces of ears and noses, and one woman is said to have carved open the man who killed her father at Badr and chewed his liver.

The Medinans had left about 70 dead, of whom 10 were emigrants, and the other side had lost about 20. The victors did not march on Medina to finish off their opponents, which turned out to be a costly mistake. They had noted that not all the tribes had joined Mohammed (particularly the powerful Jews) and they had seen Ibn Ubayy defect. Clearly, they were unwilling to antagonize anyone unnecessarily and retired in triumph. Almost immediately Mohammed rallied his forces and set out in pursuit of the Meccan army. He took good care to keep his distance, lighting as many fires as possible at night to exaggerate his strength. His purpose was largely to impress upon surrounding tribes that his situation was not as desperate as the Quraysh were bound to make out. This done, he returned to Medina.

This was a critical time for the Prophet, and his position was now seriously challenged by his opponents. Those still undecided argued that if victory at Badr had been won by the grace of God, defeat at Uhud must mean that God had changed sides. The crisis spread to the Muslim ranks when Ibn Ubayy and his followers said that their advice should have been noted and that in future experienced people should have more say in public affairs. Many of the most ardent Muslims saw this as an act of treachery, and Mohammed had to restrain Ibn Ubayy's own son from killing his father on the spot. The situation was finally resolved by revelation (Koran 3:119) and Uhud was interpreted as a test to distinguish the faithful from the faint-hearted. But the real significance of this period is that what had started for Mohammed as a purely religious issue was now taking on political and economic significance in which some of the issues were being settled by military force.

The Jewish Opposition

But Mohammed never lost sight of his original inspiration. Although he was a Prophet and not a scholar, the presence of the strong Jewish community in Medina must have been a constant reminder to him of the intellectual strength of the faith he was challenging. For their part the Jews of Medina had enough knowledge of their scriptures to realize that the claims of Mohammed were incompatible with Judaism. Their argument was that the Koran was mistaken on a number of issues raised in the Old Testament. Therefore it followed that the Koran was not the word of God. This being so, Mohammed could not be His Prophet. Something had to be done about such fundamental opposition.

The Jewish settlements throughout Arabia were numerous and well organized. Their life was based on skilled agriculture, and their communities were exclusive and tightly knit. In Mecca, Jews seemed to have been comparatively rare, and were viewed with a mixture of curiosity (because of their strange habits and taboos) and apprehension (because of their energy and success). Both Christians and Jews viewed the Arabs with some contempt. They were seen as primitive and uncivilized, having neither moral values nor an organized church. Both referred to the Arabs as *hanif* (pagan or infidel), and it may have been inverted snobbery which eventually, after the triumph of Islam, led the Muslims to adopt the label of *hanif* as a badge of superiority.

Mohammed's attitude to both religions was not that their faith was intrinsically wrong or that their prophets, including Jesus, were mistaken. They were serving the will of the same God, but Mohammed's message to them was that his revelations superseded all previous revelations, and the preaching of all previous prophets. Yet he found an intellectual justification for his cause in the Bible itself: Ismail was the father of the Arabs, and his brother Isaac the father of the Jews. This being so, their father Ibrahim (Abraham) was, strictly speaking, not Jewish at all. He had faith in one almighty God, but, as he preceded both the Christian and Jewish religions and was the first to submit to the will of God, then surely he was the first Muslim:

> And they say, 'Be Jews or Christians and
> you shall be guided'. Say thou: 'Nay, rather
> the creed of Abraham, a man of pure faith:
> he was no idolater'.

> (Koran 2:129)

Mohammed was told that Abraham had settled some of his people in a barren valley near the holy Temple of God, and his son Ismail had built this temple and made it a place of pilgrimage and asylum. Furthermore, he asked God to select one of the future inhabitants of this place as a Messenger to tell people of his revelations and wisdom. At this point the Voice instructed Mohammed that the faithful should turn towards the *Kaaba*[1] in Mecca to pray, not towards Jerusalem. Thus at one stroke Mohammed formally and irrevocably announced his break with the Jews, and at the same time absorbed the Arab's ritual of the pilgrimage to Mecca.

This altered the status of Islam in relation to the other two religions. It was no longer an uncivilized and barbaric people being led by the untutored Mohammed, usurping the tradition of revelations given by Moses. It was the faithless Jews who were now accused of rejecting the Message which, according to their own tradition, had been addressed to their ancestors. They were accused of having neglected and persecuted their own prophets for preaching the Message, of having rebelled against Moses, of disobeying the commandments they had been given, and of continuing to do so. As the Christians had testified, they had failed to believe in Jesus, killed him and slandered his mother. This ideological conflict was given common meaning by focusing on the Jew's dietary laws. Was it not a fact that their law forbade them things that were perfectly good to eat? How could this be if it were not, as the Koran said, a punishment for their sins? It is interesting that the Christians had used the food issue to make their own break with the Jews 600 years earlier.

The War of the Ditch

Meanwhile the Quraysh, under their new leader, Abu Sufyan, had no intention of letting matters rest. The threat posed by Mohammed and his Muslims to their position and power was now clear to them and they resolved to destroy the movement in Medina. To do this they needed an army much larger than the one at Uhud, and they set about recruitment of the Bedu tribes. Mohammed heard of these intentions, and retaliated with his new power and wealth. There followed a period of minor raids, assassinations and intrigue. Mohammed became convinced that the Jewish tribe of Banu n-Nadir were plotting his assassination, and he ordered them to leave the oasis. He gained the consent of the Medinans that the Jews' land should be divided up among the Meccan immigrants so that they would no longer be a burden upon the community. The produce would be used for the maintenance of the destitute.

1. Arabic for cube: the centre of the pilgrimage in Mecca.

The final confrontation with the Quraysh began when Abu Sufyan, at the head of three armies with a total strength of 10,000 men and 600 cavalry, marched on Medina. Mohammed had time to prepare for the assault, but as he could raise no more than 3000 men, there was no question of meeting Abu Sufyan's army in the field. Except to the North the oasis was protected by hills from cavalry attack. On their exposed side the Medinans dug a huge fortified ditch, and took up their positions behind it. The Meccans approached the ditch, halted, and did not seem to know what to do next. Tradition has it that both sides stood hurling insults and arrows at each other for two or three weeks (sic) with few casualties on either side. Abu Sufyan tried to resolve the matter by intrigue in urging the last Jewish tribe left in Medina, the Qurayza, to strike Mohammed from the rear. The Muslims responded by sowing dissent among the tribes in the coalition facing them. The siege dragged on and the attackers seemed reluctant to do anything that would involve too many casualties. When it became clear that nothing had been achieved, and little could be done about it, they went home.

For Mohammed it was a triumph. The eyes of Arabia had been upon him, and he had shown that he was not to be moved by force. If an army of 10,000 men could not shift him, nothing could.

Massacre of the Qurayza

Immediately afterwards the Prophet took action against the last group in Medina to cause him any anxiety: the Jewish Qurayza. His supporters besieged them in their fortified village and called upon them to surrender. After 25 days they offered to depart on the same conditions as the Nadir. He refused and insisted on an unconditional surrender. After some hesitation the Qurayza gave in. Mohammed offered them their lives if they would submit to Islam: only one Jew agreed. Mohammed was besieged by them and their allies asking for mercy, but he had his answer ready. Would they accept that one of their own allies should decide their fate? If so, all must abide by his decision. When this was agreed the arbitrator from the Aws tribe pronounced that all adult males were to be executed, the women and children sold into slavery and their property divided. The next day the sentence was carried out and over 600 men were massacred. It was May AD 627.[1]

It has been suggested by some European scholars that Mohammed adopted this policy of clearing the Jews from Medina just because they were Jews, but this is inconsistent with his general policy of seeking

1. This traditional view of the incident has been challenged in the recent work of Barakat Ali.

allies wherever possible. Mohammed attacked them because they criticized the Koranic revelations, thus undermining the foundation of the whole Islamic community, and gave support to his political opponents. In the end he turned on them not as Jews, but as an opposition. It is significant that in places where the Jewish communities were too small to be effective, or where they did not generate hostile activity, they were allowed to live unmolested.

Truce with the Quraysh

For some while after the siege of Medina, neither side took any military initiative. The Prophet changed his tactics and announced his intention of going to Mecca for the ritual of *umra* — the traditional ceremony connected with processions around the *Kaaba* — and he invited his followers to go with him. It was to be a peaceful expedition of several hundred men and a few women. The Meccans, believing it to be an attack, met the force outside their city, but after negotiations a treaty was concluded between the two sides which denied the Muslims access to the *Kaaba* on that occasion, but conceded access to Mecca the following year.

Many of Mohammed's supporters were disappointed by this apparent reversal, but Mohammed had obtained the diplomatic concession he wanted. In making a treaty with the Muslims the Meccans had recognized both Mohammed's authority and that his followers were part of the traditional cult associated with the city.

The Jews of Khaybar

Having secured a non-aggression pact with the Meccans, the Prophet turned his attention to his other enemies, this time in the North. The Jews of Khaybar had broken up their alliance with the Quraysh and the Bedu tribes; thus there was an opportunity to move against Khaybar while the Jews were isolated. At the head of 1600 men, Mohammed attacked and beseiged the forts one by one. Each surrendered in turn and had to accept the Muslims' terms. Mohammed's task was made easier because there was no central authority among the Jews, and they had been abandoned by their Bedu allies. This time, apart from taking some prisoners, the Muslim terms concentrated on property. The Jews had to surrender the better part of their possessions, and hand over half of the date harvest. As, one by one, the Jewish colonies of the region surrendered, they were given better terms, and were allowed to keep their possessions on payment of a tax. All religious opposition was now crushed and the Jews would present no further obstacles to the spread of Islam.

Fall of Mecca

The following year, sure of his position in Medina and clear of all other effective opposition, the Prophet fixed his eyes firmly on Mecca. At the same time the Quraysh, after a period of long and painful adjustment, faced up to the realities of the situation. Their leader, Abu Sufyan, had reached the conclusion that it was in their best interests to come to an understanding with Mohammed, and in the end the majority agreed with him.

The siege of Medina had shown that the Muslims could not be moved by force. Mohammed's victories over the Jewish tribes, his expeditions to the North, and his treaties with the Bedu had all increased his power. His activities were still seriously interfering with trade, which was the life blood of Meccan existence. The Muslim pilgrimage to the *Kaaba* had greatly impressed the Meccans by its discipline and intention. Clearly, Mohammed was not set on destroying their institutions, but on the contrary seemed to be trying to reinforce them, albeit with a different perspective and to the exclusive glorification of Allah. What is more, the religious and military success of the Muslims had been reinforced by material success and wealth. The Meccans were above all businessmen, and they recognized that a practical accommodation had to be found with the new movement and its ideology.

Abu Sufyan was sent to Medina to open negotiations. Ostensibly he was there to negotiate about the blood feud that involved the two sides and seemed irreconcilable. There are different interpretations of what went on during the negotiations, but it is undisputed that immediately afterwards Mohammed began preparations for an armed expedition. The story was circulated that the expedition was bound for the North, but when the Prophet had assembled an immense army of 10,000 men he marched them south. This was 10 Ramadan, Year 8 (1 January 630). On the way he collected recruits, including many of his old enemies from the city of Mecca itself. Two days from Mecca the army camped and lit 10,000 fires. The city panicked and sent Abu Sufyan to the Muslim camp to negotiate. Whilst with them he was formally converted to Islam and returned to Mecca announcing Mohammed's terms: the city was in no danger if it welcomed the conqueror peacefully. The lives and property of all those who surrendered would be safe. They must lay down their arms and either stay in their houses or take refuge with Abu Sufyan.

After allowing time for the terms of the ultimatum to be understood, Mohammed broke camp on Thursday, 20 Ramadan 8 (11 January 630). The Muslims entered the deserted city in four columns. There was only token resistance which was quickly put down with very few casualties.

Mohammed went straight to the *Kaaba* amid the jubilation of his supporters and, watched by the Qurayshites, he touched the Black Stone and pronounced in a loud voice the supreme exhortation of Islam: '*Allahu akbar*' ('Allah is greatest') and 10,000 voices took up the call. His second act was to have all pagan idols thrown from the shrine, and the frescoes removed, save, it is said, those of Abraham, Jesus and the Virgin Mary. He then made a speech urging the Qurayshites to acknowledge him as the Messenger of God, and to come forward and swear allegiance.

Mohammed stayed barely two weeks in Mecca, and the only people who suffered persecution were the propagandists and poets who had satirized his claim to prophethood. He took the opportunity to borrow some large sums from the wealthy Qurayshites in order to distribute compensation to the Muslim soldiery who had failed to gain any booty, and over 2000 of the most needy men were given 50 *dirhams* each. He had all idols destroyed, but otherwise seemed content to leave things much as they were. There were now considerable advantages to being a Muslim, and, having physically established authority over the two most important towns, he had created a climate in which the adoption of his religion could take its own course. Social pressures now worked in favour of Islam rather than paganism, and in a few years paganism in Mecca was a thing of the past.

Unification of the Tribes

Mohammed had quickly to face a challenge from an unexpected quarter. A large confederation of tribes called Hawazin had risen against him. They were in alliance with other tribes centred on the city of Ta'if, and were old enemies of the Quraysh. They saw Mohammed's rise purely in tribal terms and saw his new power as a Qurayshite threat. Both sides raised huge armies which met at Hunayn. After a fierce battle, in which Mohammed himself took a major part, the Muslims were victorious. The defeated withdrew into their fortified town and, after a brief siege, Mohammed withdrew to divide the spoils of the battle. This almost turned into a riot, and after considerable difficulty Mohammed restored order, and shocked his old Companions by his generosity towards the new converts. Even the pagans were given something. He was now in a position to return to Medina where, eight years before with a few Companions, he had sought sanctuary from persecution.

Paradoxically, it was the almost simultaneous events outside Arabia that made the subsequent unification of the country swift and complete. The Roman Empire in the West had been overrun by barbarians. In the East it had survived under the style of the Byzantine

Empire with its capital at Constantinople, but it had fallen into confusion, partly because of attacks from without, and partly because of internal conflicts and inefficient rule. The serious rival to Byzantine was the Persian Empire of the Sassanids in the East, which stretched from Iraq to·Afghanistan. Following 50 years of uneasy peace, a long and decisive war began in AD 602. For almost 30 years the conflict raged across the Middle East, first one side and then the other gaining advantage. The sack of Jerusalem and the carrying off of what was believed to be the true Cross caused consternation among Christians throughout the Byzantine Empire, and provided a rallying point for their forces. Eventually, the Persian resources were exhausted by the long struggle, and in June 629 Constantinople was occupied in triumph. The Holy Rood was restored to Jerusalem in March 630. To the civilized world the triumph of Christianity seemed assured. The defeat of Persia meant the decline of Persian influence in southern Arabia and the Persian Gulf. The political vacuum left the field open for the inspired sword of Islam.

In the years following, Mohammed made the most of this situation. There was a constant exchange of envoys between the Muslims and the tribes in the far corners of Arabia. The Prophet undertook a complicated diplomatic and military task. Alliances were made in which acknowledgement was given to the power of God, and through which peace, security and the benefit of trade would accrue at home. Spoils were to be generated from abroad. Each tribe had to embrace the faith, promise not to attack other tribes which had made alliances with Mohammed, and furnish troops when required. The system had proved itself in both effectiveness and prosperity, and converts flocked irresitibly to the creed which had set its sights on an Arab state with an Arab ideology. For all practical purposes Arabia was united.

Within a year of the fall of Mecca there was the last great expedition, to Tabuk in the North. Its purpose was to test the limit of the Prophet's influences, and treaties were signed with local princes, Jewish settlements and one Christian king.

The Farewell Pilgrimage

Since his entry into Mecca Mohammed had been content to allow the ritual pilgrimage (*hajj*) to be attended by Muslims and pagans alike. In AH 10 (AD 632), however, he decided to remove all pagan influence from this ritual. Mohammed was accompanied by all his wives and the most eminent of the Companions. With a great crowd around him he performed the *umra*, the processions round the *Kaaba* and the seven journeys between Safa and Maraw. On 8 Dhu L-Hijja, the ceremonies of *hajj* began. He performed the traditional rites at Mina, Arafat and

Muzdalifa: the prayers, pauses, the casting of stones and the sacrifices. But he made it clear that the acts were dedicated to God alone and not to the divinities that had been associated with these sanctuaries. On the tenth day he had his head shaved according to custom and performed the ritual depurification. In the days of the *hajj* he made speeches and had dialogues with people. These were later collected into one great speech. In it Mohammed forbade usury and blood feuds for crimes committed during paganism. He laid down the organization of the calendar, the four sacred months, and its lunar structure. He defined the mutual duties of husbands and wives, urged the proper treatment of slaves, and preached brotherhood among all Muslims. With the ceremonies completed, he immediately returned to Medina, and he was never to see his native city again. The visit was to become known as the Farewell Pilgrimage, and from that day to this only Muslims have been allowed to enter Mecca.

Death of Mohammed

Shortly afterwards the Prophet became ill. He was planning another campaign to the North which had to be entrusted to Usama, a negro youth who was his son by an Abyssinian freed woman. Mohammed was suffering from severe head pains and fever, and took to his bed. His illness grew worse and he began to suffer from fainting fits. Some two weeks later on 13 Rabi (8 June 632) he recovered enough to show himself to the faithful in the courtyard. His family and Companions were delighted and the word began to go round that the Prophet was better. But by that same afternoon he had to take to his bed once more as he became steadily weaker and delirious. Before nightfall Mohammed the Prophet, Messenger of God, was dead.

The Prophet's Successors

Mohammed made no provision at all for a successor after his death, following the Arabic custom that the leader emerges according to the consensus of the community. In the absence of any revelation to the contrary, Mohammed allowed matters to take their course. According to tradition, Abu Bakr had been asked by the Prophet on his deathbed to lead the community in prayer as *imam*. As he was also the Prophet's father-in-law and a leading member of his following, it would have been easy for him to assume the right to succeed Mohammed as *Khalifa* (Caliph) or 'substitute'. But he did not take the initiative. In the confusion following the Prophet's death it was Omar, son of Al-Khattab, an outstanding personality in the Quraysh, who saw the need to resolve the question of the leadership quickly. He gave Abu Bakr the *bay's,* the clap of palm on palm, which for the first time was used to acknowledge sovereignty, and Abu Bakr became the first Caliph.

His role was naturally more limited than that of Mohammed. He had certain religious duties such as acting as *imam* at prayer, but any respectable Muslim can perform this function. It is God and not the Caliph who directs religious affairs. Nevertheless, the Caliph clearly had great political power, which increased in scope as the Empire of Islam spread.

The appointment of the Caliph without reference to the community was a significant departure from Arab custom, and this did not go unnoticed. When Omar himself became Caliph, having been nominated by Abu Bakr on his deathbed, he wrote a letter to the Governor at Basra:

> People have an aversion to their rulers and I trust to God that you and I are not overtaken by it . . . See to the execution of the laws . . . Strike terror into wrongdoers and make heaps of mutilated limbs out of them. Visit the sick among Muslims, attend their funerals, open your gate to them and give heed in person to their affairs, for you are but a man among them except that God has allotted you the heaviest burden.

Omar nominated a council of six to elect his successor. The council chose Uthman ibn Affan, a member of the Umayyad clan, who had been one of Mohammed's sons-in-law. By this choice, however, they passed over another of the Prophet's sons-in-law, Ali, who was also his cousin. Ali, and many other members of the community, considered that he who was nearest in blood to the Prophet had a stronger claim to be Caliph. This conflict was to divide Islam permanently. Ali was elected Caliph when Uthman was assassinated, but the Umayyad clan held Ali responsible for the assassination and refused to accept him as Caliph. One of the Umayyads, the governor of Syria, proclaimed himself the true Commander of the Faithful, thus precipitating the split of the Islamic community into two principal sects, the Sunnis (who accept the legitimacy of the first four Caliphs) and the Shi'ites (who favored Ali as nearest in blood to the Prophet).

Ali met his death at the hands of a group of purists, the Kharijis or Seceders, who considered both Caliphs usurpers on the grounds that neither had been raised to the leadership of Islam by the free choice that Arab custom demanded. These democratic tribesmen, detesting the family rivalries at Mecca and the struggle for political power in Medina, disputed the need for any *imam* or head of state so long as the divine law was carried out. They saw the struggle for power between the rival factions as irrelevant, and dangerous to the purity of Islam, and therefore vowed to assassinate both Caliphs. Their attack on the governor of Syria, however, was not fatal.

Under the first four Caliphs the unity of Islam was more or less maintained by a central leadership, but within the first 100 years of its foundation, the territory it controlled became too big to be managed by a central administration. As the pace of expansion increased, the driving force for controlling and administrating the new society became local in character. Various powerful families inside and outside Arabia embraced the new religion and became its champions by exporting it to new territories and founding new dynasties. The first of these was the Umayyad based in Damascus. After a thousand years in which dynasties flourished and foundered from Spain to China, the three great Muslim empires—the Ottoman in Turkey, the Middle East and the Mediterranean; the Safayid in Iran; and the Moghul in India—flowered in the 18th century. By the 19th century all three were either destroyed or seriously weakened by the imperial expansion of the European powers. However, it was only the power and wealth of these Empires that was challenged by Europe. The religious faith that underpinned them remained unchallenged, and has provided the foundation for the revival of Islam in modern times.

Class Structure Under Islam

The unification of Arabia under Islam, and the organization required to spread it far beyond, brought about the structural changes in tribal society where a man's position was virtually determined by his birth. The Koranic revelations superseded the authority of the tribe which had previously determined its own beliefs and way of life. Islam substituted a detailed code of moral and social behaviour, affecting every aspect of a person's life. This code provided not only the cohesion of a new religion, but also the elements of an embryonic nation. Henceforth the authority for the doings of the community rested not with the chief or the collective voice of the people, but with Mohammed and, beyond him, with God. This introduced an idea foreign to the Arabs—that of a central authority.

The tribal aristocracy established by birth still persisted and continues to be important[1], but it exists, as it were, in parallel with the idea that all Muslims are equal within the brotherhood of Islam. In its early days one of the most subversive aspects of the new creed was the notion that any Muslim was not only equal to any other in the eyes of

---

1. See Koran 6:165:
   'It is He who has appointed you viceroys
   in the earth, and has raised some of you
   in rank above others.'

God, but also equal to the unbelievers who ruled society by right of centuries of established custom and tradition. The element of hope embodied in Islam is one of the main reasons for its spread (for example, in India where it offered a social refuge to the Hindu untouchables).

In Mohammed's Farewell Pilgrimage, when preaching brotherhood among all Muslims, he is said to have stated that all men are equal in Islam and that the Arab has no superiority over the foreigner, nor the foreigner over the Arab, save in fear of God.

Yet in spite of the Prophet's own preaching he has won a place in the hearts of the masses which has eclipsed even the most noble birthright. Since his day even the slightest kinship with his tribe, the Quraysh[1], has been held in the highest esteem. A Qurayshite would be honoured above the highest nobleman, and even an adopted member of the tribe would have precedence over the offspring of an old sheikhly family.

The question of class arose most sharply when marriage was involved. It was the responsibility of the father or guardian of the girl to become her *wali* (literally: protector) and it was his duty to see that the suitor was of equal birth and that the match was suitable in other ways. When Islam abolished distinctions of birth it became theoretically possible for a slave to ask to marry a girl from a distinguished family although this is unlikely to have occurred any more often than a serf asking for the hand of a lord's daughter in medieval England. People knew their places, and gradually society arranged customs to ensure that the ideas of equality did not get out of hand. The Quraysh became the new élite and the rest of the Muslims were in an equal class irrespective of their tribe. In marriage a non-Arab Muslim was equal to an Arab if both his father and grandfather had been Muslims before him, but even so he was obliged to provide an adequate endowment. Nevertheless, tribal tradition, directly contrary to Koranic doctrine, strongly discouraged the marriage of an Arab with a non-Arab woman in early Islamic times.

Although Mohammed made important reforms in tribal customs and brought about significant changes in the treatment and rights of slaves, like other religious leaders before him he took slavery as part of the natural order of things. Nowhere in the Koran is there any suggestion that it should be otherwise. Mohammed encouraged the humane treatment of slaves and urged their emancipation, and as Islam matured the stigma attaching to the status of the slave slowly

1. In modern Arabia the descendants of the Prophet are known as *Ashraf* (plural of *Sharif*). They are often large landowners, forming separate communities, and generally marry within their own clan. In no sense do they have authority as a religious community.

diminished. Quite early on the principle was established, even though it is not laid down in the Koran, that Muslims were not to be taken as captives or slaves.

Slaves might be acquired by sale, gift, inheritance or capture. As it became illegal to sell a free Muslim into slavery, parents were forbidden to sell their children, although this has not always been observed, even in modern times. Legislation provided for the sale and purchase of slaves as for any ordinary goods with certain restrictions in the case of females who had borne children by their masters, and of the children themselves. Slaves had very few legal rights, their labour and their bodies being the property of their master to do with as he liked. Household slaves were very rarely sold, and were often adopted as members of the family. In exceptional circumstances slaves had opportunities to acquire great wealth and power. There was a slave king of Delhi and the Manluk sultans of Egypt were originally slaves. A whole series of dynasties was founded in the Middle East during the 12th and 13th centuries by the Turks, whose original slave bodyguards were appointed to high office, and eventually became kings who founded dynasties.

The spread of Islam by conquest gave rise to a unique class. These were named Mawali, converted Muslims of the subdued territory outside Arabia. They became affiliated to one of the Arab tribes from among their conquerors, owing allegiance and receiving protection. They were not always well treated by their conquerors, were often made illegally to pay tax and suffered harassment and contempt. In Kusa they had to have a mosque of their own; and under the Umayyad régime, even when they fought for Islam, they were sometimes deprived of their share of the spoils. Nor was this poor treatment confined to backward communities. It was not long before the religious scholars of Persia and Turkey, taking their new faith seriously, became expert in its doctrines and traditions, and the most learned doctors in Islamic theology. But far from this gaining the respect of the Arab invaders, it simply encouraged them to regard the conquered people as inferior beings fit only for studying culture and science. This treatment of the Mawali led eventually to their adopting fabricated Arab identities, changing their names and inventing family trees. Eventually Persian political influence became strong in the middle of the eighth century, and both theological and political pressure redressed the balance.

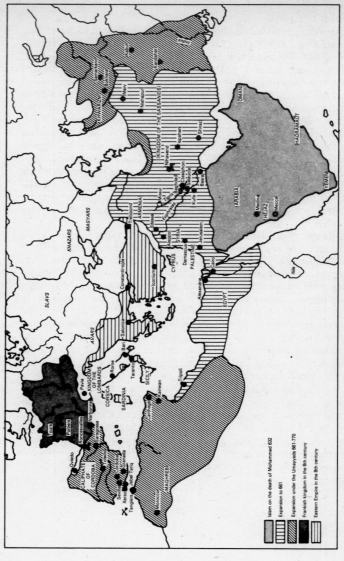

The spread of Islam in the eighth century

Islam on the death of Mohammed 632
Expansion to 661
Expansion under the Umayyads 661-770
Frankish kingdom in the 8th century
Eastern Empire in the 8th century

Chapter 2

The Message

> Today I have perfected your religion
> for you, and I have completed My blessing
> upon you, and I have approved Islam for
> your religion.

(Koran 5:8)

'Religion' is translated from the Arabic word *din*, but this does not convey the proper meaning to the Western mind. For *din* does not mean simply the spiritual fulfilment or enlightenment of the individual, it means all matters pertaining to a way of life. *Din* encompasses theology, scripture, politics, morality, law, justice and all other aspects of life relating to the thoughts or actions of men. For the Westerner, used to viewing religion as a matter of private conscience, this is the fundamental point to grasp in trying to understand Islam. It is not that religion dominates the life of a faithful Muslim, but that religion, in this comprehensive sense, *is* his life.

His faith is based on the belief that literally everything in life is the predetermined will of God, and that His will has ruled and does rule absolutely from always to eternity. Not only is every aspect of each individual's life predetermined but also 'not a worm weeps in the earth, not a leaf falls from the tree except by the decree and will of God'[1]. Giving unto Caesar that which is due to Caesar is an idea alien to Islam.

This does not mean that the Islamic faith has no structure. There are fundamental beliefs, 'pillars of faith', which form the core of the religion, and to which all other aspects of life are ultimately related. But first it is useful to consider a few basic definitions in order to establish a foundation upon which to build.

Allah. Allah is Arabic for God, the Supreme Being of the Muslims. The first article of the essential Muslim creed states *'La illah il-Allah'* — 'There is no god save Allah'.

Islam. Islam means submission to, and therefore being in the proper relationship to, God.

1. F A Klein, *Religion of Islam*, Curzon, 1972.

Muslim. Muslim means submitter.

Prophets. Prophets are recognized as Apostles or Messengers who are divinely sent for particular nations or communities, and who bear witness to the divine message. Noah, Abraham, Lot, Ishmael, Isaac, Jacob, David, Moses, Shu'aib and Jesus are among them.

Mohammed. Mohammed is the Messenger of God, to whom God revealed His word and His law in such a manner and in such detail as to supersede all other revelations and previous interpretations of his Word, and upon whom He placed the ultimate Seal of the Prophet. It was Mohammed who first called upon the Arabian tribes to submit to the will of God and to commit themselves afresh each day and each moment to His service. But no degree of divinity is conferred on Mohammed, in spite of the special place that the Prophet holds in the hearts and minds of Muslims; such a suggestion is considered blasphemous. God is unique and alone.

Koran. Koran means recitation; it is the sacred book of Islam. It is the uncreated and direct word of Allah and is coexistent with Him. It is a discourse on what God has uttered, and describes itself simply and finally as 'the best of histories' (12:3). It is held that the Torah of Moses, the Psalms of David and the Gospel of Jesus were all sent down by God, but that the Koran is the last and final word of God.

Revelation. The idea of revelation is central to Islam. It has been described as the flashing of divine light on the soul. The Koran explains that

It belongs not to any mortal that
God should speak to him, except
by revelation, or from behind
    a veil,
or that he should send a messenger
and he reveal whatsoever He will.

(Koran 42:50)

The Five Pillars of Islam

The basic duties of Muslims towards Allah are known as the Five Pillars of Islam.

Shahada

The first duty is recitation of the *shahada,* or short creed: 'There is no God but Allah, and Mohammed is His Prophet.' This profession of faith said in public is enough to gain recognition by the community.

Salat

The second pillar is *salat,* the devotional worship. The usual translation is prayers, but worship or formal prayer gives a better indication of its meaning. *Salat* is essentially an acknowledgement of God's might and power, and does not consist of asking Him for favours. It is both an adoration and an act of submission, a physical act which is repeated at least twice and finishes with the worshipper touching the ground with his forehead. Muslims worship five times a day—at dawn, midday, mid-afternoon, sunset and after nightfall. The call to prayer is uttered from the minaret of the mosque by the muezzin (*mu'adhdhin*):

> 'Allah is most great,
> There is no God but Allah, and
> Mohammed is His Prophet,
> Come to prayer, come to salvation,
> Allah is most great, there is no
> God but Allah.'

And in the morning: 'Prayer is better than sleep.' The Shi'ites always add 'come to the best of work'.

Ritual ablutions must be performed before *salat,* including the washing of hands, face and feet. If water is not available, sand is used. The prayers themselves are ritualized and include recitations of the first *sura* and other verses from the Koran. Preferably prayer should be performed in congregation, although it is valid in private, and may be seen all over the Muslim world in airports, shops, offices, building sites and streets.

On Fridays congregational prayers take place at noon in mosques (*masjid,* or place for prostration). Prayer is led by an *imam* (president) with the worshippers standing in ranks behind him. At least 40 faithful are required to form a congregation, and it is obligatory for all adult males to attend. Hence Friday mosques, roofed or not, must be large enough to hold the whole male population. Women normally take no part in these proceedings.

Generally before the prayers, the *imam* delivers from the pulpit an address in which the teachings of Islam are expounded.

Friday is not regarded as a day of rest, and there is no prohibition on work. Particular emphasis is placed on the midday prayer on Fridays, but, this aside, it is not considered a special day.

The direction of prayer is called *qibla* and is generally marked in a mosque by a niche in a wall which indicates the direction of the city of Mecca in Arabia. More specifically it is the *Kaaba,* a black cubic shrine sited in the courtyard of the Great Mosque. By tradition the *Kaaba* had been established by Abraham, and was the centre of worship for the Arab tribes, but was subsequently usurped by idolators. Mohammed deemed that the *Kaaba* should be established as the direction of prayer, which had previously been Jerusalem.

Imams (and in some places *sheikhs*) are appointed to certain mosques and orders, but this does not confer on them any exclusive right to lead prayer. The leadership may be taken by any good Muslim if he is acquainted with the nodalities of worship.

In spite of the communal character of some Islamic institutions, worship for a Muslim remains essentially something that takes place between an individual and God. If it is convenient and appropriate to do so, Muslims pray together, but the duty of the prayer devolves directly and unambiguously upon the individual. Even if there were only one Muslim in the world, there would be nothing to prevent him from carrying out all the requirements of the Islamic faith, and every Muslim understands that on the Last Day he will be judged alone.

Zakat

The third pillar is *zakat*, the obligatory tax for the needy.

> And what you give in usury,
> that it may increase upon the
> people's wealth, increase not
> with God; but what you give in
> alms, desiring God's Face,
> those — they receive recompense
> manifold.

(Koran 30:38)

In the days of Mohammed payment of *zakat* was possibly the clearest external sign of adherence to Islam and encapsulates the old Semitic ideas of sacrifice. Each believer is required to contribute a fixed percentage (usually 1/40th) of his income or property to the needy and wayfarers. Normally there are no formal arrangements for the collection of *zakat* and the custom has declined in many places. A notable exception is Saudi Arabia, where *zakat* is levied as a formal tax, and even foreign companies are not exempt from payment on behalf of their Saudi employees.

Sawm

The fourth pillar is *sawm*, the fast during the month of Ramadan. The Koran commands that for the entire lunar month Muslims must refrain from all food and drink and other sensory pleasures during daylight hours. The fast begins with the red of the dawn and ends with sunset. By tradition, during the nights of Ramadan it is customary to sit in the mosque or at home praying and reciting the Koran.

Travellers, pregnant women, the sick and the aged and some others are exempted from the fast. When the month of Ramadan falls in summer it is especially difficult for people in the hot and humid countries of the Middle East and it is common for shops, offices and government departments to open restricted hours. This is generally considered a bad time for trade and business.

The start of Ramadan is determined by astronomical observations, so that the calendar date may be flexible within a day or two. The exact start is usually announced near the day. At the end of Ramadan there is a day of obligatory feasting followed by a festival of several days (*eid*) when people visit one another bearing gifts. In strict Muslim countries during Ramadan it is decidedly bad manners, if no more, for foreigners to eat, drink or even smoke in public.

Hajj

The fifth pillar is the pilgrimage, or *hajj*, to the *Kaaba*, the holy shrine in Mecca. *Hajj* means 'to set out for a definite purpose'.

> It is the duty of all men towards God to come
> to the House a pilgrim, if he is able to
> make his way there.

(Koran 3:92)

Thus every able-bodied Muslim is expected to make the pilgrimage at some time, and to many it is the climax of a lifetime. Only minors, slaves and the poor are exempted.

There are various ceremonies connected with the *hajj*, including wearing a special garment called *ihram*, circling the *Kaaba* seven times (*tawaf*) and kissing the black stone in the corner of the shrine. One of the pilgrim's important duties is to sacrifice an animal on the 10th day of the month. This sacrificial festival is celebrated at the same time throughout the Muslim world. The climax of the pilgrimage is the 'standing on Arafat', a hill and plain to the east of Mecca. The time for this is from midday to sunset on the ninth of the month.

The Prophet forbade access to Mecca for unbelievers and the interdict has generally been held to apply to Medina also. Very few unbelievers have penetrated either, and then only in disguise and at considerable risk.

The numbers of pilgrims are increasing each year, and in 1979 totalled over 2 million, the majority of whom also visit Medina to pray at the tomb of the Prophet.

The Koran

The language of the Koran is Arabic, and because it is the uncreated work of God many consider that it cannot and should not be translated into other languages. When it is rendered into another tongue, however skilfully, the words are no longer those spoken by God, and therefore no longer the Koran. Certainly, most educated Muslims will have a working knowledge of Arabic, and even the illiterate are likely to know some words through learning passages by heart.

The Koran is not organized in any chronological or sequential manner. Although some of the text was written down under Mohammed's supervision, it is agreed that it was completed in its present form at the time of Uthman the Third Caliph (AD 644-656). Its contents reflect the manner in which God revealed His message to the Prophet over a period of 20 years. On close examination it becomes clear that there is a structure, which reflects an intention to demonstrate that aspects of life should not be seen separately, but accepted as a whole based on the divine will.

The fragmentation of the text also reflects the fact that those who collected Mohammed's revelations after his death were not concerned to preserve their chronological order.[1] Muslim historians agree that parts of the same revelation are sometimes widely separated in the pages of the book.

It seems probable that for some years the revelations were retained only in the memories of Mohammed and his followers, although some scholars believe that much of the Koran was written down by the Prophet himself. When early Christians and others challenged Muslims to point to any miracle of Mohammed's that would demonstrate his prophethood, the orthodox reply was that the Koran itself was his miracle, since he could neither read nor write. It is still widely held among Muslims that the Prophet was unlettered and that he recorded the Holy Book under divine inspiration. Some modern Western scholars argue, however, that there is no evidence to show that Mohammed could not write, and that, given his experience in Meccan trade, it is possible that he could write as well as the average merchant.

Reason plays an important part in the Koran. In it God is always discussing, arguing and appealing to reason, and it continually expounds the rational proofs of Allah's omnipotence. Christians are called upon not to exceed the bounds of rationality:

> People of the Book, go not beyond the bounds
> in your religion, and say not as to God
> but the truth. The Messiah, Jesus son of Mary,
> was only the Messenger of God.

(Koran 4:169)

1. The exact state of the Koran at Mohammed's death, however, remains uncertain, although it is clear that the revelations could not have been collected in any final form so long as the Prophet was alive and adding to them.

Repeated some 50 times in the Koran is the verb *aqala* which means to connect ideas together, to reason, to understand an intellectual argument. A reasoning passage is frequently followed by the phrase 'have ye then no sense?'. Infidels who are unconvinced by Mohammed's preaching are regarded as 'a people of no intelligence', incapable of the intellectual effort required to cast off routine thinking. It has rightly been said that Mohammed comes close to considering unbelief as an infirmity of the human mind. The Koran is peppered with exhortations to people to re-examine the beliefs of their fathers, to recognize and understand the signs which God is displaying through revelations to His Messenger. Those who will not believe are not only ignorant but wilful. Perhaps the ultimate appeal to reason lies in the fact that God has taken the trouble to send his preaching in Arabic so that 'haply you will understand' (Koran 43:1).

The Koran is roughly the size of the New Testament. It is divided into 114 *suras* (chapters), each of which bears the name of something contained in it. The *suras* are divided into *ayat* (verses). The *suras*, with one exception, are arranged roughly in order of length, with the longest first, and it is generally agreed that the shortest ones, coming at the end, date from the Prophet's earliest days. Reverence for the Koran is evident everywhere among Muslims. The book is never laid on the ground or allowed to contact anything dirty. There is probably no other book in history, including the Bible, that has been subjected to so much study and analysis. Commentaries (*tafsirs*) on it fill entire libraries. The best known of these is by al-Tabari (d AD 923) which is a phrase by phrase analysis filling 30 volumes.

Hadith and Sunna

After the Koran the second foundation of Islam is the *Sunna*. This seeks to designate the sayings, actions and behaviour of the Prophet during his lifetime.

It was found after Mohammed's death that people faced problems that reference to the Koran alone did not solve. It was natural therefore that they should seek guidance from what people before them had done, and in particular from what the Prophet and his Followers in the ideal Muslim community of the first generation had said or done in comparable circumstances. Thus, the search for precedents became all-important.

Over the years, however, situations arose for which there was no exact historical precedent. Traditions began to be fabricated, and some believed that they understood Mohammed's mind so well that they could speak for him, perhaps because he is believed to have said 'Whenever someone says something true, it is as if I said it'. Eventually there was a reaction which resulted in systematic studies designed to sift the reliable from the fabricated. Such controversies were finally resolved by the jurist al-Shafii (d AD 820), who held that the *Sunna* of the Prophet alone is authoritative.

The *hadith* are literally oral reports going back in an unbroken chain to the Prophet. The nature, character and reliability of each witness in the chain was minutely examined by students of *hadith*, together with the action or saying in question. Eventually a vast body of biographical material was accrued to assess the strength and reliability of each *hadith*, and by the third Islamic century several great collections of *hadith* had emerged, which have since become recognized as second in authority only to the Koran. The collections are known as the Six Sound Books.

Controversy still exists about the *hadith*, however. In the last hundred years, disagreement about their reliability has emerged among Muslim scholars. Some still place full reliance on the historical accuracy of the classical method, whilst others reject the *hadith*, and seek guidance only from the Koran.

Jihad

Jihad literally means an effort or striving. It includes a religious war against unbelievers with the object of converting them to Islam or subduing all opposition (see Koran 9:5; 4:76; 2:214; 8:39). It is the sacred duty of the Muslim nation to ensure that Islam triumphs over all religions. It is considered a general duty of the nation as a whole, not of individuals. Furthermore, it is a duty which relates only to religion. It has nothing to do with economic exploitation, political repression or imperialism in any form.

In his early career Mohammed spread Islam by teaching and persuasion: several early Meccan *suras* stated that he was sent only to preach. When, at Medina, he wanted to win Jews over to his side, he stated that there was to be 'no compulsion in religion'. This attitude changed on his flight to Medina, when he declared that God had allowed him and his followers to defend themselves against infidels, and later when he proclaimed that he had divine leave to attack them and set up the true faith by the sword. Mohammed himself fought in nine battles and ordered many more. It is still the duty of the *imam* to order war against infidels on every suitable occasion. If he neglects to do so he commits a sin, unless his forces are not strong enough to subdue the enemy. Detailed rules are laid down about such matters as the declaration of war, who can be spared the sword and under what circumstances, who may keep their religions, how taxes are levied and how the spoils of war are to be distributed.

Jihad is to be taken very seriously. It is one of the few areas in which the Koran criticizes the judgement of the Prophet:

> It is not for any Prophet to have prisoners
> until he make wide slaughter in the land.

(Koran 8:68)

Dar al-Islam and Dar al-Harb

The world is therefore divided into two — *Dar al-Islam*, (the seat of Islam) and *Dar al-Harb* (the seat of war, which is inhabited by pagans, Christians and Jews).

Sacred Places

The *Kaaba* is the most sacred place for believers. Much more than a mosque, it is believed to be the place where heavenly power touches the earth directly. The Prophet's mosque in Medina is the next in sanctity. The third is Jerusalem as the first *qibla* (direction of prayer before it was changed to the *Kaaba*), which, according to tradition, is the place where Mohammed made his ascent to heaven. For the Shi'ites, Karbala in Iraq (where Mohammed's grandson Husayn was martyred) and Meshed in Iran (where Imam Ali ar-Rida is buried)- are special places of pilgrimage. For the masses the Sufi shrines are particular objects of veneration despite the fact that this is against Islamic teaching. In Baghdad, the tomb of the greatest saint, Abd al-Qadir al-Jilani, is visited by pilgrims from all over the world.

Sacred Days

The two festivals kept are: *Eid al-Fitr* (breaking the fast) which immediately follows Ramadan, starting on the first day of Shawwal and lasting three days, and *Eid al Adha* (sacrifice) which begins on the 10th of Dhu-l Hijieh, when the pilgrims perform their sacrifices, and lasts three or four days. The noon prayer on Fridays, with its accompanying *khofba* (homily) is a weekly event.

In addition to the Five Pillars, Muslims celebrate important religious occasions. On the Prophet's birthday meetings are held, speeches made and prayers offered. Shi'ite Muslims hold a great festival on the 10th of Muharram commemorating the martyrdom of Husayn, the Prophet's grandson, in the battle of Karbala (61/680). Parades are held with symbols of the slain Husayn, and the worshippers weep and flail themselves. There are also dramatic performances of a passion play to show the martyr's suffering.

Sin

According to the Prophet, there are seven ruinous sins:

1. Associating anything with God
2. Magic
3. Killing people without reason
4. Taking interest on money
5. Taking the property of an orphan
6. Running away from battle when *Jihad* has been declared
7. Accusing an innocent woman of adultery.

Some sects add to these: disbelief, fornication, sodomy, cuckolding, refusal of alms, despairing of God's mercy, disobeying parents, disavowing of kinship, swearing a false oath, fraudulent measuring or weighing, drinking alcohol, postponing the *salat*, suppressing evidence, theft, bribery, eating pork, breaking the fast of Ramadan, treachery and fighting believers.

It is the duty of a Muslim to show repentence for sins immediately; any delay in itself constitutes a sin. There is no place in the system for discussion or ambiguity. Canonical punishment for sins is stipulated in the Koran, and such punishment, when administered, automatically confers forgiveness.

Death

The sheer scale of the obligations set upon an orthodox Muslim's life and the difficulties that might be found in keeping them, are acknowledged by the rewards that await the faithful after death. Paradise, which offers unimaginable pleasure and fulfillment, is described in some detail in the Koran. There are also specific descriptions of Death, the Resurrection, the Last Judgement, and Hell, so that no one can be in doubt about their options in eternity.

Death takes place when men reach the age which God has appointed for them. After death each person will be asked by the examining angels: 'Who is thy lord, what is thy religion and who is thy Prophet?' If the person gives the satisfactory answer: 'God is my Lord, Islam my religion and Mohammed my Prophet' he is assured of the mercy of God and the delights of Paradise. If the answer is unsatisfactory, two angels beat him between the eyes and he is doomed to eternal hell-fire. Dragons will torment him to the day of Resurrection, and his grave will be made narrow to crush him. The infidel will suffer such torments forever, the disobedient believer for a period according to his sins. Prophets and martyrs are said to be not subject to examination. Angels are also exempt, but not the *jinn*.

It is written that obedient believers will go to Paradise and that infidels will go to Hell. Disobedient believers will also go to Paradise if they are penitent. If they are unrepentant God will pardon or torment them as He pleases, but He will not leave them in Hell forever because they are believers and must not be treated like infidels.

Resurrection

The exact time of the Resurrection is known only to God. At the approach of the Last Day, the Hour may be known by certain signs such as the appearance of the Mahdi,[1] who will go from Medina to Mecca, the appearance of an antichrist who will ride an ass and be followed by 70,000 Jews, and who will finally be slain by Jesus, the descent of Jesus[2], near the Mosque at Damascus during afternoon prayer, the appearance of the barbarian nations Gog and Magog who will invade the Holy Land and proceed to Jerusalem where Jesus will request God to destroy them, the rising of the sun in the West, the destruction of the *Kaaba*, and other inescapable signals.

The Hour

The sign of the imminent coming of the Hour will be the sounding of the trumpet which will strike terror into the hearts of all creatures; all buildings and mountains will be levelled, the heavens will melt, the sun will be darkened, and the seas will dry up. This will be followed by a second blast when all creatures in heaven and earth will die. Between the two blasts all creatures will be in an intermediate state between insensibility and death for 40 years.

Judgement

At the sound of the blast of Resurrection all souls will repair to their bodies and mankind will go to the place of assembly for Judgement. The graves of the dead will open up and their occupants will join the assembly. God will appear and, according to tradition, Mohammed will rise first and place himself on the throne at God's right hand. All the other Prophets will then take their places under him.

All creatures will be questioned, and a balance will be set up to weigh the books of good and bad actions. Each man will be handed his

1. A ruler who will appear in order to preside over the earth's last days. The Shi'ites say he has already appeared as the 12th *imam*, and resides in some secret place until the end of the world. The Sunnis say he has yet to appear.
2. It is prophesied that Jesus will marry, beget children, die at 40, and be buried at Medina.

own account and will be asked to read it. A good man is said to be given his book in his right hand. After each account is rendered and each man's actions weighed, sentence is pronounced according to whether the good actions outweigh the bad. A bridge will then be spread over the midst of Hell and all will have to pass over it. All men without exception will pass through Hell. Believers will pass through quickly, while infidels remain there forever.

The judgement is passed on the individual and is not influenced by a man's position, kinsmen or wealth. Tradition has it that in earlier times whole communities went to Hell because they showed solidarity in rejecting the prophet sent to them. In the later passages of the Koran, however, the issue is belief or unbelief: man must not only fulfil the will of God, he must also believe in it.

Paradise and Hell

The result of the Judgement is either everlasting bliss or everlasting torment. There is no intermediate condition. Some scholars have interpreted certain Koranic passages as implying that a state of Purgatory exists, but it is universally accepted that there are only two *final* destinations, Paradise and Hell.

There are many names for the place to which the condemned are sentenced — the most common is *an-nar*, the Fire. The torments of the damned are depicted with a wealth of detail. The overseers of Hell are angels instructed by God to administer punishment, and since all water is in Paradise, the damned of Hell must beg for it. The righteous, having crossed the bridge, will enter Paradise and enjoy all sensual and spiritual pleasures.

Paradise is described as abundance and luxuries of many kinds for the gratification and enjoyment of the blessed. The recurring image is that of believers reclining on silken couches, in surroundings perfect in every detail. There is an abundance of fruit and wine served by ever-youthful boys. The reference to wine is interesting in view of the prohibition on alcohol, but its quality is such that it does not befuddle the mind or pain the head. The setting is quite specifically a garden with rivers of pure water, milk and honey.

The imagination of both East and West has made much of the *houris* of Paradise, and there are several passages in the Koran describing the maidens who are to be companions of the believers. They are spotless but amorous virgins resembling pearls, ruby or coral, with swelling breasts unseen and untouched by men or *jinn*. Their eyes are cast down in modesty and they are perpetually enclosed in pavilions.

But Paradise does not consist only of bodily and sensual pleasures; it also includes spiritual delights. The believers experience forgiveness, peace and the satisfaction of the soul in God, and ultimately they receive the most precious gift of all — seeing the face of God.

The relevance of all this to men is quite clear. What is intended for women is not so clear. The Koran says:

> Whosoever does an evil deed shall be
> recompensed only with the like of it,
> but whosoever does a religious deed,
> be it male or female, believing — those shall
> enter Paradise, therein provided
>   without reckoning.

(Koran 40:43)

Again, we are shown the faithful 'busy in their rejoicing, they and their spouses, reclining upon couches in the shade' (Koran 36:55). Dark eyed *houris* are promised to each man as brides and it seems likely that women, or at least those who survive the Judgement, will be transformed to occupy the place allotted to them in Paradise. Just as each man will be perpetually 36, so each woman will be a uniform but unspecified age, and will be endowed with considerable physical charm.

What is true of women in Paradise is true also of children. They are mentioned in the general scheme of things as 'immortal youths' (Koran 76:19) and the Koran states

> ...those who believed, and their seed followed them
> in belief, We shall join their seed with them

(Koran 52:21)

It is not stated whether children are subjected to the Last Judgement, or at what age a person becomes responsible for his actions.

The eighth century scholar Abu Hanifa, founder of the Hanafi school of religious law, gave no answer to the question of whether the infants of disbelievers will have to answer for themselves on the Day of Judgement, or whether they will go to Hell or Paradise, and there are contradictory traditions. One tradition says that every child is born into the law of God, and therefore will enter Paradise. A follower of Hanifa has said 'I am certain God will not commit anyone to the punishment (of Hell) until he has committed sin'.

However, it is not sensible to seek a single consistent picture, as the images suggest what it is beyond man's capacity to conceive. The fundamental message is that Paradise holds the means to satisfy man's deepest relationships and most profound spiritual needs.

Kalam (Theology)

There is no church in Islam, no hierarchy, and no central See directing affairs. *Kalam* literally means speech (of God) which is the Koran. It also has a technical meaning — the process of advancing reasoned arguments to support religious beliefs. A practitioner of *kalam* is called a *mutakallim*.

It is probably true that in Islam theology does not occupy such an important place as in, say, Christianity. Mohammed was, after all, a Prophet not a theologian, and he belonged to a people with no previous philosophical or intellectual tradition. Indeed, in early times the problems facing theology were political rather than religious, involving the leadership of the community. Following the murder of the third Caliph Uthman, the issue of political power took the form of religious discussions among the contending parties: the first problem was that of predestination and free will, and the second that of major and minor sins, and whether a sinner is excluded from Islam.

The question of predestination and free will is clearly raised in the Koran:

> Surely your Lord is God, who created
> the heavens and the earth in six days,
> then sat Himself upon the Throne,
> directing the affair...
>> Will you not remember?

(Koran 10:3)

> And beware a day when no soul for another
> shall give satisfaction, and no counterpoise
> shall be accepted from it, nor any
> intercession shall be profitable to it,
>> neither shall they be helped.

(Koran 2:117)

Embodied in these two verses are the twin teachings that God alone is responsible for conducting the affairs of the universe, but that every individual is personally responsible and personally accountable for his actions.

These matters were first raised in a critical sense by the establishment of the Umayyad family dynasty over the Muslim world in Damascus in 661. Their rise had been accomplished by the defeat of some of the most respected of Mohammed's followers, including his son-in-law and cousin, Ali. The Umayyads justified their rise to power by stating that all things happen according to the will of God. Against this government propaganda, factions arose to argue that man has free will and controls his own destiny; therefore to oppose a government was not to oppose God.

The arguments become more sophisticated as Islamic scholars met Christians in such centres as Damascus in the second and third Islamic centuries. Christian scholars, armed with a more developed theology, stimulated Muslim thinkers to attain a better grasp of their religious convictions in order to defend their faith. This, together with contact with Greek analytical thought, absorbed by a group called Mu'tazilites, gave birth to the *kalam*.

Good and Evil

The Mu'tazilites claimed that human reason, independent of revelation, is capable of distinguishing good from evil, and that revelation confirmed the findings of reason. Man is therefore expected to do right even if there were no prophets and no divine revelation. Revelation must therefore be interpreted in accordance with rational ethics, and its function is twofold. First, God's aim is to aid man in making the right choice between good and evil (for which reason He sends prophets). Secondly, revelation is necessary to make clear the positive obligations of religion, such as prayers and fasting, which would not be known without revelation.

The most significant and lasting contribution to the *kalam* was made by al-Ashari (born 260/873) who marshalled sophisticated arguments in defence of conservative Islamic doctrines. His views with slight modifications represent the theological stance of most Sunni Muslims today.

Free Will and Predestination

Perhaps the most subtle and difficult of these stances is the relationship between free will and predestination. Every Muslim must believe in God's absolute decree and predestination of both good and evil, and that God has from eternity predetermined and decreed literally everything — good, bad, belief, unbelief, and that everything that has been or will be depends on His will. At the same time Muslims believe that man is responsible for his actions and deserves reward or punishment for them. These apparently contradictory ideas are reconciled in theological distinctions between man's and God's spheres of power. Man's actions are of two kinds — voluntary and involuntary. Both are created and produced by God alone, and man has no influence whatever over them. But because God causes both power and choice to exist in man, man's actions as created are ascribed to God, but as produced are ascribed to man. In any event, no man can question that he will be judged by his evil doings, even though all is created by God, because, ultimately, no man has the right to question the doings of God.

Muslim Sects

Although the Koran warns against discord and emphasizes that believers should not allow themselves to be divided into factions, no one leader emerged after the fourth Caliph to hold Islam together. After the death of Ali, differences in interpreting doctrine arose, largely as a result of political pressure, and differing groups appeared.

Mohammed is said to have prophesied that his followers would divide into numerous sects and the number of Muslim sects today exceeds even those of the Christians.

The four main divisions are derived from the schools of law, and these have produced an immense number of commentaries and other works, all differing on a variety of points but coinciding in general principle.

Sunnis or Sunnites

The majority of Muslims are Sunnis — followers of the *Sunna*, the orthodox and traditional doctrine. The Sunnis recognize the legitimacy of the first four Caliphs as leaders of the community and upholders of the law. They used to see the Caliphate as the property of the Quraysh tribe, the tribe of the Prophet. From the Quraysh the man of the most profound faith and outstanding ability would become leader. But religious authority rests wholly in the Koran and the *Sunna* and on the interpretation based on the consensus of the community, the *ijma*.

Shi'ites

After the death of Mohammed, one party (*shia* means party) contended that the succession should remain with the closest relative of the Prophet. They therefore favoured Ali, his son-in-law. Shi'ite is derived from Shiat Ali, the party of Ali. Although Ali eventually became Caliph, he was preceded by three other men and soon lost his rule to the Umayyads. A central religious belief fo the Shi'ites is that God has chosen a series of *imams* for the leadership of the community and endowed them with special knowledge providing a source of living guidance. Therefore the Shi'ites believe that true Islam cannot be known and practised without the guidance of the *imam* God has chosen. To the Sunnis this confers a degree of divinity upon leaders and is blasphemous. Similarly the Shi'ites do not recognize the *ijma* (consensus).

Some would argue also that the leadership conferred on the *imam* allows a more flexible attitude to social, economic and political change, as interpretation of the faith is given an emphasis which is not matched in the Sunni doctrine.

The Shi'ites are well spread throughout the Islamic world and are most numerous in Iran, Iraq, Southern Arabia and the Indian subcontinent.

Ismaili

The most important of the smaller sects is the Ismaili, who hold that the Prophet will be followed by seven *imams* who will interpret the will of God to man.

Kharijites

Another important group are the Kharijites (the seceders or rebels) who are strict conformists. They asserted that the Caliph could be any Muslim, irrespective of race or tribe, provided that he had the purity to make him the finest.

The Kharijites held that any who committed a grave error or sin and did not repent ceased to be a Muslim. The profession of faith alone did not make a person a Muslim unless his faith was accompanied by righteous deeds. This aggressive idealism was accompanied by the belief that *Jihad* was among the cardinal pillars of Islam and the Kharijites interpreted 'enjoining good and forbidding evil' to mean the vindication of truth through the sword. This inflammable combination resulted in almost constant rebellion against nearly every established authority and led to their virtual extinction during the first two centuries of Islam, although a moderate group of Kharijites have survived in the form of Ibadis, who retain the beliefs without resorting to the aggressive methods.

Although the differences between Muslim sects are often deeply felt and sometimes lead to conflict and violence, they should be viewed by the outside world as domestic quarrels. The overriding belief and faith is that Islam is true, monolithic and indivisible.

Sufism

Orthodox Sunni Islam is a relatively austere intellectual faith. It lacks ceremony, authoritarian leaders and outward passion. Its sophistication has little appeal to the emotional needs of the rural masses far removed from the centres of learning and the great mosques. A subtle streak of mysticism has been present in Islam for centuries in the form of Sufism, which offers a new dimension to the religion of the mosque and the law courts. Sufism, or mystical Islam, named after the crude woolen garments (*suf*) of itinerant holy men, has appeared within all theological schools of Islam and is, in a sense, independent of them. It represents an alternative approach to the divine.

The highest point of veneration for the Prophet was reached among the Sufis. Many Sufis regarded Mohammed as the eternal manifestation of the very force which created and sustains the universe, and through which alone God may be approached and known. The effect of this piety was to confer on Mohammed supernatural qualities which both he and orthodox belief were careful to avoid.

As in other mystical sects, Sufi ascetics cultivated the ecstasy of intimate union with God through discipline and overwhelming love for the divine. They developed their philosophy of the faith from the eighth century through defining mystical experiences, and by the 12th century orders of Sufics were organized throughout the Islamic world. A Sufic order was known as *tariqa*, or way to attain union with God. Each order was headed by a *sheikh*, the arbiter of spiritual knowledge, who with his followers maintained an establishment similar to a monastery where members lived out their régime of discipline and meditation.

These were important social institutions because common people had access to them, not only for spiritual advice, but also for food, medical care and even financial assistance. Some orders became very powerful, notably the Safawid order, which became the nucleus of the Persian Safawid Empire, and the Baktashi order of Turkey. Each order was distinguished by the special ceremony of worship and meditation, perhaps the most famous of which is the dance of the Turkish Malawi order, the whirling dervishes. A later development of Sufism was the designation of saints and this aspect still appeals to ordinary Muslims. These Sufi masters are believed to possess spiritual power and the ability to perform miracles.

Great reverence is paid to saints and when one dies his tomb becomes a place of pilgrimage. Reverence for saints has led to some abuses in Sufism and modern Muslims seeking to purge Islam of superstition have caused a decline of Sufism among the educated throughout the Islamic world, but it retains its hold on the masses.

*   *   *

The notion of love for one's neighbour, in a Christian sense, is not enshrined in the Koran. There are certain prescribed duties towards the disadvantaged, the poor, widows, orphans, slaves and the vanquished, but these are of a practical nature, and no emotional commitment is required or expected. There is also the concept of Muslim brotherhood. He who accepts the faith and becomes a believer is automatically accepted as a Muslim brother without question. This confers certain rights of treatment which do not apply to unbelievers.

This underlines the essentially practical nature of the Islamic faith. God's will is interpreted as a series of rules for all occasions, and either one conforms to them or one does not. Conforming to them has certain consequences, breaking them has others. This rigid simplicity is the underlying structure of Islamic thought, and will be present, whether open or hidden, in all circumstances, from international affairs to trivial domestic matters.

Chapter 3
Islamic Law

Apart from the status of women in Islam, nothing seems to excite a more hostile reaction in the West than what are thought to be the standards of its traditional law. In many ways the heart of Islam is its law, but this law includes much more than any legal system devised in the West. Not only does it deal with matters of religious ritual, it also evaluates every aspect of political, social and private life.

The Sharia

The general term for law in Arabic is *sharia*, which can be roughly translated as 'the path in which God wishes men to walk', and every human deed without exception falls under the perspective of the law. There has been no more far reaching effort to lay out a complete pattern of human conduct than the Islamic *sharia*.

The general assumption underlying the *sharia* is that men are incapable of discriminating between right and wrong by their own unaided powers. It is for this reason that guidance was sent to them through prophets. God, who is all powerful, revealed a path for men, based upon his unrestricted sovereign will. His will is not to be judged by human reason, and it must be obeyed in total and without question. For a Muslim the *sharia* represents divine and eternal law, and is consequently completely trustworthy. It is the basic institution of Islamic civilization, and underpins the certainty that Muslims have always felt about the correctness of their way of life. Law is therefore linked in the Muslim mind with a comprehensive set of rules for life which, if followed, please God in this world and earn salvation in the next.

In all Western systems law is associated with the state, applies to all within its territorial boundaries, and is enforced by a police power. None of these facts holds true of Islamic law. It is binding primarily upon individuals who stand directly in a relationship with God, and it is not enforced by the state. Although there are some rules for non-Muslims, most of the provisions of the *sharia* apply to Muslims living in Islamic territory, and can become inoperative in foreign lands.

The limit of Western systems of law is generally to regulate man's relationship with his neighbour and with the state, but the *sharia* includes also his relationship with God and his own conscience. Usually, the first chapters in the legal manuals deal with basic religious duties and ritual practices. The *sharia* is as much concerned with ethical practices, and what man should or should not do in conscience, as with what he is entitled or bound to do in law. These acts are divided into those which are praiseworthy (and therefore find divine favour) and those which are blameworthy (and therefore bring divine disfavour) but in neither case is there any legal sanction or punishment, nor any reward.

Another major distinction between the *sharia* and Western systems is the Muslim belief that law expresses the divine will. On Mohammed's death God's revelations ceased, which meant that the form and content of his revelations were fixed and unchangeable. The result of this is that when the *sharia* law was crystallized and recorded in the medieval manuals it became a rigid and unchangeable system. In sharp contrast to the Western secular systems of law, which grew out of social circumstances and change in society, Islamic law moulds and fashions society itself.

The Basic Features

None of the modern classifications or distinctions between categories of law exists in the religious law of Islam[1]; there is even no clear separation of worship, ethics and law in the Western sense. Consequently, although it is convenient for the Western reader to consider various aspects of the law under separate headings, the subject matter is in fact continually overlapping, and there is no sense of systematic distinction.

The fundamental principle underlying the whole of Islamic religious law is intent. Originally this applied to the ritual worship, which is not considered valid unless it is accompanied by pious intent. Silence cannot be taken to replace a declaration of consent, except in a few special cases. In theory, evidence in writing is accepted unconditionally only from a mute person, and from others with considerable reservations, but modern practice has considerably modified this traditional view. In matters of fraud there is little inclination to protect the victim. The effect of duress is given considerable scope, not only in removing the penal sanction but in making the act itself permissible. For instance, drinking wine or having illegal intercourse under threat of death or injury is permissible; indeed, refusal would be sinful.

1. See Joseph Schacht, *An Introduction to Islamic Law,* Oxford University Press, 1964.

Under the law all men's actions are divided into five categories: obligatory, recommended, indifferent, disapproved, and forbidden. Islamic law does not recognize institutions or corporate bodies as entities in their own right. Government is not recognized by the traditional law, and therefore the Ministry of Financial Affairs, for example, is owned not by the government but by the Muslim community, (ie, the sum total of individual Muslims).

The capacity to transact legally belongs to a person who is *rashid*. Technically this means of prudent judgement and is normally associated with reaching puberty. Both sexes are said to have reached puberty by the age of 15, but in no case can a boy attain puberty below the age of 12, or a girl below the age of nine. People who are not *rashid*, because of minority or deficiency, are placed under interdiction and their affairs are managed by a guardian.

A fully responsible citizen is a free Muslim who is sane and of age. Legally a women has fewer rights and duties from the religious point of view. In respect of blood money, evidence, and inheritance she is counted as half a man. In marriage and divorce she has fewer rights than a man. She is equal to a man in terms of the law of property and obligations, and may act as a *qadi* (judge) in certain matters. The legal rights of slaves are as carefully defined by the law as those of free men.

The legal position of non-Muslims in Islam relates to the law of war; they must either be converted (not by force)or be subjugated or killed (except women, children and slaves). By tradition, under a treaty of surrender Muslims may undertake to safeguard the life and property of non-Muslims who are called *dhimmis*. By this arrangement the non-Muslims live and work under certain disadvantages, but their freedom of religion is guaranteed and they are free to observe their own customs. A non-Muslim who is not protected by a treaty is an enemy alien and his life and property are completely unprotected by the law. In criminal law the *dhimmi* is liable to *hadd* (see page 62) and discretionary punishments as far as they are not specifically Muslim. Thus, a *dhimmi* would not be subject to *hadd* for drinking wine, but would be subject to discretionary punishment. Non-Muslims have complete legal freedom provided they do not interfere with the religious interests of Muslims. Freedom in matters of religion is explicitly guaranteed.

The Concepts of Islamic Law

In spite of its divine origin, Islamic law does not claim universal application. Inside Islamic territory it is binding in full for the Muslim, but outside its application is more limited. For example, according to the Hanafi school it is legal for Muslims to indulge in *riba* (interest)with non-Muslims in enemy territory. Furthermore, the law takes for granted the decadence and corruption in contemporary society. It has an inbuilt, matter-of-fact view of human fallibility, and has not remained immune from such practices as the bribing of witnesses and *qadis*, or tolerating the abuses of corrupt governments, and highly placed individuals, over whom the *qadis* were powerless. Islamic law considers valid the appointment of a *qadi* who is not 'of good character', nor does it question a judgement based on the evidence of a witness who is not of good character, or even the appointment of a *qadi* by a political authority which is not legitimate.

As in the field of worship, obligatory acts are accompanied by others which are only recommended. For instance, heirs can be recommended, but are not obliged, to pay the debts of the deceased, and even the next of kin who has the right to demand retaliation for murder is recommended to waive it against the payment of blood money.

Joseph Schacht[1] has pointed out that it was the first legal specialists themselves who created the system of Islamic law; they did not borrow it from pre-Islamic sources, although these sources did provide many of its material elements. Similarly, the development of Islamic law can be distinguished from that of Roman law in a fundamental way. In Roman law it was the growing importance of commercial life which called for the creation of corresponding legal forms; in Islamic law it was the religious zeal of a growing number of Muslims which demanded the application of religious norms to all aspects of behaviour. If the Roman jurists were to be useful to their clients they had to try to predict the probable reactions of the magistrates and judges to each transaction; if the earliest Islamic lawyers were to fulfil their relgious duty, as they saw it, they had to search their consciences in order to know what good Muslims were allowed or forbidden to do. In Islamic law even the two formal legal concepts valid and invalid are continually pushed into the background by the Islamic concepts of allowed and forbidden. The aim of Islamic law is to provide concrete and material standards, not to impose formal rules on the interplay of contending interests, which is the aim of secular law. Consideration of good faith, fairness, justice, truth and so on play only a subordinate part in the system. The rules of Islamic law are valid by virtue of their existence and not because of their rationality. If, for example, a boy is mutilated accidentally on being circumcised, the full blood money is paid, but if he dies only half the blood money is paid. This is because half of the cause of death is attributed to the circumcision itself (because this alone may cause death) and only half to the mutilation. Only this second half creates liability because the performance of circumcision

1. Ibid.

(which is recommended or obligatory according to the school of law) does not in itself create liability. If the owner of a wall which threatens to collapse sells it after he has been asked to demolish it, and it them collapses and kills someone, neither the seller nor the buyer is liable; not the seller because he was not the owner at the time it collapsed, and not the buyer because he had not been asked to demolish it.

However it it not unknown for Islamic law to diverge from a formally correct decision for reasons of fairness or appropriateness. But according to some Western lawyers this principle, both in theory and application, occupies too subordinate a position for it to be able to influence positive law to any considerable degree. Further, although Islamic law possesses an impressive number of legal concepts, they are, generally speaking, derived not from the realities of legal life but from abstract thought. For instance, a finder may use found property if he is poor, but not if he is rich; if he is rich he is entitled to make it a charitable gift (*sadaqa*). Even this is not strictly applied however, because if the finder's parents or children are poor he is entitled to give it to them.

It is important to understand that public powers are, as a rule, reduced to private rights or duties, and the essential duties of the Islamic state are seen not as functions of the community but as duties to be fulfilled by a number of individuals. The whole concept of an institution is missing.

The idea of criminal guilt hardly exists and, apart from religious expiation and one or two other exceptions, there is no fixed penalty for any infringement of the rights of a human being or the violation of his person and property, only the exact reparation of the damage caused. Monetary fines are unknown. Also the execution of the judgement in this sphere is, in principle, a matter for the party in whose favour it is given.

The Schools of Law

Although the basis of the *sharia* is the Koran, the holy book is in no sense a comprehensive legal code. A relatively small number of verses deal with strictly legal matters and these cover a wide variety of topics. Their main effect was to introduce many new rules and to simplify and modify the existing Arabian customary law. When Mohammed was alive he was the supreme judge of the community and resolved legal problems as they arose by interpreting the provisions of the Koran, as did the Caliph of Medina after his death. This served the community well when it was small, but it would not do for the vast empire that came into being shortly after the Prophet's death. An organized judiciary evolved with the appointment of judges (*qadis*) to the various provinces and districts. In the absence of a detailed documented legal code the *qadis* had considerable discretion in applying the law. Their decisions were based upon the rules of the Koran wherever these were relevant, but where there was no clear parallel or precedent they interpreted the law as best they could, very often absorbing elements from Roman and Persian law in the process.

Early in the eighth century groups of pious scholars began to debate whether the law was being administered in accordance with the religious ethic of Islam. These early jurists reviewed all current legal practice in the light of Koranic principles, and established an Islamic code as part of their ideal scheme of law.

The two most important schools of law were founded by Malik ibn Anas and Abu Hanifa, and became known as the Malikis in Medina and the Hanafis in al-Kufah. Because the early law schools wrote independently from each other and were subject to different influences and social pressures, it is not surprising that they came to different conclusions on certain issues. Perhaps the most important of these was the deep conflict of principle which emerged between those who maintained that outside the terms of the Koran scholars were free to use their reason to ascertain the law, and those who insisted that the only valid source of law outside the Koran lay in the precedents set by the Prophet himself.

The third school of Sunni law was founded by the jurist al-Shafii (died 820) who tried to produce a greater uniformity in the law by eliminating conflicts and defining the exact sources from which the law must be derived. He taught that proper knowledge of the *sharia* could be found only through the divine revelation either in the Koran or in the divinely inspired precedents (*Sunna*) of the Prophet as ascertained through authentic reports (*hadith*). Human reason was to be employed only in cases not specifically answered by divine revelation, confining itself strictly to arguing from the principles of closely parallel cases to be derived from the Koran or *Sunna*. Al-Shafii's reliance upon the importance of the *Sunna* triggered off remarkable and intensive activity to establish as accurately as possible all the sayings and actions of the Prophet in order to compile a complete catalogue of precedents covering as many aspects of behaviour as possible. As very little, if anything, was written down at the time of the Prophet, this immense undertaking had to be carried out by personally interviewing descendants of the Prophet, and his Companions and Followers. The character and reliability of each person interviewed had to be assessed and documented. Each facet of each story (evidence) had to be checked back through preceding generations, and at every point the character of the person passing on the information had to be investigated.

As a result of al-Shafii's work the legal process had crystallized in the 10th century into a specific procedure. The jurist must first consult the Koran and the *Sunna*. When a specific solution cannot be found from these sources, he must deduce precedents for the situation and take into account the public interest. The results of this process must then be evaluated against *ijma*, or the consensus (of scholars). The result of these deliberations could be either a tentative conclusion or conjecture on the part of individual jurists, or, if there was unanimous agreement, a certain and infallible expression of God's law.

The consensus view was originally permissive in the sense that it allowed the validity of different opinions in man's attempt to define the *sharia*. Later it became restrictive, because once the consensus had agreed on the variations that were legitimately possible, the subject was frozen and any further variations or opinions were bordering on heresy. Once the *ijma* had been concluded and the result recorded in the legal manuals, further individual speculation and interpretation ceased, and subsequent jurists were bound to follow the doctrine as it was recorded in the 10th century. This method of finding out the precise terms of the *sharia* is known as *fiqh* (understanding).

The division between the various law schools became geographically defined as the *qadis'* courts favoured the doctrine of one school above the others. In this way Hanafi law became predominant in the Middle East and India; Malaki law in North West and Central Africa; Shafi'i law in East Africa and the southern parts of Arabia, Malaysia and Indonesia; Hanbali in Saudi Arabia.

Apart from the four schools of Sunni or orthodox Islam there are the minority sects, the Shi'ites and Ibadis, whose interpretation of the *sharia* is considerably different from that of the Sunni. In particular the Shi'ite view that the *imams* are divinely inspired, and are therefore the natural rulers of the community, gives rise to a different balance within the law. Shi'ite law is applied in Iran and in the Shi'i communities of India and Africa; Ibadi law applied in Zanzibar, Oman and parts of Syria.

Procedures

The rules of procedure and evidence in *sharia* law are quite different from any Western system. Traditionally the court is administered by a single *qadi*, who is the judge of the facts as well as the law. When confronted by a difficult issue, he has discretion to seek the advice of a professional jurist or *mufti*. There are no superior courts or systems of appeal. The court procedure is simple and without ceremony and is controlled by the *qadi* through his clerk. The parties usually appear in person, although legal representation is permitted.

The *qadi's* first responsibility is to decide which party bears the burden of proof. The initial legal presumption attaching to each case is that the accused is innocent, and the burden of proof rests with the prosecution or the claimant, but the burden of proof might shift between the parties in a case where counter-claims are made. The standard of proof required is a rigid one and basically the same in criminal and civil cases. If an admission of guilt by a defendant is not forthcoming, the prosecutor or plaintiff is required to produce two witnesses to testify orally to their direct knowledge of the truth of the charge. Circumstantial evidence or written evidence, even if overwhelming, is not normally admissible. Two male adult Muslims of integrity and reliability are required to give oral testimony. Women witnesses are allowed, but two are required in the place of one man. In claims of property one witness is often enough, together with the plaintiff's own solemn oath as to the truth of his claim. The prosecutor is given judgement if he produces proof in the required form. If his evidence is not substantial, the defendant will receive judgement in his favour. In cases where the evidence is not conclusive, or not properly given, a sworn oath by the defendant can win him the judgement, but if he refuses to take the oath, judgement is given to the other side. The importance of the sworn oath, and consequently the reliability of a person's word, can be gauged by the importance attached to it by the courts. Two witnesses are the prescribed number; no advantage accrues to the side producing more than two.

Stringent demands are made of witnesses in terms of qualifications and the content of their statements, particularly in the evidence on unlawful intercourse where four male witnesses are required instead of the normal two. They must testify as eye witnesses, and in order to qualify for the *hadd* punishment a confession of unlawful intercourse must be made on four separate occasions. A further safeguard lies in the fact that if the witnesses, or any one of them, are found to be false or there are discrepancies between them, they are all in principle liable to the *hadd* punishment themselves.

There is no official prosecution or punishment for murder, bodily harm or damage to property, only a guarantee of the right of private vengeance. In these cases pardon and amicable settlement are possible, but repentance has no effect.

In most cases the simple procedures of the *qadi* court give rise to an almost automatic process. In this traditional system, once the matter of the burden of proof is settled, witnesses are or are not produced, the oath is or is not administered and sworn, and the verdict follows automatically.

However, although the *sharia* doctrine was always the focal point of the legal system, it was never exclusively authoritative, and has always recognized jurisdiction other than that of the *qadis*. The *qadis'* courts have a cumbersome system of procedure and evidence, and did not prove satisfactory in all cases; very rough justice was often done, particularly in respect of criminal, land and commercial law. Accordingly, other courts were set up, known collectively as *mazalin*, for these purposes, and the jurisdiction of the *qadis* was generally confined to private family and civil law.

Punishment

The penalities prescribed by Islamic law fall into two groups; private vengeance, and punishment of crimes against religion and military discipline. In Islamic law the first group has survived almost intact. Crimes against religion are: unlawful intercourse; its counterpart, false accusation of unlawful intercourse; drinking wine; theft; and highway robbery. The punishments prescribed for them are fixed and are called *hadd*. According to the offence, punishment can vary from death to flogging. There are no fines in Islamic law.

The *hadd* is the right of God, so no pardon or amicable settlement is possible. Prosecutions for false accusation of unlawful intercourse or theft take place only on the demand of the persons concerned, and the applicant must be present both at the trial and at the punishment. In the case of unlawful intercourse the witnesses play the major part; if they are not present (and if they do not cast the first stone) the punishment is not carried out. The religious character of the *hadd* punishment is shown by the part played by active repentance; if the thief returns the stolen goods before prosecution, or repents from highway robbery before arrest, the *hadd* lapses. In cases of unlawful intercourse and drinking wine it must be proved that the act was voluntary. Only one *hadd* is applied for several offences of the same kind. Proof for *hadd* offences is made difficult. Confessions can be withdrawn, and the *qadi* should suggest this possibility to the accused, except in a case of false accusation of unlawful intercourse.

Witnesses are recommended not to testify against accused people, and the judge is obliged to give full weight to all the circumstances extenuating the guilt of the guilty. By contrast, where punishment established by the law of *hadd* is concerned, the judge has no choice and must execute the prescribed punishment. In these cases even a plea for mercy by or on behalf of the accused is not allowed. However, in order to establish guilt, very difficult legal proof is always required, and the rules allow everybody the opportunity for escaping punishment. In cases involving *hadd* a confession of guilt is required before 'determined punishment' can be executed, and consequently punishment takes on the character of penitence.[1]

Preventive or punitive action may be taken under the law for reasons of public policy. Muslims who refuse to obey the *imam* are forced into obedience and are not subject to any special penal sanction. A male apostate from Islam is condemned to death, but he is normally reprieved for three days to give him an opportunity to return to the faith. A woman who commits apostasy is imprisoned and beaten every three days until she returns to Islam. There are no legal penalties for offences against religion, even for neglect of the ritual prayer. There is no punishment for perjury or for giving false evidence; it is simply given publicity, and in certain cases liability arises for any damage caused.

There exists no general concept of penal law in Islam. The concepts of guilt and criminal responsibility are little developed, and that of mitigating circumstances does not exist. On the other hand the theory of punishments, with its distinction of private vengeance, *hadd* punishments, *tazir*[2] and coercive and preventive measures, shows a considerable variety of ideas.

Hadd Punishments

Hadd means an unalterable punishment prescribed by canon law which is considered a right of God.

There is no concept of marital fidelity in Islamic law. Married people are not required to be faithful *to each other*, and sexual intercourse outside the legal bounds is not a violation of the married partners' rights, but an offence against God. In unlawful intercourse (*zina*) a distinction is made between people who are *muhsan*, and those who are not. In the category of *muhsan* is a free person who has concluded and consummated a valid marriage with a free partner, or who is able to do so. Such a person, if convicted of unlawful intercourse, is subject to the punishment of death by stoning. The penalty for a person outside this category is 100 lashes (50 for a slave). Unbelievers cannot be *muhsan*, but strictly speaking they are subject to the Islamic law and the punishment of flogging.

The *hadd* punishment for drinking wine, and this includes being drunk and incapable for whatever cause, is 80 lashes (40 for slaves) though the application of this punishment is made difficult by the required proof that the act was voluntary. This means that the *hadd* cannot be applied automatically to a person found drunk and incapable, and further proof of intent is required.

1. This is not to say that these provisions of Islamic law have always been recognized by Muslim authorities. Arbitrary and self-interested punishment has been, and still is, inflicted under Islam as under any other code of law.
2. A punishment intended to prevent the culprit from relapsing, to purify him.

Theft is defined as taking by stealth something of the value of at least 10 *dirhams* for which the culprit has neither the right of ownership nor custody. Excluded from the category of *hadd* punishments are all those things found in Islamic territory which are not strictly speaking owned, such as wood, grass, fishes, birds; provided that ownership is not obvious, as in the case of wood in the form of a chair. Also excluded are easily perishable things like meat and unharvested fruit. It excludes also things which cannot be objects of property such as a free person, wine, and musical instruments, and things of which the accused is part owner, such as public property.

The stiplation of custody excludes theft from a near relative, from a house which the accused has been permitted to enter, and embezzlement. Property has to be removed from its legal ownership, therefore a thief caught, say, within a house, according to some, is not subject to *hadd*.

The punishment consists of cutting off the right hand and, in the case of a second theft, the left foot; in the case of further thefts, the thief is imprisoned until he shows repentance.

The crime of highway robbery is related to both theft and murder, and the penalties inflicted differ according to the facts of the case. If only theft is involved, and the value of the property when divided by the number of culprits satisfies the requirement for *hadd*, the right hand and the left foot are cut off; if murder alone has happened, execution with the sword is the penalty; if both plunder and murder have happened, execution by crucifixion is the sentence (Koran 5:33). These punishments are awarded to all accomplices regardless of their individual involvement, except that if one of them for any reason is exempt from *hadd*, for example because he is a minor, the *hadd* for highway robbery lapses for all, although each remains criminally responsible for his individual acts.

Retaliation

Offences against the person from murder to assault are punishable by retaliation (*kisas*) in which the offender is subject to precisely the same treatment as his victim. However, this kind of offence is not technically regarded as a crime since it is not the state which has the right to prosecute, but only the victim or his family.[1] For this reason, these offences have been described as civil injuries and the victim's family may opt for compensation or blood money (*diyah*) in place of retaliation.

1. As retaliation is a matter for the next of kin, when there are several equally related in a family, the demand for *kisas* has to be unanimous among them, otherwise it does not apply. *Kisas* is not applied in the case of accidental killing.

For *kisas* to be applied certain conditions must be fulfilled. For instance, the killer must be a Muslim, adult and in full possession of his faculties. Other conditions are sometimes imposed, but these are disputed in various law schools. For example, when several people commit a murder, and one of them for one reason or another cannot be put to death, the others also escape *kisas*. In addition to these conditions, three of the law schools demanded that before *kisas* can be allowed, the murdered person is at least the equal of the murderer in respect of Islam and liberty, whilst the Hanafis take no account of this. *Kisas* can be applied only in Islamic countries, or in countries under Islamic control.

The penalties for murder vary according to the degree of culpability. A distinction is made between deliberate intent with or without a deadly implement and between killing by mistake and indirect killing. In cases of bodily harm, retaliation takes place for specific injuries. There are rules laid down when a murder is committed and the culprit is unknown. Where a body is found in an inhabited or occupied place, the inhabitants of a street, for example, must swear 50 oaths that they did not kill him. If there are less than 50 people involved then some must swear more than once. If a body is found in a mosque, the public treasury pays the blood money; if it is found in open country, his blood is not avenged.

Although it is the exclusive prerogative of the victim or his next of kin to claim retaliation, Islamic law recommends waiving it. In this case, penance by the culprit can take the form of the freeing of a Muslim slave, or fasting for two consecutive months.

The Koran lays down the principle of retaliation in two different ways. Referring to the Torah given by God to the Jews it reiterates:

> We prescribed for them:
> 'A life for a life, an eye for an eye,
> a nose for a nose, an ear for an ear,
> a tooth for a tooth, and for wounds
> retaliation'
>
> (Koran 5:48)

And:

> O believers, prescribed for you is
> retaliation, touching the slain;
> freeman for freeman, slave for slave,
> female for female.
>
> (Koran 2:174)

It is not surprising that difficulties have arisen in interpreting these two passages. For example, is it intended that a free man can be put to death for the murder of a woman? Although some jurists will insist that this cannot be so, general practice allows this form of retaliation. However, the life of a free Muslim cannot be had in retaliation for the death of a slave, nor can *kisas* be applied to any Muslim for the murder of an unbeliever.

Kisas can be applied only after deliberate proof of guilt is produced. The procedure of proof in a murder trial is the same as in any other case, and the *kasasa*, or solemn oath, plays an important part. The execution of *kisas* is open to the avenger of blood and takes the form of either beheading with a sword, or, within certain limitations, the murderer is put to death in the same way as his victim. If somebody deliberately and evilly inflicts a fatal wound, he is legally liable in principle to similar treatment. If *kisas* is not permitted, or the person entitled to it voluntarily forgoes his claim, compensation may be demanded for an unlawful injury; a form of blood money or *diyah*. A woman receives between one-third and a half of the man's rate depending upon the school of law. A minor or insane person is not liable to pay compensation in ordinary circumstances. The *diyah* for the latter is paid by the state. If a minor and a person of age together kill a Muslim intentionally, the latter is put to death, the former pays half the *diyah*.

Women and children are not liable to pay *diyah*. Employers are liable for injury to employees. Owners are responsible for their animals. People who cause accidents are responsible for the consequences.

Property

Although Islamic law does not define property it recognizes several graded categories on which restrictions are placed in legal transactions.

There are things which by definition cannot be property, and the sale of which is null and void. These include a free person, animals not ritually slaughtered and blood. There are things in which ownership is not vested at all, such as big rivers and public roads; everyone is entitled to use them provided the public interest is not prejudiced. A third category is things in which there is no separate ownership, which means things that do not yet exist independently, such as flour from corn or milk in the udder. (This means that something that has a potentially separate existence, such as un unborn animal, cannot be sold or bartered until it has a separate existence). This includes constituent parts of a whole, such as columns supporting a building (but part of a building, like an apartment or suite can be owned separately). There are things that are defined as property, but on which there are restrictions concerning disposal.

Ownership

Ownership is defined as the right to the complete and exclusive disposal of a thing and is called *milk*. The legal categories of ownership and possesion are numerous and detailed, and often differ from Western ideas. For example expectation can play an important part in acquiring ownership. If a man plants an orchard in order to harvest the fruit, and a bird nests in one of his trees, anyone who takes the eggs, the nest, or the bird for that matter, acquires ownership of them, even though he takes them from land belonging to another. Similarly the owner of land does not have exclusive rights to any minerals or treasure found in it. One fifth must be paid to the public treasury, as is the case for booty taken in war. Ownership can never be acquired by finding. If something is found, a public notice is posted, and if no claim is made the finder is entitled to make a charitable gift. Only if the finder is poor is he entitled to use the object himself, and even then he holds it in trust. If this intention is lacking the finder becomes a usurper. It is an assumption of the law that any property or treasure dating from Islamic times is not ownerless, and must be regarded as found property. In Arabia today articles can be left unattended in the towns for days, and in country districts, or in the desert, for years, the assumption being that one day the owner will return to collect his property.

The concept of public property is restricted in scope by a certain logic. A thoroughfare, for example, is public because it leads somewhere, whereas a blind alley is not, because it does not. To some extent use of public property is free to every person, either for its intended purpose, or sometimes for private use. An individual may loiter, sleep, or trade in the street, or even erect a shelter providing it does not prejudice the public interest. Similarly every person can sue for its removal. Land in the vicinity of an inhabited place is considered a common for the inhabitants.

Land which has no determined owner and is not put to use may be cultivated by anyone on obtaining a license from the *imam*. The license lapses if the applicant fails to cultivate it within three years. In real estate land can be sold, but the right to build upon it cannot.

By tradition the ownership of land seems to have been less important than the acquisition of money. This situation came about by the circumstances of the Arab conquests. Vast areas of cultivable land became available which the conquerers were either unable or unwilling to work themselves. Consequently they extracted revenues in the form of rent and taxes which were controlled by the Caliph who distributed funds among those with a right to payment; a proportion being reserved for the expenses of state and to provide help for the needy as described by the Koran. As a result the idea came into being that real property had to be cultivated or developed thereby generating an income. The right of ownership had to be deserved, and although the right of ownership was not lost through land remaining idle, it could vanish if someone else bought it under cultivation. Although this perhaps explains some of the traditional Muslim attitudes towards ownership it has to be said that custom varied from place to place, and since the 19th century most independent Muslim countries have simply adopted Western land law; in colonial countries reforms were carried out to the benefit of the occupying power.

The common right to water has always been an important issue in the Middle East and on this subject Islamic law has its origins in Iraq rather than Arabia. Big rivers are public property, and small water courses are the joint property of the riparian owners. The right to use water is separated from the land to which it belongs, and although a canal might be privately owned everyone has the right to drink from it, or to use it for the ritual ablution, but he must not trespass on another person's land except in cases of necessity. Water is only considered private property if it is in a container.

Contracts and Obligations

Unjustified profiteering and unjustified risk are both rejected on ethical grounds, and these general prohibitions pervade the whole of the law. Islamic law provides for certain fixed types of contracts within which there is considerable scope for varying terms. Custom plays an important part in contracts, and transactions are allowed only in so far as they are customary. There is no general term for obligation; the nearest approximation to it is care as a duty of conscience. The conclusion of a contract is eesentially informal. The contract is a transaction that requires an offer and an acceptance, which are both normally made in the same meeting. An offer can be withdrawn before acceptance.

In a number of places the Koran prohibits unjustified enrichment, or receiving a monetary advantage without giving a counter value, and he who gains in this way must give the proceeds to the poor as a charitable gift. This applies in particular to reselling a commodity at a higher sum before payment has been made for it, or reletting a hired object for a greater sum (for example a house). The general prohibition applies in the first place to sale and barter, but also to exchange. It is directed against speculation in food and in precious metals.

Based on the Koranic prohibition of a certain game of hazard (*maysir*), Islamic law insists that there must be no doubt concerning the obligations undertaken by the parties to a contract. The object of the contract must be determined or known. This requirement is directed particularly at objects which can be measured or weighed; the quantity must be determined exactly even if the price of a unit of weight or measure is stated. For the same reason it is forbidden to sell unripe fruit to be delivered when ripened, or a house from the architect's drawings, because it is not known whether the fruit will ripen or the house be completed.

The elimination of risk or chance was aimed primarily at forbidding gambling which was a great passion in ancient Arabia. This general principle has been expanded to cover lotteries of any kind, and the award of prizes for any performance. There are only two exceptions to this rule; prizes are allowed for the winner of a horse race, on account of the importance of training horses for Holy War, and for the winners of competitions relating to the knowledge of Islamic law.

The definition of liability is complicated, but in general it arises from either the non-performance of a contract, or from tort, or from a combination of both. Liability is here distinguished from negligence.

Negligence

There is no concept of negligence in Islamic law. The general principle is that it is a person's responsibility to look out for himself. If someone digs a hole and another falls into it, the person who dug the hole is not liable if he did it with permission of the land owner. If somebody erects a building on public property, and another falls through a faulty staircase balustrade no liability arises. If a wall threatens collapse, its owner is only liable if any person (like an adjoining owner) who might suffer has asked him to demolish it.

Interest

All transactions in Islamic law are bound by the doctrine of *riba*. Strictly this is a prohibition on usury, but it was extended to preclude any form of interest on a capital loan or investment. Coupled with the law forbidding gambling transactions, *riba* law in principle does not allow any transaction or speculation the results or benefits of which cannot be forecast precisely.

Waqf Foundations

A unique feature of Islamic law is that relating to *waqf* foundations. This is a procedure whereby an owner relinquishes his right to real estate property which henceforth belongs to God. The income or benefit accruing from such an arrangement is normally invested in some charitable institution, but might include the founder's own family.

Marriage

The family is the only group based on affinity which Islam recognizes. Islam is opposed to tribal solidarity, because the solidarity of believers should supersede the solidarity of the tribe.

Marriage is a contract of civil law. The bridegroom concludes the contract with the legal guardian (*wali*) of the bride and he undertakes to pay a price (*mahr*) or dower directly to his wife, and the amount must be stated in the marriage contract. The contract must be concluded in the presence of free witnesses, two men or one man and two women: this has the double aim of providing proof of marriage, and of disproving unchastity. The contract is the only legally relevant act in concluding marriage. The *wali* is the nearest male relative in the order of succession; he can give his ward in marriage against her will if she is a minor, but when she comes of age she has the right to rescind. Some hold, however, that she does not have this right if her father or grandfather gives her in marriage. Similar rules apply to the bridegroom if he is a minor. A free woman who is fully responsible may give herself in marriage, but the *wali* has the right to object if the prospective husband is not of equal birth.

When the woman has been married previously her consent is necessary, but it is still her father or guardian who contracts the marriage on her behalf. In Shi'ite and Hanafi law only minors may be contracted in compulsory marriage, and adult women contract their own marriage, providing they do not marry beneath their social status.[1] Men may be maried to a maximum of four wives at the same time, but a woman is restricted to one husband. A husband is obliged to support the wife, provided that she is obedient to him in domestic and social matters. A wife who leaves the family home without cause forfeits the right to maintenance.

Divorce

A divorce may be effected simply by the mutual agreement of the spouses, known as *khul*, in which case the wife pays a financial consideration to the husband for her release. In all except Hanafi courts a wife may obtain a divorce on the grounds of some matrimonial offence committed by the husband, such as cruelty, desertion or failure to maintain.

1. See also Chapter 7.

The wife's rights in divorce are strictly limited to the above situations. A unique feature of Islamic law is the right given to the husband unilaterally to terminate a marriage at will by repudiation (*talaq*) of his wife. *Talaq* is an extra-judicial procedure and is not subject to the scrutiny of the courts or any other body. A marriage can be finally and irrevocably dissolved by a repudiation repeated three times. After the first *talaq* a waiting period of three months begins, known as the wife's *idda*, which establishes whether or not she is pregnant. If she is, the *idda* is extended until the birth of the child. During this waiting period a single *talaq* may be revoked at will by the husband and the marriage remains valid.

Legitimacy

A child is indisputably legitimate if it is conceived during the lawful wedlock of its parents, and the legal position of children in respect of inheritance, maintenance and guardianship depends on their legitimacy. There is no legal relationship between a father and his illegitimate child in Sunni law; but for all purposes there is a legal tie between a mother and her illegitimate child. For example, care and control of the person for the purposes of education and marriage, and the property of minors, belongs to the father or a close male relative; the right of custody of young children, if parents are divorced or separated, belongs to the mother of the female paternal relatives.

Inheritance

The law in respect of inheritance is strictly laid down. Two-thirds of the estate passes to the legal heirs of the deceased under the compulsory rules of inheritance. An individual may dispose of the other third at his discretion.

There is a fundamental difference between the Sunni and Shi'ite systems of inheritance. Sunni law is essentially a system of inheritance by male relatives who trace their descent from the deceased through the male line. A share is laid down for each male relative according to class, degree and blood tie. The females among the relatives take half the share of the male relative of the same class, degree and blood and none of them can exclude from inheritance any male agnate, however remote. There is a complicated system of dividing the estate between those entitled to inherit, and the proportion each one receives is determined exactly by the rules laid down, but the system is designed to favour descendants through the male line. If, for example, the deceased is survived by his wife, his daughter's son, and a distant agnatic cousin, the wife will receive a quarter of the estate, the grandson will be excluded altogether, and the cousin will inherit the remaining three-quarters.

Shi'ite law rejects the dominance of the agnatic tie and does not distinguish between male and female connections. In this system the surviving spouse always inherits a fixed portion, as in Sunni law, but all other relatives are divided into three classes: parents and descendants; grandparents, brother and sisters and their children; uncles and aunts and their children. Any relative in class one excludes any relative in class two, who in turn excludes any relative in class three, and a full-blood excludes the half-blood. As a result, although in principle females still receive only half the share of a corresponding male, in general they are much more fairly treated. In the example mentioned above, the wife's position would remain unchanged, but three-quarters of the estate would go to the daughter's son, or indeed a daughter's daughter rather than to the cousin.

Law Reform

There are two important changes of direction within the history of Islamic law: one was the introduction at an early date of a legal theory which not only ignored but denied the existence in it of all elements that were not in the narrowest possible sense Islamic, and which reduced its material sources to the Koran and the example of the Prophet; the second, which began only in the present century, is modernist legislation on the part of contemporary Islamic governments, which does not merely restrict the field in which the sacred law is applied in practice but interferes with the traditional form of this law itself.[1]

Modern criticism is directed against traditional Islamic law not as a religious law as such, but against the body of doctrine developed in the Middle Ages and regarded subsequently as unchangeable.

The *sharia* law is still applied in its entirety in the Arabian peninsula[2], but in other parts of the Muslim world it has been restricted from the beginning of the 20th century into family law, including the law of inheritance, and the singular institution of *waqf* endowments. But the criminal and general civil law in most Muslim countries is now based upon European models, with a system of secular courts to apply them.

Modern reform of Islamic law started with the Ottoman Law of Family Rights of 1917 which was later repealed in Turkey but remained in force in Lebanon, Palestine, Syria and Jordan.

From 1920 onwards the legislative impetus moved to Egypt where reforms have been enacted in family law, the organization of the *qadi* courts, the law of inheritance, legacies and culminating in 1955 in the

1. Joseph Schacht, *An Introduction to Islamic Law*, Oxford University Press, 1964.
2. The Shi'ite form has been applied in Iran since the revolution in 1979. See Chapter 4.

establishment of unified administration of justice in the hands of secular courts. Other reforms on divorce and a code of personal status are in draft form. This activity has inspired similar movements in the Sudan, Jordan, Lebanon, Syria, Iraq and Libya; in some cases the laws enacted go further than those in Egypt.

Outside the Arabian peninsula even the *sharia* family law is not applied in the traditional manner. Throughout the Middle East it is now generally expressed in the form of modern codes and it is only in the absence of a specific code that recourse is made to the traditional manuals. In India and Pakistan much of the family law is now embodied in statutory legislation, and the authority of judicial decisions has superseded that of the legal manuals. The *sharia* as a central entity has been abolished in Egypt and Tunisia, and *sharia* law is administered through a unified system of national courts, as is the case in India since partition. The rules of evidence of the *sharia* have been modified in many countries. In the Middle East circumstantial and documentary evidence is now generally admissible; witnesses are put on oath and cross-examined, and the general procedure, whereby one side produces witnesses and the other takes the oath of denial, has been largely superseded. In India and Pakistan, the courts apply the same rules of evidence to cases of Islamic law as in civil cases generally.

In the 20th century, the dominant issue in the Middle East concerning the reform of the *sharia* has been the need for justification on a jurisitic basis. That is, given the social and political desirability of reform, the overriding factor has become the justification for change in terms of Islamic jurisprudence, so that the change appears as a new, but orthodox, version of the *sharia*. Reform has been effected by the secular state in some cases, without challenging or altering the *sharia* in any way. One example of this flexibility of the Muslim mind is the attempt in Egypt to prohibit child marriage. In 1931 a law was enacted that the court was not to entertain any disputed claim of marriage where the marriage could not be proved by an official certificate of registration, and no such certificate could be issued if the bride was less than 16 or the bridegroom less than 18 years old at the time of the contract. The effect of this law was not to say that a marriage contracted of a minor was invalid, but as it would not be registered all legal rights would be forfeited. Another example is that as traditional Hanafi law was enforced in Egypt, a wife was not allowed to petition for divorce under any circumstances. However, by substituting the Maliki law in this area a wife's right to the judicial dissolution of her marriage could be obtained through her husband's cruelty, failure to provide maintenance and support, and desertion. By contrast, the British administration in India met the problem head on, and in 1929 enacted that the marriage of girls below the age of 14 and boys below the age of

16 was illegal under pain of penalties, while the Dissolution of Muslim Marriages Act, 1939, was modelled on English Law, allowing a Hanafi wife to obtain judicial divorce for cruelty, failure to maintain and other standard grounds. The only two countries to abandon the *sharia* completely[1] are Turkey, which in 1926 adopted the Swiss Civil Code and Albania, which in 1967 made all religions illegal.

Since the 1950s, in parts of the Middle East, pressure for legal reform has been growing. Modern jurisprudence has claimed the right to challenge the interpretations of the medieval jurists placed upon the Koran and the *Sunna*, and to interpret for itself, in the light of new circumstances, the original texts, and to re-open questions that had in theory been closed since the 10th century.

One example is the Syrian law of personal status, 1953, which has reassessed the terms under which a man may take more than one wife. The Koran instructs a man to treat all his wives equally, and if for any reason he is not able to do this he has to restrict himself to one wife. Traditionally, this qualification has been left to an individual's conscience, but the Syrian interpretation insists that it is a legal economic requirement. Coupled with the requirement that marriages must be registered, this enables the *qadi* to withhold permission from a married man to take a second wife until he can show that he can support them both in equality. The Tunisian law of personal status, 1957, goes further and argues that the Koranic injunction refers not only to economic equality, but also to equal treatment in all other respects. Since under modern conditions total equality and impartiality is impossible to achieve, the essential conditions for polygamy cannot be met, and Tunisian law therefore prohibits polygamy.

Syrian law also challenges the traditional right of a husband to divorce at will, and subjects the husband's motives to the scrutiny of the court. The Koranic requirement that husbands should make a fair provision for divorced wives and retain wives with kindness or release them with consideration has by tradition been left to the conscience of the husband. In Syria the court is now empowered to order a divorced man to pay a maximum of one year's maintenance if he has abused his powers. But in this matter also Tunisia has gone further. The reformers here rest their justification on the Koranic passage which urges the appointment of arbitrators between husband and wife in the case of matrimonial discord. They argue that if a divorce is imminent there must clearly be discord, and arbitrators must be appointed. Who better to arbitrate dispassionately than the courts of the land, having, as they do, trained judges to sift evidence? The law thus withholds from a husband the extra-judicial right to divorce, taking this duty

1. This applies also to the republics of Southern USSR and the Muslim communities in China.

upon itself, and declaring that divorce outside the court is without legal validity. Although the court must dissolve a marriage if a husband persists in his repudiation, it has unlimited rights to compensate a wife for damage she has suffered as a result. In Pakistan the traditional *khul* divorce, where by mutual consent a wife pays compensation to her husband, has been modified to give a Muslim wife the right to obtain a divorce by payment of suitable compensation, whether a husband agrees or not.

It would, however, be a mistake to give the impression that in modern times the reform of Islamic family law is a formality, or that it proceeds apace. Changes in the law in Algeria, for example, have been relatively rare and mainly concerned with the guardianship of minors and the formalities of marriage and divorce. In 1959 an ordinance was laid down that marriage is concluded by the consent of husband and wife, fixing minimum ages for marriage, and decreeing that the marriage can be dissolved only by a judicial decision on certain grounds at the demand of husband or wife, or at their joint demand. A final court of appeal was established in the Court of Appeal in Algiers. This court has on occasions diverged from the strict doctrine of Islamic law when it appears to conflict with Western ideas of fairness, justice and humanity.

In some countries like South Yemen, Somalia and Tunisia, the state has been able to break from the strict provisions of the *sharia* in issues relating to marriage, divorce, abortion, etc, and has promulgated new laws which have abolished polygamy, restricted a husband's right to divorce, legalized abortion, and provided women with the same share in inheritance as men. The Somali state has even gone so far as to exempt government workers from fasting during Ramadan, in order to keep up production.

In Saudi Arabia the *ulama*, who regulate religious practices, argue that the law comes only from God, therefore the government, through the king, issues decrees. In modern times justice is administered by a mixture of secular institutions and the traditional *qadi* courts. In the case of an industrial accident, for example, claims for compensation are decided by the Ministry of Finance, whilst the *qadi* gives judgement concurrently on the question of blood money. In the case of a road accident the police investigate and decide on the guilt, if any, of the driver, and the *qadi* then allots the blood money on the basis of their decision. Various decrees provide for fines and imprisonment as punishment, which, if it is considered appropriate, are imposed in addition to the punishment prescribed in the *sharia*.

A hard core of traditionalist opinion still adamantly rejects the process of re-interpreting the basic texts of divine revelations, and great problems of principle and practice still have to be solved. The traditionalists maintain that the function of law is to fulfil the will of God and not to suit the changing needs of society. By contrast, modern jurisprudence bases itself directly on the tradition of the early medieval jurists, who were interpreting the Koran and the *Sunna* against the social and political needs of the time. They argue that neither the Koran nor Mohammed forbade subsequent interpretation, and that much of Islamic law has social origins.

Chapter 4

Society and Politics

In the upheavals which have rocked the Middle East since the Second World War the conflicts seem to have been as violent between Muslim states as between any others. Yet there are threads of Islamic principle linking them together on a political as well as a religious level.

This chapter, rather than analyzing the political and military conflicts between Muslim countries, discusses briefly the extent to which the teachings of Islam are reflected in their political and social institutions.

Islamic Principles: Theory

Politics and the Individual

The function of Islamic society is to fulfil the divine will, not through the activity of the community or the organizations and institutions within it, but through each individual understanding his duties. There is an important distinction between being individually responsible, and acting in isolation. Muslims are expected to fulfil certain communal functions, as is shown by the importance attached to the Friday *salat*, the giving of alms, and the consensus of the (Sunni) community (*ijma*). However, these are not seen as communal responsibilities, but as the responsibilities of an individual acting with other individuals. The underlying theology is man's ultimate responsibility to God for all his actions.

In all Sunni communities the only social unit recognized by authority is the family, and a believer is discouraged from forming loyalties to any other group, including the tribe. In strict Islamic terms the only other body to which a Muslim belongs is the brotherhood of believers — in other words the Islamic nation. In this important respect, Islam has from its inception been not simply a religion, but also a state, and by definition has always had an inherent awareness of the political process. Furthermore, the Islamic state has within it everything required for life, its own assessment of what is important and what is not. The relationship between economic relationships and political power was recognized by Mohammed from the very beginning; he was not only Islam's founder and Prophet, but its first lawyer and statesman.

But the intellectual void left in society between the family and the state means that for historical and cultural as well as religious reasons a Muslim will not organize or associate with political parties as readily as his counterpart in Europe.

Thus, for the past 150 years, political development inside Islam has either been stagnant or, more recently, has developed quite differently from any Western model. This has to be explained not simply in terms of Islam's former colonial status, but also by its political image of itself.

It is useful to refer here to A Universal Islamic Declaration made in London in 1980.[1] It is the first document of its kind in modern times, and sets out some fundamental political aims:

> A universal order can be created only on the basis of a universal faith and not by serving the gods of race, colour, territory or wealth.
> The ideal of man's brotherhood seeks and finds its realization in Islam.
>
> Establishment of justice on earth is one of the basic objectives for which Allah sent His prophets and His guidance. (Koran 57:25).
> All human beings have rights on all that Allah has provided, and as such Allah's bounties are to be shared equitably. The poor and the needy have the right to share in the wealth of the rich. (Koran 51:19). It is the religious duty of Muslims to harness these resources and to serve the ends of justice, to promote goodness and virtue, and to eliminate evil and vice. (Koran 3:110). Allah's resources must not be allowed to become instruments of oppression and exploitation by any individual or section of society or state.
>
> It is only the mandate of Allah which confers legitimacy on governments, rulers and institutions, and legitimate power and authority can be derived only in accordance with the mandate laid down in the Koran and *as Sunna* of the Prophet Mohammed (Peace be upon him).
>
> Any system of government is Islamic as long as it upholds the mandatory principles laid down by the Koran and *as Sunna*. Apart from this mandatory requirement there is considerable flexibility in the form which an Islamic government may adopt. It is through this flexibility that Islam caters to the requirements of every age and place.
>
> The primary duties of the state are to establish justice in all spheres of life and to nurture and strengthen the unity of the *umma*[2].

1. *The Times*, 14 April 1980.
2. The community

These objectives can only be achieved when the full expectations of people are fulfilled; and when differences in rank, power, wealth and family ties are not permitted to undermine the socio-political process of Islam.

Islam aims at creating a model society. Its strategy is to mould the individual in accordance with the tenets of Islam, to organize and mobilize within a social movement for progress and development, and to establish an Islamic Order by building society and state, their institutions, and policies at national and international levels.

It is noticeable that nowhere in the Declaration is any mention made of individual liberty or political freedom. On the contrary, Islamic strategy is to 'mould the individual in accordance with the tenets of Islam'. This is consistent with the tradition which holds that man cannot attain the right path through his own unaided efforts, and the inference is that individual fulfillment is more likely to lead to vice and evil than anything else. Nor is anything said about abolishing poverty, or riches for that matter. In fact, the Declaration has nothing to say directly about altering the class relationships in society.

But if Islam does not subscribe to the ideas of liberty and equality, the same cannot be said for fraternity, and the first clearly identifiable political aim is brotherhood. The reference to man's brotherhood finding its realization in Islam is fundamental. The Prophet frequently discussed the question of why mankind consists of a plurality of *ummas* (communities) and has not remained a unit. He saw the ultimate reason for this in God's Message 'Mankind were only one nation, then they fell into variance' (Koran 10:20).

At first Mohammed regarded the Arabs in general as a closed *umma*. But in time his *umma* came more and more to consist exclusively of his immediate followers — the Muslims. One of the consequences of the spread of Islam was Mohammed's ruling that once a man embraces the faith he becomes a member of the community and must not be attacked by his Muslim brothers. This edict turned the tribal aggression of the Arabs outwards, which in the course of time brought together very different races and nations to form a Muslim brotherhood.

The second social objective of Islam is to uphold justice, which is seen clearly as part of the socio-political process. It is perhaps under this heading that the greatest scope is offered for discussion of changing political ideas in Islam:

> Indeed, We sent Our Messengers with
> the clear signs, and We sent down
> with them the Book and the Balance
> so that men might uphold justice.

(Koran 57:25)

Finally, the Sunni doctrine of *ijma* must be considered. Literally, *ijma* means 'agreeing upon'. Originally this was interpreted as agreement of those people who have a right, by virtue of knowledge, to form a judgement of their own. After Mohammed's death, these were his Companions; later it meant the religious scholars. But the idea is open to, and has been given, other interpretations. The fundamental tradition from which the *ijma* is derived quotes the Prophet as saying 'my people will never agree in an error'. In consequence, it is argued, there is in the consensus of the people as a whole a power to *create* doctrine and law, and not simply to stamp with approval that which has been handed to them. The *Shorter Encyclopaedia of Islam* gives two examples of the power of *ijma* expressed by the community. The first is that the cult of saints has become practically a part of the *Sunna* of Islam, in spite of its being disapproved by purists and religious scholars; and even stranger is the popular belief in the infallibility and sinlessness of Mohammed, in spite of clear statements in the Koran to the contrary. In these cases the *ijma* has not simply shown its flexibility on certain points, but has changed settled doctrines of the greatest importance. The idea therefore that the consensus of the community can be used as an instrument for political change has a respectable pedigree. There is some controversy, however, as to whether this means that the Muslim people can made Islam whatever they, as a whole, wish.

These, then, are some of the theoretical building blocks from which all modern Islamic societies are constructed. Just as the Western democracies have used, with varying degrees of conviction, the ideas of the French Revolution, liberty, equality and fraternity, Islam has generated from its own internal resources the alternative slogan of brotherhood, justice and the right of the community.

Islamic Principles: Practice

The Ottoman Empire

In spite of prohibitions, there is nothing new about Muslims fighting each other. Almost as soon as the Arab invaders broke out of Arabia in the seventh century their conquests became too extensive to be administered and controlled from a central source. The result was the rise of various Muslim dynasties that sought to extend their power and influence over the Islamic world by intrigue and conquest, until the expansion of the European colonial powers in the 18th and 19th centuries.

At the beginning of the 16th century, Arabia, Iraq and Syria, and Palestine lost their importance as the trade routes between Europe and

Asia, when Europe discovered an alternative route by sea round the Cape of Good Hope. Ironically, this was made possible by the Arab researches in physics, astronomy, geography and other sciences brought back by the Crusaders 500 years earlier. The medieval gloom from which Europe was emerging was soon to descend on the Arab regions because of their diminished economic importance, and the domination of their fellow Muslims by the Ottoman Turks, who were to rule the region until the First World War. International trade bypassed the Arabs for four centuries, and the Middle East was transformed from a cosmopolitan and international trading centre based on a capitalistic money economy to an insular and regressive backwater with a feudal political structure. Just as Europe was reconstructing the whole of its intellectual, economic, political and social life, the Middle East, under Ottoman rule, was embarking on a reverse course. Ottoman society, dominated by inflexible religious leaders, was encasing itself in a rigid code of Islamic law.

European Imperialism

By the end of the 18th century the stagnation and corruption of the Ottoman Empire made it ripe for conquest by European imperialism, and all aspects of the Middle Eastern life were materially affected for the next 150 years. It is impossible to understand the development of modern Islam without understanding the colonial role ascribed to it by the European powers.

France made the first move when Napoleon sent an expeditionary force to invade Egypt, and eventually French influence extended along the North African coast and into Palestine and Syria. Initially, Britain's interest was to secure the sea route around Africa, and in order to control the Indian Ocean she set up, by various means, bases in Iraq, Persia and along the coasts of the Arabian peninsula. When the Suez Canal was opened in 1869, Britain expanded its imperial interest to the eastern Mediterranean. In putting down a minor Egyptian revolt in 1882, she took control of the Suez Canal from the French and occupied Egypt to become the dominant colonial power in the Middle East.

In the meantime Austria and Russia had cast covetous eyes on the Eastern European and Western Asian parts of the Ottoman Empire, and when Germany and Italy began to make their imperial interests felt, the Ottoman government had its hands full. The economic and strategic exploitation of the Middle East by Europe had other and equally important consequences for its people. Throughout the second half of the 19th century European dominance dragged in its wake cultural influences and technical changes which lifted the dead hand of the Ottoman régime. The most important and ironical consequence of this was that the conditions were created for the re-emergence of the Arab identity. The Ottoman Empire was no match for the tide of events, and out of its ruins the Arabs constructed a new sense of identity, based on their own heritage, but rationally supported by the political and nationalist ideas formulated in Europe.

The present day geographical boundaries of the Middle East did not exist under the Ottomans; the region was identified as provinces of the Ottoman Empire. But even more significant were the differences between the Muslim sects. The Ottoman Turks had imposed on Islam the rigid orthodoxy which became its official version, or *Sunna*. Those who accepted this view came to be known as Sunni, or Sunnite. However, there remained a large minority of believers who refused to accept this interpretation of Islam. They maintained the belief of the early Shi'ites, who had founded the Baghdad Caliphate. The Shi'ite stronghold became Persia, the birthplace of the movement, but others were scattered throughout the Arab world. They believed that the leadership of the Muslim world, and consequently the interpretation of the divine will, could only be assumed by the direct descendants of Mohammed, through his son-in-law, Ali. The Ottomans tried but failed to put down Shi'ite aspirations to justify their own power in the Muslim world, which was not descended from the Prophet.

There also arose in the 18th century a division within the Sunni movement itself. This was led by Abd'al-Wahhab, a religious scholar, and a local tribal warrior chief called Mohammed ibn Saud. They formed an alliance in the Arabian heartland to challenge and reject the Ottoman theology. The Wahhabis preached and practised a brand of Islam that was basically simple and harsh, and the movement gained control of central Arabia and shut off the routes of the pilgrimage to Mecca. These conflicts between Muslim sects were another factor affecting the political balance within Islam, and persist to this day.

But although the internal tensions within the Ottoman Empire had real significance, it was the rivalry between the French and the British from the beginning of the 19th century that was largely responsible for the turn of events, and still influences the course of Middle Eastern politics.

The first 40 years of the 19th century saw the internal struggle of Mohammed Ali, the viceroy of Egypt, who sought to expand his power and territory at the expense of the Ottoman Sultan. Britain and France intervened at various times and took sides to neutralize each other's influence. At the same time, Russia cast predatory glances at the accessible regions of the tottering Empire and the conflict of imperial interests subsequently brought about the Crimean War (1854-55). Although the Ottomans won the war against Russia, this was only done with the support of Britain and France, and the price paid for victory was the domination of their Empire by the economic and political interests of these two powers. Subsequently the Ottoman government fell steadily into decline and bankruptcy. After the British occupation of Egypt to gain control of the Suez Canal, the Ottoman régime no longer had the economic power, political will, or military strength to control its Empire. When militant nationalism, born out of the French Revolution, filtered into the consciousness of its minorities, from Greece to Egypt, its decline was complete.

Towards the end of the 19th century small but important secret Arab societies had sprung up in Egypt, Iraq and Syria, preaching political independence. At the same time a new political movement, Zionism, was being formed in Europe, based on the idea of a Jewish state. The Pan-Arab movement gathered strength, and in 1905 in Paris a book was published called *The Awakening of the Arab Nation*. It envisaged an independent Arabic speaking nation extending from the Fertile Crescent to the Suez Canal.

By the beginning of the 20th century France was already in control of the provinces of Algeria and Tunisia and was moving into Morocco. Britain was established firmly in Egypt and the Arabian peninsula. Italy had scarcely been born as a state before she wanted a share of the pickings and selected the North African province that became known as Libya. Italy invaded in 1911 and triggered off a local war with Turkey that eventually led to the Balkan Wars of 1912-13, and indirectly contributed to the tensions underlying the outbreak the First World War in 1914. The end of that war brought the dissolution of the Ottoman Empire.

Arab Nationalism

In 1902 a revolt was launched in Arabia by Abdul Aziz ibn Saud, a descendant of the original ally of Wahhab, which was essentially directed at the corruption of the Ottomans. National independence movements were proliferating throughout the Empire, not just in the Arab regions, but also in its Eastern European and Western Asian territories. The repression of these movements by Constantinople had the effect of forcing them underground, and societies dedicated to revolution and national self-determination were formed in most major cities, including the Arab cities of the Fertile Crescent, but before full expression could be given to these new movements the war of 1914 erupted.

The First World War had some profound effects on Islamic politics and society. First, as a result of a series of big power manoeuvres, the Ottomans found themselves allied with Germany, and therefore on the losing side. Secondly, the waging of a modern war brought to the Middle East a military presence and civil support of a strength not seen in the region since the Crusades. The indigenous population came into direct contact with new ways: new organizations, new weapons, new transport and communications, and, above all, new social relationships. Furthermore, intervention by the allies was largely welcomed, rather than resented, by the politically conscious factions: the British and French were fighting the Turks who had become the primary target for emerging Arab nationalism.

The British took the initiative in the fight against the Ottomans and arranged a deal with the Grand Sharif of Mecca, Hussein ibn Ali. The arrangement was that in return for Ali organizing and leading an armed rebellion against the Turks, thereby helping the British war effort, Britain would be prepared to recognize and uphold the independence of the Arabs in the region consisting of the Fertile Crescent, excluding Egypt, and virtually the whole of the Arabian peninsula. In the meantime, France had begun to make proposals of her own to divide up the Ottoman Empire between the Allies, including Russia, at the conclusion of the war, which it was assumed they would win.

Britain, in order to maintain her allies' wholehearted commitment in Europe, was made to agree with their post-war expectations, and in 1916 the three concluded a secret agreement which totally ignored the British agreement with Sharif Hussein. To add to this duplicity, the Zionist movement had gained sufficient influence in British power politics for serious consideration to be given to the idea of setting aside part of the territory committed to the Arabs by London as a homeland for the Jews: namely Palestine. Upholding their end of the bargain, Hussein and his followers embarked on their revolt in a campaign that made famous the name of T E Lawrence.

Then came two events which were to have a shattering effect on Anglo-Arab relations, and which are still remembered with bitterness in the Arab world. The successful Bolshevik Revolution in Russia had unearthed in the Kremlin archives a copy of the secret agreement between the Allies. This was made public, and Britain's true position became clear to the Arabs. Shortly afterwards the Balfour Declaration was published by the British government. Although it was careful to stress the importance of safeguarding non-Jewish communities, it looked with favour on 'the establishment in Palestine of a national home for the Jewish people', and pledged Britain's best efforts to achieve that aim.

At the end of the First World War the Ottoman Empire lay in ruins, and the imperial vacuum was filled by the victorious European allies: Britain and France. For 500 years under the Turks the Middle East had had all its Islamic characteristics reinforced and entrenched by a conservative but increasingly corrupt Muslim régime. The exposure to the power politics of Europe brought new political perceptions to the region, and the geo-political processes of the West began to influence and modify the entrenched Islamic attitude.

The 20 years between the two world wars were dominated by the issue of nationalism, and the manoeuvering of Britain and France to contain it. Nationalism is a political, rather than a religious, idea, and for the first time since Mohammed's death there arose forces in the Middle East capable of ordering the course of its history but not inspired exclusively by Islam. It is still barely perceived in the West that, for example, Egyptian and Arab nationalism are not only different from each other, but are also not exclusively Muslim. Both have within them Christian minorities and even Jewish communities who regard themelves as Arabs: and it took President Nasser, at the height of his power, to convince the Egyptian people that they should not regard themselves as a separate nation, but identify with the Arab cause. Furthermore, under the Ottomans none of the geo-political boundaries which we now recognize existed, apart from the Egyptian. In particular, greater Syria consisted of what we now know as Syria, Lebanon, Palestine, Jordan and parts of Arabia, and the nationalist struggle between the wars was largely focused on the efforts of the Arabs to turn this region into a unified Arab state.

Britain and France prevented this by dividing up the Fertile Crescent, with France retaining control over Greater Syria, and Britain having the Southern part and Mesopotamia (Iraq). At the same time, Britain installed Prince Feisal, son of Hussein ibn Ali, as king of a provisional government of Syria, excluding the Syrian territories of Palestine and Transjordan (Jordan). Feisal had neither the power base nor the political programme to unite the nationalist aspirations of the Arabs. He spent his time in London and Paris, trying to negotiate the independence of Greater Syria. In the meantime, the nationalist groups at home had become increasingly restive and had organized independent guerilla groups. When sporadic fighting broke out between the groups and the French in 1920, and it became clear that Feisal was unable to control his people, the French overturned his provisional government and set up their own puppet régime.

Thus, a split developed in the nationalist movements of French Syria and British Palestine, in response to the different policies being pursued by the colonial powers. Those in central Syria focused their attention on the French occupation, whilst those in Southern Syria concentrated on the British and the Zionists. 60 years later these events still have an effect on the interplay of nationalist interests in the Middle East, and particularly on the conflict between the Palestine movement and Jordan about the future status of the Palestinians.

The kingdom of Jordan, like Feisal, is Hashemite. When Feisal instructed his people in Damascus to stay out of the struggle that was developing in Palestine with the Zionists, he demonstrated his inability to lead the Pan-Arab movement, and played into the hands of the Franco-British policy of creating small manageable national states.

The French occupation encouraged the Christian minority of Northern Syria to congregate on the Mediterranean coast where the French influence was most strongly felt. The Christians, though proud of their Arabic language and traditions, wanted to shake off Muslim domination. In 1926 France, acceding to Christian pressure, set up Lebanon as a separate republic.

After ceding Northern Syria to the French, the British set about the division of the South. In compensation to Sharif Hussein for not honouring the agreement to support his Pan-Arab state after the war, the British installed one of his sons, Feisal, as king of Iraq, and another, Abd'ullah, as the ruler of Transjordan. In addition they approved Hussein's proclamation of himself as king of Hejaz (North West Arabia). The creation of the separate states of Palestine and Transjordan gave Britain control over the routes from their oil fields in Iraq to the Mediterranean. In effect, Britain now had political and economic control over the region linking the Tigres-Euphrates, the Persian Gulf, the Nile Valley and the Mediterranean, through the hands of the ancient and respected Hashemite family.

But no sooner had Britain established itself as a dominant power in the Middle East than other factors, the seeds of which had already been sown, began to make themselves felt. The first of these was the expansion of the United States' oil interests. Other factors were the re-emergence of the Saud family dominance in Arabia, the reaction of the Arabs to the Zionist ambitions in Palestine, and the increasing strength of the nationalist movements in the region. It was not nationalist aspirations, and certainly not Muslim rivalries, which created the geopolitical map of the modern Middle East. Yet once the boundaries had been created, they took on a significance of their own, and most have survived to the present day. Once political structures had been created within these boundaries, regardless of whether the unit was economically viable or religiously compatible, another dimension was added to the ideas of Muslim brotherhood and Pan-Arab unity: patriotic nationalism.

The ascendancy of the Saud family in Arabia began in 1902 when the youthful Abdul Aziz ibn Saud emerged from exile in what is now Kuwait and recaptured the family's traditional capital, the mud-brick oasis town of Ridayh. Abdul Aziz had remained loyal to the fundamentalist Wahhabi doctrine, and had stayed aloof from the dealings of the British and the Hashemites in the North, concentrating instead on consolidating his power in central Arabia. By 1925 he was strong enough to challenge and win control of the Hashemite Hejaz, the traditional cradle of Islam. Two years later he was in control of two-thirds of the Arabian peninsula, and was in a position to demand, and get, British recognition. After overcoming a series of revolts and tribal wars he had, by 1932, brought most of the territories of the Arabian peninsula into the kingdom of Saudi Arabia. This done, he declared himself king.

The Challenge of Zionism

If the sub-division of Greater Syria into national states helped to pave the way for the creation of Israel, it also helped ultimately to create the nucleus of the strongest opposition: the national identity of the Palestinians. It was a long time, however, before this became an effective force. The immediate effect of the sub-division was to dissipate the strength of the growing nationalist movement as it was forced to concentrate on an increasing number of local issues. As a result the Palestinians felt isolated and betrayed, and left to face the mounting pressure of Zionism alone.

Zionism, a political movement founded in Europe, seeks to provide a homeland (preferably, though not necessarily, in the land of the Jews' spiritual ancestors) for the oppressed and persecuted Jewish people of the world. Originally it did not seek to establish a sovereign Jewish state.

It is a common misconception in the West that Arab unity or Arabism has been brought about largely by the threat of Zionism. This is no more true than saying that Zionism has been largely brought about by the threat of Nazism. At the end of the First World War, when the Balfour Declaration first made Zionism a real threat to Palestine, Arab consciousness was working in its own quite different way. As the Arabs saw it, there was no such place as Palestine. What had been Palestine in biblical times had long since been absorbed as part of the Ottoman province of Syria, and the people who had lived there for centuries, whether Muslims or Christians, regarded themselves as Arabs, not as Palestinians.

Muslims regard Jews as a religious group, not as a nation. Certainly for them there is no generic connection between the Jews who emigrated in waves to Palestine at the end of the First World War, and the Jews who had lived in the Middle East for 2000 years. The immigrants had come almost exclusively from Eastern Europe and Southern Russia and their ancestors had been converted to Judaism in the eighth century: none had originated in the Middle East. Muslims in general, and Arabs in particular, make a distinction between the possibility of a Jewish homeland as part of an Arab state, which might in principle be acceptable, and a politically Western oriented Zionist sovereign state, which is not.

Living in Palestine in 1919 there were about 60,000 Jews and 10 times that number of Arabs. Under the British administration, Jewish immigration increased, and the Jews began to make it clear that their eventual aim was the establishment of an independent state. This triggered off a series of riots, in which the Arabs struck back at the nearest available target: the Jews. In the years leading up to the Second World War much blood was shed on both sides, but Jewish immigration proceeded apace, and their achievements in building up their nation were impressive. With the help of massive injections of foreign (mostly Jewish) capital and the immigration of skilled European and American Jews the homeland became a prosperous miniature state on the European model. By the mid 1930s the Arab population were becoming increasingly concerned by the prospect of total Jewish control. The creation of a Jewish state by partition was being openly canvassed, and this threat, reinforced by the national frontiers surrounding it, strengthened the notion of Palestinian nationalism.

The Second World War, and the events leading up to it, concentrated the minds of Arabs, Jews and British alike. At the start of the war the open hostility between Arabs and Jews in Palestine had reached dangerous proportions. Arab resentment of Zionism was no longer centred exclusively in Palestine but had spread throughout the Arab world. In the meantime, the persecuted Jews of Europe were desperately looking for sanctuary, and for many a natural refuge was Zionist Palestine. When the danger of war with Germany became real, Britain dramatically reversed its policy which had for so long favoured the Jews. A White Paper was published, drastically limiting Jewish immigration, and stating flatly that it was not British policy that Palestine should become a Jewish state. Britain's intention was obvious. Although she could not foresee that the war would leave the Middle East virtually intact (apart from North Africa), Britain clearly did not want to enter the war with the Arab nations becoming increasingly hostile to her foreign policy.

But if the Arabs in general greeted the new policy with relief, it made the Zionists into bitter enemies. It provoked the formation of a dangerous underground movement, which staged an open armed revolt against the British in 1939 when Britain refused to revise the ban on immigration to accommodate the Jewish refugees from Nazi Europe.

Even so, by 1947 there were over 600,000 Jews living in Palestine, and more than twice as many Arabs who owned 95% of the land. But the Zionist pressure eventually bore fruit as the result of the terrorist campaign in Palestine, and a propaganda campaign in the West. The break came when President Truman, abandoning Roosevelt's promise to King Abdul Aziz that the US would make no commitments regarding Palestine without first consulting the Arabs, publicly advocated the immediate admittance of 100,000 Jews into Palestine. This statement marked the beginning of the United States's political involvement in the Middle East, and signalled its ascendancy at the expense of Britain. The Arabs viewed this turn of events with despair, especially when the British Foreign Office began to make it clear that it was ready to wash its hands of the Palestinian affair. It was easy to see that the vacuum would be filled by the United States with its powerful Jewish political lobby. The Arabs argued that the events in Europe were none of their making, but their aspirations and interests were being once more swept aside in order to pacify the wave of Christian guilt which swept the world when the results of Nazi persecution became generally known.

The Arabs found themselves in the position of having to plead their case to a Western audience in terms that they would understand, and they failed. Their case was rooted in the Islamic standards of justice and the complexities of Arab history, and was constructed on a sense of the shame that the colonial powers should feel for the way they had dealt with the Arabs in the past. It was no match for the Zionist propaganda, Western in its origin and language, and based on a mixture of humanitarian ideas and pragmatic solutions carefully tuned in to a real sense of Western guilt.

Britain finally referred the whole Palestine question to the United Nations in 1947 and a special committee recommended partition of the land into separate Arab and Jewish states. The Jews accepted the idea, because by now the establishment of any kind of Jewish state was an overriding priority. It was flatly rejected by the Arabs for exactly the same reasons that they had advanced all along: the land belonged to the Arabs and had done so for centuries; the Jews were not a nation, and never had been; neither the United Nations nor anybody else had the right to dispose of Muslim territory; and no Muslim could agree to relinquishing Islamic land to the infidel without a fight.

Following intense Zionist and American pressure the UN General Assembly endorsed the idea of partition and the following year a provisional Israeli government established itself in Tel Aviv. At the same time armies from Egypt, Lebanon, Syria, Transjordan and Iraq were advancing on the frontiers of the new state. The first Middle East war was about to start, and Islam began to move back into the centre of world events.

The Arab armies were unable to overcome the poorly equipped but highly motivated Israeli forces. At the end of the war all Palestinian territory was occupied by either Israel or Transjordan, with the Gaza strip under Egyptian administration. The Palestinians were left with nothing.

National Liberation Movements

The Second World War, like the First, accelerated social change, but the changes which took place in the Muslim countries were motivated more by anti-colonial objectives than by pro-Islamic sentiment.

Yet it is noticeable that although each country has found its own way to independence, every national leader to emerge has been a devout Muslim. Furthermore, there are only two significant political movements whose constitutions aim at setting up a democratic secular state, rather than a state where, at the very least, Islam is the official religion. There are the Ba'th Socialist Party, and, paradoxically in view of the support received from Muslim states, the Palestine Liberation Organization.

Although, until the Iranian Revolution, the concept of Islam had not been used directly in national self-determination, its inherent qualities of opposition to foreign domination, anti-corruption, and justice, have always been at hand to trigger off a national response. Moreover, while various Muslim countries have shown a willingness to import selected Western ideas on social equality, collective ownership and other socialist concepts, including equality for women, all have stopped short of embracing either Communist or Marxist methods. However politically leftist have been the policies of Iraq, Syria, Egypt and Libya, their leaders, as devout Muslims, have rejected quite specifically all atheistic philosophies.

Modern Political Structures

The variety of forms of government seen in Muslim countries relates to the economic and political realities from which each emerged rather than to Koranic doctrine. These have given rise to the full spectrum of political forms: single-party states, parliamentary states, socialist states, states ruled by military junta, constitutional monarchies, parliamentary states based on Islamic and other religious groupings, and two types of fully fledged Islamic states, one pro- and the other anti-monarchy.

None of these has been remarkable for its stability. Even the oldest of them has been established for barely 50 years, and most of them for very much less. Many are subject to frequent changes, which suggests that they are moulded less in the tradition of Islam than by the political upheavals that historically accompany national independence. Even

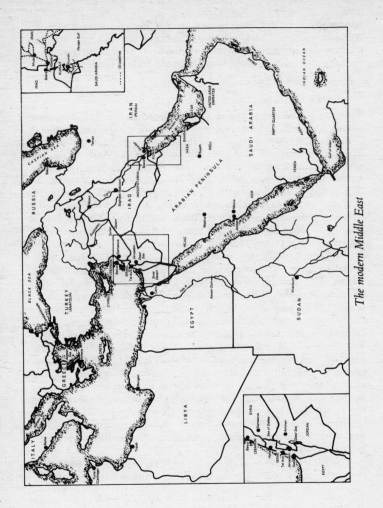

The modern Middle East

Turkey, which has not suffered from a colonial past, and is the only country to have adopted a modern Western parliamentary system, has been taken over by a military junta three times in the last 20 years. The rest, with two exceptions, appear to have more in common with newly independent non-Muslim states than they have with each other on the question of representative government. The two exceptions are the fully-committed Islamic states of Saudi Arabia[1] and Iran.

Unity and Division

There are occasions and issues on which solidarity is readily achieved among Muslims, and others which trigger off the deepest conflicts.

A distinction worth drawing is that between the Islamic concept of Muslim brotherhood, and the political concept of Arab unity. The first holds the pedigree of the Koran, the Prophet, and the *Sunna*. The second is a modern political weapon, conceived and launched by Gamal Abdul Nasser when President of Egypt. Until that time the inhabitants of the Arabian peninsula, and in particular the Bedu, considered themselves the only true Arabs, and many of them still hold this view. Until Nasser's time, many Middle Eastern peoples, particularly the Egyptians, regarded themselves as quite distinct from the Arabs. Nasser's definition, which has now become generally accepted, is that an Arab is someone whose language, and therefore culture, is Arabic. This includes not only Muslims, but the adherents of all other religions, including Christians and Jews. But by definition it excludes Muslim states such as Turkey, Iran and the Indian sub-continent.

By contrast, the concept of Muslim brotherhood automatically includes all Muslims in the Islamic community, and excludes all others. The idea is deeply rooted in the very origins of Islam. Once the Prophet had won over the communities of Medina and Mecca, he set about converting and forming alliances with the surrounding tribes. The seal of an alliance was that the tribe submitted to Islam and as a result it became an inflexible rule that those who had become believers must not be attacked. It is this principle which virtually put an end to the traditional aggressive attitude of the Arab tribes towards each other, and, with their aggressiveness turned outwards, resulted in the spectacular spread of Islam.

The great achievement of the *ulama* is that for nearly 1000 years these religious scholars maintained the structure of Sunni society vir-

1. There are a number of small states along the Arabian Gulf which have systems of government very similar to that in Saudi Arabia. These include Kuwait, Bahrain, Qatar and the United Arab Emirates. They are ruled by an Amir (ruler) rather than a king and orthodox Wahhabi law is generally less strictly enforced, although this varies from state to state.

tually intact, by insisting that there were certain matters it was not in their power to alter. This suited their rulers well enough, especially as they controlled the appointment and promotion of the *ulama*. But its significance for today is the place that this unbroken tradition of social stability has in the hearts of the masses. This resistance to change has been reinforced by intractable minority problems in many states as a result of the break-up of the Ottoman empire. The Copts in Egypt, the Sunni Kurds and the Shi'ite Arabs in Iraq, and the Christians in Lebanon have presented insoluble problems for political unity, and reinforced the underlying resistance of the Sunni communities to change. The political changes in the Middle East since the Second World War have been largely brought about by the emergence of an increasingly powerful middle class, which has been educated either in the West or, at least, within the framework of a modern educational system. This has had a far reaching effect on commercial, technical, intellectual and political life in virtually every country. Significantly, though, it has had little or no religious impact.

Race and Class

The European political idea of equality has been accepted by the orthodox Muslim mind only in limited areas. Islam is indifferent to race and colour, and although sharp distinctions are sometimes made between groups of people, they are based on class and social prejudice rather than on racial discrimination. Prejudice takes a different form from that frequently found in the West. Thesiger, travelling in the Empty Quarter of Arabia in the early 1950s, noted of his travelling companions that

> at first glance they seemed to be little better than savages...but I was soon disconcerted to discover that, while they were prepared to tolerate me as a source of very welcome revenue, they never doubted my inferiority. They were Muslims and Bedu and I was neither. They had never heard of the English, for all Europeans were known to them simply as Christians, and more probably infidels, and nationality had no meaning for them...Arabs have little if any sense of colour bar; socially they treat a slave, however black, as one of themselves... I remember asking some Rashid who had visited Riyadh how they had addressed the king, and they answered in surprise, 'we called him Abd'al Aziz, how else would we call him except by his name?' and when I said 'I thought you might call him Your Majesty', they answered 'we are Bedu. We have no king but God'.

The attitude of the Koran to slavery is similar to that of the New Testament. Both accept the social institution of slavery, and then give directions to make it more tolerable. Islam inherited slavery from ancient Arabia, and reformed its worst excesses, as it did in the case of inheritance, marriage, divorce and retribution. The basic social purpose of Islam was not to transform its essential class structure, but to carry out reforms in order to create a more stable and unified society. Thus, on the whole, slaves seemed to have been well treated. It was considered a pious act to free slaves, and in the case of unintentional killing, the freeing of a slave was the price to be paid to the community. Islam made it impossible to take a fellow Muslim in slavery, this being inconsistent with the idea of Muslim brotherhood. This was the limit of enlightenment in seventh century Islam.

Modern Islamic States: Saudi Arabia and Iran

Although there are many countries in which Islam is the official religion, in which the leaders are pious Muslims, and in which Islamic law and tradition play a prominent part, there are very few which can claim to have retained Islam in its entirety. Saudi Arabia and several of the small Gulf states are examples. But these countries retain their Islamic character by virtue of resistance to change and in particular to change inspired by Western values which might undermine the values of Islam. Other countries, on achieving national independence, have made positive efforts to retain, and in some cases to expand, various aspects of traditional life, but there is only one state which has consciously and wholeheartedly abandoned all Western influence as being corrupt, evil, and anti-Islamic and has instituted a programme to reconstitute a fully-fledged Islamic state. That is Iran.

It is interesting to examine the two constitutional and political paths down which Saudi Arabia and Iran are travelling, not so much for the purposes of comparison but to see the variety and complexity of ideas that can be accommodated within the scope of Islam.

Saudi Arabia is an orthodox Sunni state, occupying territory whose people have more or less followed the teaching of the Prophet and the *Sunna* in an unbroken tradition dating from the time of Mohammed. Abdul Aziz ibn Saud reunited the territories of Arabia with the traditional weapons of the Sword and the Message, and he won the allegiance of the tribes by the traditional diplomacy of intermarriage.[1]

Iran became an Islamic Republic in 1979. This event was preceded by waves of public protest, civil unrest, and riots against the régime of the Shah (king). At first the civil revolt had no clear aim or leadership, and involved a number of political factions, as well as the Muslim clergy.

1. He is said to have had some 100 wives and over 100 children.

The widespread and popular feeling was focused on such general issues as freedom from foreign exploitation and interference, civil rights, civil justice, and an end to corruption in public life. It quickly became apparent that the only force that was influential enough to unite the forces of revolt was the Muslim clergy who had been preaching in their mosques for years the Islamic virtues of social justice, honest dealing, and the superiority of Islam over the infidel. Once the clergy delcared themselves, they transformed the revolt into an Islamic Revolution, provided its slogan *'Allah'hu akbar'* (God is greatest), and provided the leader for the occasion: Imam Khomeini. By contrast with Abdul Aziz, Khomeini played down the role of physical force (although it was there for him to order it) and relied on the morality and justice of his message. The forces which the Shah relied upon to maintain power — the military, Savak (secret police) and in the last resort his foreign allies[1] — proved inadequate. The armed forces, even the Royal Guard, would not fight to defend the régime, Savak was decimated by popular action, and the Shah's allies did nothing.

Perhaps the most significant aspect of these events is that a cornerstone of the Shah's policy was to 'modernize' his country with the maximum speed. This involved importing Western values, as well as Western technology, at the expense of traditional values, and this policy was at the root of his struggle with the clergy. Iran was run like a private company, and every state and commercial transaction involved a 'commission' to the royal family. Political power was maintained by faith in military and para-military force alone. The expectations of the people, the dissatisfaction of the business community and the residual strength of Islam were not given enough weight in the Shah's analysis. The miscalculation was to bring about his downfall.

Saudi Arabia is an absolute monarchy and has no written constitution. Political power rests exclusively in the hands of the king, and he makes appointments to all government posts, and those of all government agencies. The king rules through a Council of Ministers by issuing royal decrees which become statute law. Each minister takes on ministerial and departmental responsibilities, similar to those in a parliamentary system. Political power and religious orthodoxy are part of each other, based upon the Koran, *Sunna* and the *hadith* as interpreted by the Wahhabi sect. There is thus no distinction between the legislature and the executive, and religious/political power is enforced by the *ulema* (religious scholars) and the *mutawwa* (secret police).

The Council of Ministers debates the policy of the state, and makes

1. The American CIA overthrew the nationalist government in 1954 and reinstituted the monarchy with the Shah at its head.

decisions which require the royal assent. A committee system based on the idea of council is common in many aspects of Saudi life. Although the decision of a committee cannot be appealed against in a higher court, every individual has the right of access to the king, and may appeal to him directly.

The country is divided into four administrative regions with appointed officials, and each region is sub-divided into districts presided over by a local leader or *sheikh*. The *ulema* have a strong influence on all national or local affairs, and it is their duty to preserve the rule of law on all issues.

There are no elections of any kind in Saudi Arabia. Political parties, trade unions, trade and professional associations and institutions are illegal. The Hanbali school of law is officially recognized. Its interpretation of the *sharia* is possibly the most orthodox and conservative, and accounts for the *sharia's* surviving virtually intact.

The economy is a capitalist free enterprise system, but because the ovewhelming wealth of the country is created through its oil deposits, the government has the power not only to direct the economy, but to control it. The king, through the Council of Ministers, controls and directs the State revenue as he sees fit, and this combined with the intermarriage of the Saud family with the tribes secures his power base. Although government agencies control development and the economy, with the notable exception of defence, they do not normally engage in direct trading. This is left to private enterprise. It is illegal for foreign interests to own land, or to hold a majority interest in Saudi companies or corporations. Official monetary policy is administered by the Saudi Arabian monetary agencies (SAMA) which have the power and functions of a bank.

Foreign investment is encouraged, and it is common for the government to employ foreigners and foreign contractors. There is no constitutional objection to a foreign military presence or base although strict conditions could be imposed in such cases on religious grounds.

As an orthodox Islamic state, Saudi Arabia is bound to support the just cause of Muslims in foreign policy. The Saudis contribute a greater proportion of their gross national product in foreign aid than any Western nation, the United States included.

By contrast, Iran has established a fundamentalist Islamic state by revolutionary change and has formalized it with a written constitution.

The official introduction to the constitution of the Islamic republic of Iran, published in 1980, states: 'the fundamental characteristic of this revolution in relation other movements in Iran in the last century is its Islamic content'.

The constitution which was approved in a referendum by 98 per cent of the electorate represents the only attempt in modern times to define an Islamic state in writing. It is considered here as an expression of the abiding faith in the eternal nature of Islam.

The introduction acknowledges the contribution made by women in the solidarity which overthrew the old régime, and defines the Islamic method of government as 'the political objective of a nation that organizes itself in order to be able to move forward to its common ideal and objective, the movement towards God'. This is to be done by:

— Participation by all members of the community in all the stages of political decision making.
— Continuous and equitable leadership of the clergy.
— Allowing women greater liberties and an assumption of higher responsibilities.
— Setting up defence forces not to protect the country's frontiers, but to carry on a crusade in the name of God until the law of God is established throughout the world.
— Establishing a judicial system, consisting of judges fully acquainted with Islamic principles... remote from any unhealthy connection with other branches of government.
— The mass media being in the service of an Islamic culture.
— Working so that the present century will witness the victory of the deprived peoples of the world and the defeat of their oppressors.

All laws and regulations are to be on the basis of Islamic principles as laid down by the Guardian Council. The Leader of the community is to be a religious lawyer, and is accepted by the majority of the people. Among his duties are: selection of religious lawyers for the Guardian Council; appointment of the highest judicial authority; acting as supreme commander of the armed forces; the appointment of all bodies responsible for the security and defence of the State; and dismissing the President if considerations of the national interest make this necessary. The Assembly of Experts has the right to dismiss the Leader.

The President is next in authority to the Leader of the nation, elected by the direct vote of the nation for four years. The three powers of legislature, executive and judiciary are independent of each other and the President is the link between them all. All are under the authority of the Leader. The legislature is the National Assembly whose representatives are elected by universal suffrage and secret ballot. Its duration is six years. Zoroastrians, Jews, and Christians will have one representative each in the National Assembly. The National Assembly cannot make laws in contravention of the official religion of the country.

The official religion is Islam. Sunni sects are guaranteed freedom of religious expression, as are Jewish and Christian Iranians (within the framework of the law). The policy of the government towards non-Muslims is based on justice and goodwill. All citizens are to enjoy equal rights with no distinction of race, colour, language or creed; men and women have equality before the law. Provided the Islamic principles of the Republic are not flouted, political parties, groups, societies, guilds, and Islamic societies are legal.

The economy of the Islamic Republic is based on the public, private, and co-operative sectors. Private ownership is fully respected. The government will appropriate all money derived from usury, bribery, theft, gambling, and illicit trade practices, and either return it to its owner or divert it into State funds.

The army of the Republic is described as an Islamic army which is an army of the people. The establishment of military bases in Iran by foreign countries is prohibited. Foreign policy is based on independence, defence of the rights of all Muslims, non-alignment with dominating and aggressive powers, peaceful relations with non-destructive powers and the rejection of every type of aggression and domination of one nation by another. The Islamic Republic shall not withhold its support from deprived peoples of the world against their oppressors. Political asylum can be granted, but not to traitors.

It is clearly the intention of the new constitution that ultimate political power should lie with the religious authorities. The popular will is given familiar expression by election of the President and the National Assembly. The judge in this matter is the Guardian Council, half of which is appointed by the Leader and half by the judiciary. The judiciary is appointed by the Leader. Effectively, therefore, the Leader controls the National Assembly. He has power also to dismiss the President. Yet it cannot be said that the religious authorities, through the Leader, control policy by formulating it: this is the function of the civil government. The Islamic element is written into the constitution to run parallel with the elected parliament, and to check that no legislation is enacted which is un-Islamic. This will seem a contradiction to those weaned on the sovreignty of parliament, but it is quite consistent with the general principle that man is in need of divine guidance, and the particular Shi'ite belief that the *imams* are divinely inspired to provide it.

Although modern Iran, Saudi Arabia and the Gulf states have relied upon the ideology of Islam for their main political features, other Muslim states have not. Moreover, there is nothing in the constitution of Islam or in its development which has prevented the formation of a privileged class of power and wealth; nor has it played any role in

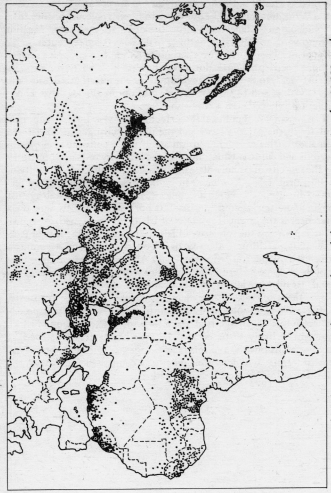

Areas of Muslim presence at the present day, each dot representing approximately 100,000 people

checking or modifying the penetration by capitalist economy in most modern states. Generally the development of the capitalist sector is low, and as a result individualistic traditions are not as deeply rooted as in the West, but this may be due more to Islam's colonial history than to its ideological stance. Similarly, the orientation of some Muslim states towards socialism has nothing to do with Islam, except in so far as the principle of Muslim brotherhood may serve to endorse a society without social privilege. But Islam had to look to Europe for its socialist ideas: to the French revolution for the idea that a democratic state is viable, and to the Russian revolution for the idea that a state without privileged classes is possible.

The alignment of political forces is changing very fast in Islam, particularly in the Middle East, and the pace of change has accelerated dramatically this century. Muslim states unite politically on certain religious and cultural issues, notably the integrity of Islamic territory and the sanctity of its holy places. Less solid and reliable is the unity of Muslim brotherhood, which can be fairly fragile in the face of territorial disputes or sectarian differences, and can result in Arab against Iranian and Sunni against Shi'ite. But both will normally sink their differences if the essential interests of Islam are threatened. A second factor supporting the solidarity of Islamic countries is the idea of Pan-Arab unity, a cultural identity based on language and a common historical heritage, and defined by Hafez Al-Assad of Syria as the struggle of the Arab peoples to achieve equality with the other peoples of the world. Its ultimate aim is the political unity of all Arabs.

But there are also issues which provoke conflict. Territorial disputes are as common in Muslim countries as anywhere else, especially if economic advantage is at stake. On social and economic issues alignment is likely to be decided by whether capitalist or socialist ideology holds power, and this factor, together with strength of nationalist feeling, will determine whether a country identifies with the Eastern or Western bloc, or with neither.

Chapter 5

Social Behaviour and Customs

The Islamic world of today is derived from seventh century Arabian society transformed by Mohammed's Message, adapted to the needs of one of history's great empires, and steeped in a thousand years of unchanging tradition. Although many of the customs and traditions can be traced back to ancient Arabia, the aim of Islam to determine the day to day course of every believer's life makes all accepted social customs in a sense Islamic. It is important to distinguish between social custom and social life. Social customs can be readily identified, but, because of the supremacy of the family in Islam, family and social life tend to be the same thing. Social life in a Western sense, embracing organizations, pastimes, clubs and other activities outside the home, exists only in a very limited form.

Traditional Hospitality and Courtesy

Perhaps the custom for which Muslims, and certainly Arabs, are most renowned is their traditional hospitality. This special kind of hospitality has its origins in the desert. Thesiger writes:

> I pondered on this desert hospitality and compared it with our own. I remembered other encampments where I had slept, tents on which I had happened in the Syrian desert and where I had spent the night. Gaunt men in rags, hungry looking children had greeted me, and bade me welcome with the sonorous phrases of the desert. Later they had set a great dish before me, rice heaped around the sheep which they had slaughtered, over which my host poured liquid golden butter until it had flowed down onto the sand; and when I had protested, saying 'Enough, enough', had answered that I was a hundred times welcome. Their lavish hospitality always made me uncomfortable, for I had known that as a result of it they would go hungry for days. Yet when I left them they had almost convinced me that I had done them a kindness staying with them.

Perhaps the most famous story of all is the story of a Bedu *sheikh*, who was known as 'the host of the wolves', because whenever he heard a wolf howl around his tent he ordered his son to send a goat out in the desert, saying that he would have no-one call on him for dinner in vain.

The Bedu take traditional hospitality to even greater extremes and it is to them that most Arabs look with admiration. As inviolable as the bond between host and guest is the bond between travelling companions in the desert. This is perhaps the strongest bond of all, transcending even tribal and family loyalties. Tradition demands that the travelling companion, be he a Christian, Jew or slave, be defended against any attack, even from Muslims, and a travelling guest will be expected to do the same.

Traditional generosity takes many forms, and sometimes the giving of presents seems to an outsider out of proportion to the occasion. To admire effusively something belonging to one's host is not good manners. This can be taken as asking for it as a gift, and a host is quite likely to insist that his guest keeps it.

An essential function in social intercourse is the exchange of views, and there is an accepted way of doing this. In answer to the usual question 'What's your news?' the reply will never be that the news is bad. Regardless of what has actually happened, until the formalities have been observed, the coffee drunk and other refreshments taken, the real news will not be discussed. Bad luck, misfortune, or even disaster may have occurred, but the telling will come in allotted time. Coffee is made with great ceremony in the desert, and many people in the towns take a great interest in serving the wide variety of blends available. An attendant serves coffee from a metal pot into a small handleless cup. The cup should always be taken in the right hand. The attendant will wait and replenish the cup when it is empty. To take one or two cups full is polite, more than three is greedy. The only way to stop the cup being continually replenished is to shake it two or three times when offering it back to the attendant.

Ritual Ablution, Bathing, Shaving

Ablution is described by Mohammed as 'the heart of faith and the key of prayer', and it is founded on the authority of the Koran:

> O believers, when you stand up to pray
> wash your faces, and your hands up to the
> elbows, and wipe your heads, and your feet
> up to the ankles.

(Koran 5:5)

Ablutions are absolutely necessary as a preparation for the ritual prayer, and detailed descriptions are laid down for washing all the prescribed parts of the anatomy. A specific prayer is recited at each stage of the proceedings. The ablution need not be performed before each of the five periods of prayer if the person is sure of having avoided every kind of impurity since the last ablution. Also laid down is the necessity to wash the whole of the body after certain periods of impurity. Brushing the teeth is a religious duty.

In all large mosques and most houses there are bathrooms both for ordinary purposes and for religious purification. According to Mohammed decency should be observed in bathing in public, and the body should not be exposed from the waist downwards.

The shaving of the beard is forbidden by tradition. The Prophet is recorded as saying: 'Do the opposite of the polytheists: let your beards grow long and clip your moustachios.' The shaving of the head is allowed providing the whole and not a part is shaven, for the Prophet said: 'Shave off all the hair of the head or let it alone'. It is the custom to shave the head in Afghanistan but not in other Islamic countries.

Food and Taboos

All religions emanating from the Middle East contained food taboos. There are several messages in the Koran directed against the pagan eating habits, criticizing the pagans for not enjoying the good things provided by God. Subsequent tradition and later generations have interpreted and sometimes expanded the original prohibitions. Some members of the pious Wahhabi sect have interpreted the ban on intoxicants to include all drugs and stimulants, including tobacco, coffee and tea.

A Muslim always eats with his right hand and avoids, if possible, touching food with his left. This is because Satan is believed to eat and drink with the left hand. Further, the left is the unclean hand which he washes after relieving himself. It is bad manners to pass anyone anything or to accept anything with the left hand. There is normally water available for washing before a meal.

There are other rules connected with eating. A Muslim pronounces the name of God over the food, and he eats what is nearest to him. Muslims will be taught not to hurry to table in advance of others, not to eat quickly or in excess, and to eat one mouthful at a time. They will be told not to study the food, but to pay attention to the other people present. The underlying virtue is self-discipline based on the idea that hunger is preferable to gluttony, and that physical appetites must be controlled.

A man must sit properly to eat, and not recline. Traditionally, all eat with the right hand from a common plate (the Bedu still do), and from this derives the exhortation to eat what is nearest. But it is permissible to pick and choose the fruit. A meal should begin and end with salt. The sexes eat separately, although it is now not uncommon for non-Muslim European women to be included as guests.

It is not considered polite for Muslims to linger at table after meals. Many have the (to a Westerner) disconcerting habit of departing without ceremony when they have eaten their fill.

All unclean things, except intoxicants, may be used as medicine, or, in extreme necessity, as food. Food must not only be lawfully slaughtered and lawfully prepared, it must also be bought with money honestly gained.

Eating is a part of religion, so food is controlled by law and the rules connected with it are codified by the moralists. The Koran says that all good things on earth may be eaten, and that bad things are forbidden (7:157). Consequently, a Muslim distinguishes not between what is edible and what is not, but between food which is lawful and food which is forbidden. A Muslim must not eat pork, nor the flesh of an animal which has not had its throat cut whilst still alive. Most of them will not eat meat slaughtered by anyone other than a Muslim, or by a boy who is uncircumcised, although some Muslims will eat meat killed by a Christian. The consumption of blood is also forbidden. An exception to the general rule is found in the case of fish and locusts, in that they are permitted without ritual slaughter because they have no blood. The Shafi'i view is that all marine creatures are permitted, but other schools of law distinguish between species. There is considerable confusion in this and other areas between the various interpretations of the law, however, and custom varies considerably from place to place.

Lawyers have tried to classify those things which were not expressly forbidden, and have formulated the general rule that anything may be eaten of which the Arabs approve. If the Arabs give a strange animal the name of a clean animal, then it may be eaten; if there is no name for it in Arabic it may be eaten if it resembles a clean animal. Classes of unclean animals are birds and beasts of prey, crawling things, those animals which men are commanded to kill and those which they are forbidden to kill.

Hunting gives very wide scope for theological hair-splitting. If the hunter evokes the name of God when he releases his arrow or sets his hound on the game, the prey is lawful food. But if the dog was not trained the prey is lawful only if the hunter cuts its throat before it dies, which is invariably done.

Drink and Alcohol

Prohibition was not part of Mohammed's original message. At first, in the Koran, we find wine praised as one of God's bounties to humanity:

> We give you to drink...
>   pure milk, sweet to drinkers.
> And of the fruits of the palms and the vines, you take
>   therefrom an intoxicant
>   and a provision fair.
>
>   (Koran 16:67)

But excesses among the believers became too disruptive and interfered with prayer, and a later revelation took a different stance:

> They will question thee concerning
> wine, and arrow-shuffling.[1] Say 'In both
> is heinous sin, and uses for men,
> but the sin in them is more heinous
>   than the usefulness.
>
>   (Koran 2:216)

This was seen as disapproval rather than prohibition, and wine was not forbidden until:

> O believers, wine and arrow-shuffling,
> idols and divining-arrows are an abomination,
> some of Satan's work; so avoid it; haply
>   so you will prosper.
>
>   (Koran 5:92)

It is not surprising that alcohol was finally forbidden as once the ritual of praying five times a day became the hallmark of the faith, it is difficult to see a time when the effects of drinking would not be present during one of the prayers.

After the conquest of Mecca Mohammed is said to have refused a present of wine, and to have had the wine poured away. W Montgomery Watt[1] suggests that if the prohibition was on wine in the strict sense (as distinct from other intoxicants) it could be interpreted as a prohibition on trading with enemies, as wine was normally imported from Syria and Iraq. A more likely reason for the prohibition, however, is the connection of wine with *maysir* (arrow-shuffling) in the verses quoted above from the Koran. *Maysir* was a pagan practice by which 10 men bought a camel, slaughtered it and drew lots for the portions. It has been suggested that the Koranic objection to *maysir* was not that it was a form of gambling, but that it

1. Gambling.

was closely connected with the pagan religion. It seems possible, therefore, that the main reason for the prohibition of wine may have been some as yet unestablished connection with pagan religion.

There are laws to be observed when drinking. In tradition blessings should be uttered before and after drinking. The cup should be held in the right hand, but opinions differ on whether drinking is permitted standing up. It is forbidden to drink out of the mouth of a water skin, nor should one drink like a dog or in other unseemly ways, nor should one drink the whole in one draught. If drinking in company, the cup should be passed to the right. It is thought that knowledge in these matters distinguishes the believer from the infidel.

Greetings

Salam alekum (peace be on you) is the traditional greeting, and the reply is *we alekum salam* (and on you be peace). This is still used universally in Arabic speaking countries, although other forms of greetings are used as Western influence grows.

Salam alekum is, according to the Koran, the greeting which is given to the blessed in Paradise or on entering Paradise. It is commanded to the Prophet:

> And when those who believe in Our signs come
> to thee, say, "Peace be upon you"

(Koran 6:154)

Shaking hands is encouraged by tradition, and is founded upon the express example of Mohammed himself. He is said to have remarked: 'There are no two Muslims who meet and shake hands but their sins will be forgiven before they separate'.

Salutation is a religious duty:

> And you are greeted with a greeting,
> greet with a fairer than it, or return it;
> surely God keeps a watchful count
> over everything.

(Koran 4:88)

Mohammed is said to have instructed people on precisely who greets whom in what circumstances: 'The person riding must salute someone on foot, and the small must salute the larger, a person of higher degree the lower', and so on. He is also said to have remarked that 'the nearest people to God are those who salute you first'. By tradition a man does not salute a woman unless she is old, although the Prophet is said to have done so.

1. *What is Islam?*, Longman, 1979.

Mosques

In the Message revealed by Mohammed, sanctuary for prayer was not a fundamental necessity; humility in the presence of God can be shown anywhere. In the beginning the *salat* (ritual worship)was performed in houses, or in any quiet place. The first mosque, literally a place for pro-stration, was built by the Prophet in Medina, but there was nothing sacred about its character. Its courtyard contained huts for his various wives, and believers and unbelievers went about freely inside. It was a general meeting place for Mohammed's followers; various tents and structures were put up at random, and in it all manner of affairs and business were conducted. Originally, therefore, the mosque was a place in which the believers assembled for prayer with the Prophet, and where he gave out regulations affecting the social life of the communi-ty. It had no specific form or content and what distinguished the earliest mosque from the Christian church, or the Meccan temple, was the absence of any specially dedicated ritual object. From this developed the general type of Muslim mosque, which, depending on circumstances, emphasized the place as a social centre or a place of prayer.

In the early centuries of Islam mosques were built in vast numbers and gradually their sanctity increased. The expression *Bait Allah* (House of God), which was first used only for the *Kaaba* came now to be applied to any mosque. As a result one could no longer enter a mosque at random as had been permitted in the time of the Prophet. The custom of taking off one's sandals before entering a mosque goes back to the early days of Islam. The believer, on entering, should place his right foot first and utter certain prayers, and when inside should perform two *rak'as* (a section of the *salat*). He should put on fine clothes for the Friday service, and rub himself with oil and perfume. It is evident from some *hadiths* that many did not want women in mos-ques, though it seems that no-one has any real authority to stop them entering. Other *hadiths* say that they should leave the mosque before the men, and sometimes a special part of the mosque was railed off for them. According to some, women must not enter the mosque during menstruation, and they should not be perfumed.

Although the mosque became a sacred place, it did not totally cast off its old character as a place of public assembly. Over the years it has been used as a place of business, and of shelter for strangers. As a result of spending the night in a mosque it naturally came about that people ate there, and in the end elaborate and formal banquets were held.

Although the *salat* can be performed anywhere, it is particularly meritorious to perform it in the mosque because this expresses adherence to the community. This is especially true of the Friday *salat*, which can only be performed in the mosque and is obligatory for every free male Muslim who has reached years of discretion.

An oath is particularly binding when taken in a mosque, and the contract of matrimony (but not the ceremony) is also often concluded there. The form of divorce effected by the *li'an* (disclaimer of paternity because of the wife's alleged adultery) takes place in the mosque.

The *qibla* is the direction of prayer, which in a mosque is marked by a niche in the wall facing the direction of Mecca. This niche is called the *mihrab*, and is often elaborately decorated. Every Friday mosque has a *minbar* — a kind of elevated pulpit located near the *mihrab*. In addition, mosques usually have a *kursi* — a wooden stand, a seat and a desk. The desk is for the Koran, and the seat for the reader. Carpets are often used to improve the appearance of mosques, and the custom of performing the *salat* on a carpet is ascribed by *hadith* to the Prophet himself. Later the chief mosques had the floor covered with a great number of sumptuous carpets, but some puritans rejected this fashion, preferring the bare ground. The Wahhabis still do.

Lighting is of particular importance, especially on ceremonial occasions, and has divine significance. In the month of Ramadan the level of illumination is increased, both inside and outside the building.

It was inherent in the character of Islam that religion and politics could not be separated. The same individual was ruler and chief administrator in the two fields, and the same building, the mosque, was the centre of gravity for both politics and religion. The Caliph was the appointed leader of the *salat*, and the appointed spokesman of the Muslim community, and as such he was the *imam*. The significance of the mosque for the State is therefore embodied in the *minbar*. When homage was first paid to Abu Bakr by those who had decided the choice of the Prophet's successor, he sat on the *minbar*. He delivered an address, and as the people paid homage to him he assumed the leadership. It was the same with the following Caliph, and this tradition was never abandoned. The Friday sermon (*khutba*) was delivered in the name of the Caliph or government and this is still so today. Gradually this system changed and the *imam* no longer represented a political office.

In modern times it is not always clear whether visitors are welcome to mosques and shrines, particularly those containing relics of the Prophet and of martyrs. It is necessary to approach a holy place with caution, and it will invariably be made clear whether unbelievers are permitted or not. According to strict religious dogma only the holy cities of Mecca and Medina are reserved exclusively for Muslims, and whether unbelievers are allowed in other holy places seems to be more a matter of local custom than religious ruling. Before crossing the threshold it is always necessary to remove one's shoes or to wear the overshoes supplied in some places.

The Prophet's Tomb

The Prophet's tomb should not be visited in the *ihram* or pilgrim dress: men should not kiss it, touch it with the hand, or press the bosom against it as at the *Kaaba*, or rub the face with dust collected near the sepulchre. Those who prostrate themselves before it are held to be guilty of a deadly sin. To spit upon any part of the mosque, or to treat it with contempt, is held to be the act of an infidel.

Dress

The Koran encourages Muslims to wear their good clothes when they go to the mosque.

According to *hadith* silk is not lawful for men to wear, but it is for women.[1] Men are prohibited from wearing gold or silver ornaments, but they are allowed a silver signet ring. Handkerchiefs must not be carried in the hand.

The Prophet said: 'Wear white clothes, because they are the cleanest and the most agreeable; and bury your dead in white clothes'. His own dress is said to have been extremely simple, and he never wore long robes to the ankle. It is said that a gold ring distracted his attention whilst praying, so he changed it for silver.

The 20th century has seen drastic changes in dress in most parts of the Middle East, largely as a result of Western influence. In most towns and cities men usually go in Western dress of some kind. An exception is in the Arabian peninsula, but even here, except for Oman and Yemen, the traditional turban has been abandoned in favour of a stylized form of traditional Bedu dress. These garments were normally worn only by the better off *sheikhs*, the ordinary Bedu for the most part being able to afford little more than simple shirts and loincloths. Nowadays stylized dress takes the form of a long shirt stretching to the ankles called a *thobe*, usually white in colour. A black *abba*, an over-garment stretching to the ground, is often worn over this by wealthy or important people. On the head is worn a kerchief called a *keffie* which is held in place by a cord round the head (*akal*), traditionally of camel hair. The headdress can by drawn across the face to shield it from sun and dust storms.

Charms

The use of amulets or charms is very widespread in Islamic countries.

1. Further details of women's dress are to be found on page 140ff.

They are often carried in small bags, lockets or purses, worn around the neck or fastened to the arm or turban. As soon as they are 40 days old, children are given amulets which may take the crude form of a shell, a piece of bone, or be made of gold or silver. Inscribed on them can be found a bewildering variety of devices, from the names of angels and verses from the Koran to magic squares and figures of animals and men. Figurative inscriptions are rarely found among Arabs, although they are common in Persia and India. The hand, usually called the hand of Fatima, is a very popular symbol among Muslims. It is carried around the neck, often cut from gold or silver, and is said to revoke the evil eye. The Shi'ites interpret the fingers as the five saints: Mohammed, Ali, Fatima, Hasan and Husain. The talisman, still known as Solomon's Seal and worn by Muslims and Jews alike, represents a six pointed star. Strictly, only the name of God or verses from the Koran should be used for amulets.

Muslim theology, which forbids sorcery, tolerates the use of amulets. They are usually made by Dervishes, who belong to the various brotherhoods, and are only of value when they are received from their hands.

Names

The teachings of Mohammed greatly influenced the names given to his followers. 'The best names given in the sight of God are Abd'allah (servant of God), Abdu'r-Rahman (the servant of the Merciful One)' ... 'You must not name your slaves Yasar (Abundance), Rabah (Gain), Najih (Prosperous), because if you ask for one of your servants and he is not present, it will mean that abundance, gain, prosperity are not in your home ... The vilest name you can give a human being is Maliku'l-amlak or King of Kings, because no-one can be such but God himself.'

Custom continued to use the names of ancient Arabia, but modified in accordance with the teachings of Mohammed. Single names are common, as Mohammed, Musa (Moses), Da'ud (David), Ibrahim (Abraham), Hasan, Ahmad. The prefix Abu means father of and Umm or Ummu means mother of. Thus Abu Issa is father of Jesus. Ibn means son of, as ibn Umar, son of Umar. Bizarre names are often found in desert regions, such as Abu Hurairah, the kitten's father. Sometimes trade names are used, for example, Hasan al-Hallaj, Hasan the dresser of cotton. Finally, people are sometimes called after their birthplace, as al-Bukhari, native of Bukharah.

Arabic names often undergo drastic modifications when the English tongue fails to get round them. For example, Saladin, the celebrated defender of Islam against the Crusades should properly be

Salahu'din, 'the peace of religion'.

Entertainments

Music, Singing and Dancing

There is an inconsistent and shifting balance between what strict religious authority lays down from time to time, and what popular custom evolves. The distinction comes out very clearly in the general area of public and private entertainment. Strict authorities believe that Islam forbids frivolous pleasures such as singing, dancing, playing and playing music of any kind. Yet it is evident that music is deeply rooted in the popular culture of North Africa, Lebanon and Egypt in particular, as well as Muslim South Africa and South East Asia. Furthermore, as if to compound the contradiction, many of the most talented and skilful performers are women.[1]

The general condemnation of music probably derives from the pious Wahhabi doctrine, and its influence on the Saud family. Certainly, the nearer one gets to the heartland of Islam, the weaker is the musical tradition, and in Saudi Arabia, where musical instruments were banned until a generation ago, it hardly exists at all.

Tradition has it that the Prophet was opposed to music, though the evidence for this is rather sketchy. This applies also to singing. It is generally held to be unlawful by Muslim theologians, and is based on a quotation from Mohammed: 'singing and hearing songs causes hypocrisy to grow in the heart, even as rain causes the corn to grow in the field'. The Sufis, who use music and song as an act of worship, say Mohammed only forbade songs of an objectionable character, but the general body of opinion is against them.

Dancing is also held to be unlawful by some authorities, although it is not forbidden either in the Koran or by tradition. According to Bukhari, the Prophet expressly permitted it on the day of the great festival. Those who hold dancing to be unlawful quote 'walk not in the earth exultantly' (Koran 17:39), although it is difficult to see how this can be used as a basis for prohibition. The Sufis dance as a religious exercise.

Whistling is mentioned in the Koran and the text is generally taken to mean that it is an idolatrous custom and is therefore forbidden.

1. The Egyptian singer, Umm Kulthum, was probably the most popular Arab in modern times, and her work was known and loved throughout the Middle East. Her death brought Cairo to a standstill, and mourners at her funeral outnumbered those for ex-President Nasser.

Theatre

Similar attitudes prevail towards theatrical performances, although the reasons here are more complex. There is in Islamic law a specific prohibition on payment for performance. In addition the segregation of women creates a major problem for the theatre.

Cinema, Broadcasting and Photography

The general prohibition on any kind of social change caused considerable problems with the introduction of photography, films, and wireless and television broadcasting. Islamic hostility to the making of images relates originally to the Koranic condemnation of the making and worshipping of idols. Subsequent religious authority in many places has expanded this prohibition to include all figurative illustration and art. The justification for this view is that God alone can create living things, and it is a sin and a blasphemy to attempt to imitate God. It is widely believed that on the Day of Judgement all those who have made images will be confronted by them and commanded to bring them to life. If they are not able to do so, they will be condemned to the fire of Hell. Consequently, in conservative Islamic countries it is quite rare to find any figurative art, what there is being confined to private houses. It is almost unknown in a public setting.

Outside Arabia the situation is different. Painting flourished under the Moghuls in India and in Persia the art of miniature painting and manuscript illustration is unsurpassed. Even so, it is quite common to see paintings with the faces despoiled by a subsequent religious purge. It is rare for a painting to show the face of the Prophet; the few artists who have painted scenes from Mohammed's life show him veiled.

All this has had consequences for photography and its development. Although photographs of heads of state are now common in all Muslim countries, this is a quite recent development. In Saudi Arabia and the Gulf States the photographing of women can provoke a hostile reaction. They were not allowed to be photographed, even for passports, until very recently, and many Muslim countries will still not ask for a woman's photograph for any official purpose. The situation is changing rapidly, but strangers taking photographs of people are sometimes unwelcome.

Wireless and television were eventually accepted because of their potential to spread the Message. Most of the air-time for Saudi television is devoted to the Koran and religious subjects, and any programme will be interrupted, without any transitional announcement, by the call to prayer.

Acceptance of public cinemas depends upon the strength of religious authority. There are none in Saudi Arabia, for example, but Cairo has many cinemas showing films from Europe and the USA, as well as local productions.

Sport

Sport appears to be the only important activity for which Islam does not lay down any special requirements, and every Muslim country seems to have adopted without qualification the sports suited to its climate and temperament. Sport is generally encouraged at all levels for both sexes, from participation in schools and colleges to international competition. The only restriction in some countries is that placed on women performing in public, and on those very few sports or games for mixed sexes.

No Muslim countries seem to have objections (except perhaps political ones) to joining all kinds of international sporting bodies, including the Olympic movement.

Animals

In Islam a dog is an unclean beast, and 'dog' is used as a term of abuse, especially when referring to unbelivers. According to the *hadith*, food which has come into contact with dogs becomes impure, and water may no longer be used for ritual purification. Vessels which have been licked by a dog must be cleaned several times and dogs make the *salat* worthless when they come into the vicinity. It is believed that angels will not enter a house where there is a dog, and that Satan occasionally appears in the form of a black dog. It is permissible to keep dogs only for hunting, herding and watching, but it is said that 'whoever possesses a dangerous dog keeps good fortune away from his house'.

Most people believe that when a dog howls without apparent cause in the neighbourhood of a house, it forbodes death to one of the residents; for the dog, they say, can distinguish the form of Azrael, the angel of death, hovering over the doomed abode, whereas man's spiritual sight is dim because of his sins.

For thousands of years the Arabs have domesticated the camel, and without it human survival would not have been possible in most of Arabia and the surrounding desert regions. In the Koran the animal given to man to ride upon is mentioned as an example of God's wisdom and kindness. Camels are a lawful sacrifice at great festivals and on other occasions, and *zakat* is payable on them. In law a driver is responsible for any damage done by the animals in his charge.

According to a *hadith*, Mohammed said: 'Cats are not impure, they keep watch around us'.

The Koran describes cattle (the title of the sixth *sura*) as being the gift of God:

> It is God who appointed for you the cattle,
> some of them to ride
> and some for you to eat.

> (Koran 40:79)

Mohammed's affection for horses is said to have been very great. The qualities of horses are much discussed in the *hadith*, even to the point of describing ideal colouring. It is laid down that in taking a share of plunder a horseman is entitled to a double share.

Bestiality is said by Muslim jurists to be the result of a most vitiated appetite and of the utmost depravity. It is unlawful but there is no *hadd*, only a discretionary punishment. According to law the beast should be killed and, if it is a lawful species, burnt.

Deportment

The traditions take some pain to explain the precise manner in which the Prophet walked, sat, slept and got up, but the accounts are not always consistent with each other. As a result, what appeared to be ordinary bodily functions turn out to have religious, if not legal, connotations. Tradition is very particular about sitting. Muslims must sit on the ground in places of public worship. In social gatherings superiors always sit higher in the order. It is bad manners to present the soles of one's feet towards a person in the company. There is even an order in which the shoes must be taken off (the right one first). Muslims are urged to sleep with their heads in the direction of Mecca. Some authors give ethical advice on how to walk and when to kneel, how to spit, and even how to blow your nose. But the overriding message is that the individual should conduct himself in public so as not to cause inconvenience or disgust to others, and in private so as to acquire good habits.

It is considered a duty to repond to a sneeze and say something like 'God be praised', which is similar to the Jewish custom. Mohammed said: 'God loves sneezing and hates yawning'.

The Prophet adopted certain ancient practices called *fitrah* (nature) which were common practice before his time. There are ten qualities of the Prophet: clipping the moustache so that it is clear of the mouth, not cutting the beard, cleansing the teeth, cleansing the nostrils with water at the ablutions, cutting the nails, cleansing the finger joints, pulling out hairs under armpits, shaving the pubic hair, washing with water after passing urine, and cleansing the mouth at ablution.

Vices and Virtues

In summary, then, a pious Muslim has a formidable list of social vices to avoid, and a daunting list of social virtues to cultivate.

According to strict custom Islam forbids frivolous pleasures (such as singing or music making), slander, lying, meanness, coarseness, intrigue, treachery, disloyalty in friendship, disavowal of kinship, ill nature, arrogance, boasting, sly scheming, insult and obscenity, spite and envy, inconstancy, aggressiveness and tyranny. According to Mohammed God has included in Islam the finest qualities and noblest virtues which are: kindliness and generosity in dealings between man and man, accessibility, free giving of what is lawful, feeding the poor, the dissemination of peace, visiting a sick Muslim, escorting the bier of a dead Muslim, being a good neighbour, honouring the aged, giving food and accepting invitations to eat with others, granting forgiveness, making peace between men, open handedness, generosity and liberality, being the first to give greeting and restraining one's anger.

A believer's word is his bond, and a Muslim must keep his promise. The Prophet is said to have hated untruths and although he was ready to accept cowards and misers as believers he refused to regard a liar as a true Muslim. Liars were classed in the same category as promise-breakers, men of bad faith and hypocrites. These are constantly denounced in the Koran, but lying as such is nowhere specifically mentioned. There may be circumstances under which it is justified, or even preferred to the truth, as, for example, where an innocent man might come to grief or danger if the truth were told.

Chapter 6
Family and Domestic Life

Family Structure

The family is the only group based on kinship or affinity which traditional Islam recognizes in law, and it is the bedrock of Islamic society. It is not surprising, therefore, that it should remain the focus and pivot of a Muslim's life. About a third of the Koran is devoted to family matters and relationships, and the importance of the family in Islam can hardly be exaggerated. The only other group recognized by tradition is the brotherhood of believers; all others, whether social or political, have been discouraged or forbidden, and this is still the case in conservative Islamic countries. Islam is the only religion which forbids the formation of groups and organizations, the justification being that it is a complete way of life, and by definition needs no man-made accessories.

The Muslim marriage is a contract in which both parties have rights and duties. It is a husband's duty to provide for his family, to treat his wives equally, and to keep them in the style to which they are accustomed. It is a woman's duty to look after her family and her husband, though not his house guests. She has control of the household, and although the religious education of the children is a joint responsibility, she often adopts a leading role here too. Grandmothers are often important in this respect. There is no community of property. A wife by law retains her own property, including her marriage dower, and has complete freedom of dealing. In rural communities she is expected to help with the cultivation of land and the care of animals. Conflicts arising from a disparity of wealth, or from expectation in terms of marital duties, are largely avoided by arranged marriages which aim at compatibility in social class.

The Koran in fact created a revolution in the status of women. Before this the women of Arabia had had no legal rights before the law. For the first time in the history of Oriental legislation the principle of women's rights was recognized.

> Women have such
> honourable rights as obligations, but
> their men have a degree above them.

(Koran 2:228)

And Mohammed said: 'Ye men, ye have rights over your wives, and your wives have rights over you'.

Traditionally, the qualities a Muslim looks for in his wife are chastity, contentment, respectfulness, submissiveness, and a humouring nature.

According to the *sharia*, a husband is not guardian over his wife except in terms of the contractual obligations of marriage. But if he does not carry out the basic duties, he is liable to imprisonment for neglect of maintenance. The evidence of a husband concerning his wife is not accepted by the Sunnis, but is allowed in Shi'ite law. Islamic law demands that a husband shall treat his wives equally and reside equally with each of them, unless one forgoes her right in favour of another wife.

A husband is legally bound to maintain his wife and her domestic servants, whether she and her servant belong to the Muslim faith or not. This is a contractual obligation of the husband, and lasts as long as the wife is subjected to the marital controls. The maintenance of a wife includes everything connected with her support and comfort, including her right to claim a home for her own exclusive use, the scale of which is consistent with her husband's means. In practice, however, these duties vary considerably from place to place.

According to tradition Mohammed said: 'That is the most perfect Muslim whose disposition is best, and best of you is he who behaves best to his wives' and 'Admonish your wives with kindness, because women were created from a crooked bone of the side; therefore, if you wish to straighten it, you will break it, and if you let it alone it will always be crooked.'

Fathers

In the Sunni law of inheritance a father receives one sixth of his son's or grandson's property. If the son dies unmarried without children the father takes the whole. According to the law of retaliation a father cannot be punished for taking the life of his son, because, as Hanifa has said, 'as the parent is the official cause of his child's existence it is not proper that the child should require or be the occasion of his father's death'. It is forbidden for a son to harm his father, even if in the army of an enemy, or to throw a stone at him if he is convicted of unlawful intercourse. In the law of evidence the testimony of a father brought against his child is not admitted in a court of law.

Mothers

Kindness towards a mother is required by the Koran. 'Be kind to parents, and the near kinsman' (Koran 4:40). Mothers cannot be compelled to nurse their children, but they are not allowed to move them to a strange place without their husband's permission.

Children

While the Koran does not prescribe rituals relating to birth, or training and instruction of the young, the subject is frequently referred to in tradition.

After the birth of a child, when he has been properly washed and dressed, he is carried by the midwife to the assembly of male relatives and friends. Someone present then recites the *azan* (call to prayer) in the infant's right ear and the *iqamah* (the second call to prayer) in the left ear. The Maulawi[1] then chews a little date fruit and inserts it into the infant's mouth, a custom said to have been founded on the example of Mohammed. After this alms are distributed and prayers recited for the health and prosperity of the child. According to tradition the amount of silver given as alms should be the same weight as the hair on the infant's head: the child's head being shaved for this purpose. After this the house is open to friends and neighbours to bring presents and congratulations.

The child should be named on the seventh day, the name being taken from either some member of the family, or saint, or some name suggested by the astrological situation. Also on the seventh day Mohammed established a ceremony of sacrifice to God. In the name of the child two goats are sacrificed for a boy, and one for a girl. The goats must be under one year old and without any blemish. The animal is dressed and cooked and, while it is being eaten, the assembled offer a prayer, although modern custom varies.

The mother is ritually purified on the 40th day, after which she is free to go about as usual. As soon as the child is able to talk, or when he has attained the age of four years four months and four days he is taught the *Bism'illah*, the first words of the Koran: *Bism'illah ir-Rahman ir Rahim* (in the name of God the Merciful, the Compassionate).

Children, and particularly, sons, are considered a blessing. There is no hierarchy of birth; the eldest son enjoys no privilege of either treatment or inheritance. Older children are expected to set an example,

1. From *maulà*, a term generally used for a learned man.

and to teach the younger ones such things as the ritual prayer.

Children are taught what is expected from them, and what they can expect in return. They learn to respect older people, to be helpful to neighbours and generous to guests. As a result of the strong family bond, crime rates generally are very low in most places, and non-existent in others. If necessary families will act together to defend their rights; and their commitments, such as marriage and funeral expenses, are treated as a joint responsibility.

In pre-Islamic times the principle ruled that 'the child follows the bed' — that is, its paternity was reckoned to be the husband of its mother at that time. Bearing in mind that marriage and divorce were both frequent and swift, paternity was frequently not given to the natural father. Islam modified the principle by laying down that a pregnant woman, when widowed or divorced, could not re-marry until the child was born. As a general rule a child born in wedlock is considered legitimate, and is recognized by the husband, providing it is born more than six months after cohabitation begins. A husband may, but is not obliged to, acknowledge a child born in less than six months. The legitimacy of a child born after cohabitation ends varies with various sects. For the Shi'ites the time limit is 10 months, Hanafi law makes the limit two years, and the Shafi'ite and Malikite codes provide for a period of four years.

The law that the child follows the bed is linked with the *hadith* stating that 'the adulterer gets nothing'. A child therefore belongs to its mother's husband even if he is not the natural father. In these circumstances, Shi'ite law gives paternity to the husband unless he disallows it formally by pronouncing the *li'an* (see page 108) against his wife. This may be withdrawn later if the husband wishes to acknowledge paternity. In any case, an adulterer cannot claim paternity of a child.

In general, therefore, Islam places few obstacles in the way of recognizing the legitimacy of children. Only if a Muslim man knows he has no right to a woman as his wife or as his concubine, or if a Muslim woman marries a non-Muslim are the children of such unions declared illegitimate. Consequently, at the present day, except in Iran, 'bastard' will very rarely be heard as a term of abuse, but 'son of a whore' is not uncommon.

By a curious anomaly in Islamic law, kidnapping a freeborn child does not incur the *hadd* punishment of amputation, because a free person is not property. However, the scholar Abu Yusuf adds that if the child has jewellery or other valuables attached to him worth more than 10 *dirhams*, then property is violated, and amputation is the punishment. Amputation is also inflicted for stealing an infant slave, because a slave is property.

Although in Islamic law of inheritance all sons share equally, in cases of chieftainship or monarchy, the eldest son normally has perference; but his is not automatic and he must demonstrate that he is equal to and fit for the position. Very often when the eldest son is passed by, because he has not satisfied the community of his suitability, a younger brother is selected as ruler. If none of the children is considered suitable to inherit the leadership or the crown, a brother might be selected for the position.

In the case of orphans, under the *sharia* law the burden falls upon the widow to manage as best she can. The tribe will not have more than a general obligation to provide for the destitute, and a new husband is under no compulsion to feed extra mouths if he does not want to. Charitable and pious foundations exist to take charge of children without parents or kinsmen, and they then become a charge on the community.

A male child is not required to observe all the customs of the Muslim law until he has reached puberty, but it is the duty of the parents and guardians to teach him the prayers as soon as he has been circumcised. When a child has finished reciting all of the Koran once through the occasion is marked by the scholar presenting his tutor with presents.

The Koran lays down few regulations on bringing up children. Where parents are married and cohabiting they are jointly responsible for rearing their children, the father providing the material necessities, and the mother taking charge of their physical well-being and religious training. In the case of a dispute the mother has custody of children during their infancy. The exact period of custody is not specified in the Koran and the various schools of law have different ideas on the subject. The Shi'ites, for example, specify two years in the case of a boy, and seven years for a girl. The Shafi'ite school, on the other hand, specified seven years as a general rule, at which age the child is considered to be able to discriminate and can choose with which parent it wishes to live. However, the mother in such cases must be respectable, stable, and unmarried.

The extended family is as important as the family unit. It is an important day when a son is married, because the family is increased by the addition of a daughter-in-law, who is received by, and under the protection of, the bridegroom's family. Similarly, when a daughter is married, she passes into the care of another family, although she does not change her family name. This is retained as a symbol of her status in the new situation, and as a link with her blood relations, to whom in the last resort she can turn for protection.

Unlike the Christian and Jewish religions, there are in Islam no religious ceremonies connected with birth, marriage, death, circumcision, attainment of adulthood, or even commitment to and acceptance of the faith. Such ceremonies as exist are prescribed by custom, rather than religion, although prayers may be said, and an *imam* might take part in the various ceremonies.

Birth

Although there is no ceremony connected with birth there are legal definitions relating to childbirth. According to Hanafi law a married woman's claim to motherhood of a child must be supported by the testimony of one woman. In the case of a father, his testimony alone is accepted.

The testimony of a midwife alone is valid in respect of birth, but legal parentage is established by the fact of the mother of the child being the wife of the husband. According to *hadith*, if the woman is in her *idda* (suspended divorce), the testimony of the midwife with respect to birth is not enough. The evidence of two men, or one man and two women, is required.

Contraception is a relatively modern social concern, and there is no guidance in either the Koran or the *Sunna* for modern Muslims. However, in recent times various religious authorities[1] have considered the question and have concluded that contraception is permissible under Islamic law. Although one of the functions of marriage is procreation, this is conditional upon the availability of the means to bear the cost of a child's education and training, so that he can be properly brought up, and not develop anti-social ways. There are genuine traditions which allow methods for restricting procreation, and these are seen as no different from the use of pharmaceutical contraceptive methods. Equally, it is not considered right that pregnancies should injure the health of a woman or weaken her unduly.

Mohammed is often quoted as saying that 'the greatest catastrophes are many children and meagre sustenance', and this is often used as a slogan in Islamic family planning organizations. The fact that the Prophet allowed coitus interruptus has encouraged the legal schools to sanction it, but the Maliki school insists that the wife must agree to this procedure, whatever her age. Similarly in Iraq, Pakistan, Afghanistan and Syria, the Shi'ite Ga'afareyz condone this method if it is agreed with the wife at the time of marriage. According to the Prophet withdrawal should not be practised with a free woman unless she agrees.

Muslims distinguish abortion from contraception, because it is an assault on life and therefore could be a criminal act; they believe that it

1. The Grand Mufti of Jordan, December 1964, and the Fatwa Committee, Al Azhar University, March 1953.

is a crime after 'quickening of life' has taken place — that is when the movement of the foetus can be felt. This is consistent with tradition which has special rules concerning an assault on a pregnant woman and subsequent damage to a foetus. After the quickening as taken place, a foetus has human rights in law including the rights of inheritance and blood money. However, if the mother's life is endangered by the pregnancy, the lesser evil is to be allowed and the mother must be saved. The only other ground for abortion appears to be if there is a strong possibility that the baby will be born deformed. The underlying assumption, therefore, is that the foetus has a right to live, but that it is not an absolute right.

Throughout the Middle Ages it was common for Muslim physicians to advise their patients on contraception. One of them, Avicenna (ibn Seena) (died 1037 AD), in his *Laws of Medicine* described 20 methods of contraception, most of which had apparently been used for hundreds of years.

The attitude of modern Islam towards birth control varies according to population size, birth rates and economic and material resources. In Kuwait and Saudi Arabia contraception is advised only for medical reasons. In Tunisia and Egypt[1] the governments officially approve and encourage birth control. This is true also of Pakistan and Turkey, and the reasons for adopting the policy are economic rather than religious.

A clear distinction is made between contraception and permanent sterilization, which all authorities agree is not permitted.

Circumcision

Circumcision of both males and females seems to have been common in early Arabia, and the custom was absorbed by Islam. It is not mentioned in the Koran, but a *hadith* describes it as *sunna* (traditional, customary) for men and honourable for females.

For males the operation is described as cutting off the whole of the skin which covers the glans, and for females as cutting off a small part of the skin in the highest part of the genitals to expose the clitoris[2]. The age at which circumcision takes place varies according to local custom. In *hadith* it is said that Ibrahim (Abraham) was circumcised at the age of 80. In Mecca children are circumcised between the age of three and seven years, girls without festivities, and boys with great ceremony. In Egypt boys are, or were, circumcised at the age of five or six years. Sometimes the operation is performed in groups of children, the

1. Egypt currently has one of the world's biggest growth rates, projected to double within 30 years.
2. This operation is not unknown in the West.

richest family paying the whole cost. The formal procession is led by a boy who is, obscurely, dressed with ceremony and pomp as a girl. It is common for the local barber to perform the operation. In North Africa a child born with a short foreskin is considered a great blessing.

In the circumcision of females it is particularly important to distinguish between what Islam prescribes and what is accorded to local custom. The *Shorter Encyclopaedia of Islam* gives the following translation of al-Nawawi (1283AD):

> Circumcision is obligatory according to al-Shafi, *Sunna* according to Malik and the majority .... As regards females, it is obligatory to cut off a small part of the skin in the highest part of the genitals .... The second view within the limits of our school is that circumcision is allowed, but not obligatory.

This description is a far cry from the mutilation practised in some countries up to modern times. In Egypt, according to Nawal El Saadawi, an Egyptian woman doctor, circumcision meant the amputation of the whole or part of the clitoris of young girls in a primitive operation. In the Sudan it was even more drastic, with the removal of all the external genital organs: the clitoris and the inner and outer lips (*labia majora* and *minora*). The wounds were then stitched up. No-one seems able to give a reason for these rituals, and certainly no justification can be found in any of the legal manuals of Islam. In recent years these practices have declined.

The treatment of circumcision in general does not have a prominent place in the books of Islamic law, but importance and value is still attached to it in popular opinion. Its merits and demerits are still contested by physicians: some consider it a barbaric ritual and others a hygienic operation, some believe it heightens sexual gratification, and others that it diminishes it.

Collective Responsibilities

An individual is responsible to the family for social behaviour, and the family is responsible to society for the behaviour of the individual. If an individual does harm, the family will be held responsible for the consequences, and if wrong is done to an individual, his family will automatically support him. This has important consequences, particularly in respect of upholding the law. The violence and lawlessness of Western cities is a source of continuing amazement to Muslim communities. They are surprised the police cannot find lawbreakers, when they know that in their own community they would be found and punished within a few days. Their young men are more afraid of what the family will do or say than they are of the police. An individual is therefore very cautious in his dealings and behaviour because it will be subject to the scrutiny of his relatives and his community, all of whom will be involved in any wrongdoing. The reputation of an individual man or woman reflects upon the family.

If trouble occurs between families, there are in some countries customary procedures to be followed as well as legal ones. For example, in the case of a road accident in which a boy is knocked down, even if the police vindicate the driver this will be irrelevant so far as the driver's family is concerned. The first thing for them to do is to visit the boy's family and arrange a truce, so that the boy's family will not retaliate to restore family honour. If the boy dies, the driver's family has to pay a fixed sum in compensation for accidental death. If he recovers, the truce ends and there is a ceremonial feast which representatives of both families attend. The driver's family will give thanks to God for the boy's wellbeing, and the boy's family will express forgiveness, acknowledging that it was an accident. Documents are signed to say that peace is restored.

The ultimate responsibility of the family, then, is to defend its honour. This includes the way all members behave in society and particularly includes the chaste behaviour of its women. A family is responsible for the esteem with which it is regarded, and it is the unavoidable duty of its men to defend and preserve the honour of the family.

If family honour is violated the shame attached to it can be a harder punishment to bear than any prescribed by the law. Even in cases of *hadd* offences, the pressure of social opinion can not only modify the punishment, but also inflict an alternative which is meant to be as severe. For example, the legal penalty for unlawful intercourse in Oman is stoning to death, or one year's imprisonment and the accompanying shame. In North Yemen, if stoning is ordered, the stones are always pebbles, cast from a distance where they will inflict only shame.

Respect for Elders

In Islam there is a profound respect for knowledge and experience. As these qualities are normally associated with age, respect for one's elders is deeply ingrained. This veneration derives in part from the fact that Islam is a legalistic system which necessitates knowing the rule for each occasion. Equally, the stability of the family depends on, among other things, stable judgement and guidance, and both of these considerations establish the elderly in a privileged position.

A sense of hierarchy is particularly strong in the family. A younger person will automatically rise to his feet when an older relative comes into the room. If he wears a traditionally cut *thobe* (see page 109) with loose sleeves he will hide his hands as a sign of deference.

The respect for knowledge is demonstrated by the power and authority of the *ulema* (religious scholars), who derive their position from their knowledge of the Koran and *Sunna*, or, in the case of the Shi'ites, from the *imams*, on whom the community relies for guidance in all aspects of human behaviour.

Neighbours

The Sunni define neighbours as those who worship in the same mosque. The Shi'ites generally refer to a neighbour as one living in close proximity (40 cubits)[1], whilst others maintain that the term covers the occupants of 40 houses on either side. This can be important in matters of real estate. A neighbour has the next right after a partner in the sale and purchase of houses and land. The Prophet laid down that a neighbour has a superior right to purchase a house (next to an immediate relative), and this applies also to land. If the neighbour is absent the owner must wait until his return before selling.

The Koran urges kindness to neighbours, and tradition has it that 'he is not a perfect Muslim who eats his fill and leaves his neighbour hungry'.

According to tradition there was a man who once said to the Prophet 'There is a woman who worships God a great deal but she is very abusive to neighbours'; the Prophet replied 'She will be in the fire'. The man then told him 'But there is another woman who worships little and gives but little in alms, but she does not annoy her neighbours with her tongue'; the Prophet said 'She will be in Paradise'.

Houses and Homes

Muslim family relationships, whether through observance of the religious laws or through custom or both, have a direct bearing on the layout and design of houses.

In the first place, a typical Muslim will be keen to live in very close proximity to the homes of his brothers and other close male relatives. The private and secluded nature of family life makes it an advantage for members of an extended family to be readily accessible. If a man is away from home, or some misfortune befalls him, he is secure in the knowledge that there is a trusted man on hand to protect and look after his family.

Secondly, houses and apartments were, and are, designed to suit the way of life of the family. There are separate entrances for the men and

1. A cubit is the length of a forearm, ie about 18-22 inches.

for the women and children. In rural districts, and in some suburban settings, there are often separate huts, or buildings for the two parts of the family. If the family is rich, there might well be separate palaces within a common enclosure or estate. The nature of the establishment and the degree of luxury does not alter the principle. The men's apartment will always have a *majlis* (literally 'a meeting of the parties'). In prosperous households, each adult male will have his own *majlis*. The *majlis* is used for entertaining relatives, guests, and business acquaintances. The favourite time for gathering is after sunset, and normally there are regular times at which the heads of families, or leaders of the community can be found in their *majlis*. This means that families and friends can congregate regularly, to discuss the events of the day, and the nearer the group is to its Bedu origins, the more the gossip will hinge on the minutest detail of events. In accordance with Islamic tradition and tribal custom, there is little or no formal ceremony in the *majlis*, although politeness and courtesy are indispensable. The courtesies are exactly the same whether a king is entertaining a head of state, or a *sheikh* is listening to a grievance from his poorest follower. Provided there is physical room, access is readily available to all. Even a total stranger will be entertained, and he will not be asked his business: he must broach the subject first in his own time.

The traditional style of furnishing was described by Sir Richard Burton[1] in the 1880s:

> The *diwan* — it must not be confused with the leathern perversion which obtains that name in our club smoking room — is a line of flat cushions ranged around the room...varying in height unto the fashion of the day...It should be about three feet in breadth and slope very gently from the outer edge towards the wall for the greater convenience of reclining. Cotton stuffed pillows with chintz for summer and silk for winter are placed against the wall and can be moved to make a luxurious heap. A seat of honour is denoted by a small square cotton stuffed silk coverlet placed in one of the corners which the position of the windows determines, the place of distinction being on the left of the host.

The reference to the windows relates to their positioning to give efficient cross ventilation of air. Before the invention of air-conditioning, window sills were normally built to the floor for the benefit of the *majlis'* reclining occupants. Nowadays modern chairs are normally used.

A dining room is usually located next to a *majlis* offering direct access. Adjacent will be found facilities for guests to perform ablutions before and after a meal. In a prosperous household, living accommodation for guests is attached to the *majlis*.

1. *Personal Narrative of a Pilgrimage to Al Madinah and Meccah,* Dover Publications, NY, 1887.

The women's entrance gives access to the family rooms, the kitchen and the bedrooms. Access is forbidden to this part of the house to all men who are not close relatives. *Haram* is Arabic for forbidden, and *harem* is a derivation. Gardens and outdoor spaces are normally surrounded by high walls.

In a traditional house there are no rooms set aside specifically for sleeping. Male visitors and friends will sleep in the verandas, or in the *diwan* on the first floor. It is also common to sleep on the roof in hot weather, and wide staircases are often built up to this level so that beds can be carried out. Masonry parapets at roof level are often built to screen the roof from public view, but are normally perforated to allow the cross circulation of air. Apart from being used for sleeping the flat roofs are often used for a variety of household purposes such as drying corn, linen and fruit.

Houses with wind towers are a Persian invention, but can often be found on the Arabian side of the Gulf. The wind towers project above roof level and are so designed to catch a breeze from any direction and direct it down into the dwelling. This system of natural ventilation is quite sophisticated, and is controlled by a series of opening shutters set in the external walls, which may be adjusted to give the best conditions at different times of the day.

It is distinctly uncivil behaviour to enter a Muslim's house without his permission, as both the Koran and tradition stress. It is, strictly speaking, necessary for a man to ask permission of his mother to see her, even if they live in the same household.

Mohammed had very firm views about money and real estate. He is reported to have said 'verily the most unprofitable thing that eateth up the wealth of a believer is building'.

Death and Burial

Death occurs at a time appointed by God. Precise preparations are made to prepare the body for the wait for the Resurrection and the Day of Judgement.

When a Muslim is dying, after having made his will, a learned reader of the Koran is sent for to recite *sura 36*, in order that, by hearing it, the spirit of the man might experience an easy release.

The Koran says nothing about funerals, but the manuals of law describe the ritual in minute detail. As soon as a Muslim is dead, he is laid on a stretcher with his head in the direction of the *qibla* (direction of prayer), after which begins the ritual washing. The body is then wrapped in shrouds, the number and nature of which depends upon custom, but the colour is generally white. After this the *salat* for the dead is performed which includes an additional prayer for the deceased and must be meticulously followed. This ceremony takes place in the house of mourning, not in the mosque or in the graveyard (which is considered too polluted for the sacred book). The nearest relative is an appropriate person to recite the service, but it is usually said by the family *imam*. It is forbidden to perform the *salat* to an unbeliever, nor may he be washed, but he must be buried. A martyr is not washed, in order not to remove traces of blood which are the hallmark of his martyrdom; nor is it necessary to pray for his soul. Keeping watch over a dead body is not prescribed in the manuals of law, although it is common in Egypt. Tradition disapproves of the old Semitic custom of burning a light by the side of the deceased. The dead are seldom interred in coffins, but this is not forbidden.

The burial service was established by Mohammed and varies little from place to place, although the ceremonies connected with the funeral procession vary according to local custom. In Egypt and other places, for instance, the male relations and friends of the deceased precede the corpse, whilst the female mourners follow behind. In India and Afghanistan women do not usually attend the funeral, and relatives and friends walk behind. There is a tradition among some Muslims that no-one should precede the corpse, as the angels of death go before it.

The stretcher is carried to the burial place by men, even when the deceased is a woman. The corpse of a woman must be hidden from the eyes of the public. Whether bystanders stand up at a funeral procession depends upn the school of law. Some do in the presence of the angels of death, and others do not because it is a Jewish custom. It is recommended to follow a funeral procession, but it is forbidden to do so on horseback, since the angels of death go on foot.

It is considered meritorious to carry the bier, but unlike Christians who customarily walk slowly to the grave, Muslims carry out the procession quickly. Mohammed is reported to have said that it is good to carry the dead quickly to their graves so that the righteous person arrives sooner to happiness; if the deceased was unrighteous, it is well to put wickedness away from one's shoulders. There is merit in attending a funeral whether it be for a Muslim, Jew or Christian.

The burial itself is performed by an odd number of men; the body is laid down in the grave with the head in the direction of the *qibla*, after which the bystanders each cast three handfuls of earth on the grave. Either on the deathbed or in the grave, the confession of faith is recited into the deceased's ear. This is to remind him to give the right answer when the angels interrogate him in his grave.

The manuals of law specifically disapprove of any ornamenting of graves, even by an inscription, although the location of the head may be marked by a stone or piece of wood. In spite of this prohibition, elaborate tombs have often been constructed out of popular esteem especially over the graves of saints. The grave of a woman is covered with a garment.

On the third day after the burial it is usual for relatives to visit the grave and to recite selections from the Koran. If they can afford it, they pay learned men to recite the whole of the Holy Book. During mourning the relatives do not wear any bright clothing nor do they change any soiled garments.

Before and after the burial, visits of condolence are paid, and the manuals of law give detailed prescriptions on exactly what one should say. It is recommended to hold a banquet after the burial, but not on the same day. On this occasion passages from the Koran are recited, and the good works of the deceased are remembered.

Suicide is not mentioned in the Koran but it is forbidden in tradition. Mohammed said 'whosoever shall kill himself shall suffer in the fire of Hell'. It is also related that Mohammed refused rites to a suicide, but it is nonetheless usual in Islam for them to be performed. He is said also to have refused the *salat* unless debts of the deceased had already been paid. In law therefore the mourners are recommended to settle debts quickly. The *hadith* is contradictory as to whether Mohammed held the *salat* on behalf of those who had been legally executed.

The burning of the dead (or the living) is strictly forbidden, although there is nothing to confirm the impression that the burning of the corpse in any way prevents his soul from entering Paradise. Tradition has it that a dead body is as fully conscious of pain as a living one.

Weeping and excessive lamentation at the graves of the dead is clearly forbidden by the Prophet, who is reported to have said 'whatever is from the eyes (tears) and whatever is from the heart (sorrow) are from God; but what is from the hands and tongue is from the Devil. Keep yourselves, O women, from wailing, which is the noise of the Devil'. However, the custom of wailing at tombs of the dead is common in all Muslim countries.

Chapter 7

The Status of Women

The Status Defined

> Men are the managers of the affairs of women
> for that God has preferred in bounty
> one of them over another, and for that
> they have expended of their property.
> Righteous women are therefore obedient,
> guarding the secret for God's guarding.
> And those you fear may be rebellious
> admonish; banish them to their couches,
> and beat them. If they then obey you,
> look not for any way against them.
>
> (Koran 4:38).

In these few words, God has made known the status of women in relation to men. In relation to other matters the status, rights and duties of women are defined with various degrees of rigidity, but in this the message is clear, finite and complete; it is not a matter for discussion or compromise. The Koran also states:

> Your women are a tillage for you; so come
> unto your tillage as you wish.
>
> (Koran 2:223).

Women in this context means wives, and clearly they are to be seen as subject to a husband's control. To what extent this attitude was a legacy of pre-Islamic times is unclear. Some authorities have suggested that among many tribes in ancient Arabia a form of polyandry had existed in which government was by matriarchy. This may have been true either if property was not inherited, or if such as there was was inherited through the female line. It is also possible that the harsh realities of the desert encouraged the restriction of the numbers of females; certainly the burial of unwanted girls at birth seems to have been common. One of the significant changes brought about by the Koran was the unconditional forbidding of this practice. Islam also recognized poverty as a cause of this and other abuses, and sought to relieve this situation by compulsory giving of alms. At the same time the doctrine that no believers were to be taken captive prevented the taking of Muslim prisoners and led to the gradual disappearance of marriage by capture. That custom was still widespread in the Prophet's time and, although women taken into captivity might be treated with great consideration and even regard, the possibility of marriage by capture reduced the general status of women to chattels. Personal freedom and independence, however, were hardly burning issues in ancient Arabia. Apart from the ability to possess and dispose of property,[1] and the choice of a marriage partner (the two matters are not unconnected), men were in a similar position to women in this respect. Even so it seems to have been rare, though not unknown, for women to exert their will on questions of marriage, and it has been suggested that the cases which are often quoted to prove that the status of women was high are those of exceptional people, and have been preserved for that reason.

In the early Muslim era there seems to be little doubt that the woman was subordinate either to her husband, or to her nearest male kinsman. His rights over her were the same as over any other property, but an interesting corollary was that, like his other property, he had to watch over it. His wife's honour was entirely in his hands, and it was his responsibility to see that it was not violated. If he failed in his duty to mount suitable protection over her, no stigma attached to the woman for alliance with another man. Proprietry marriage carried with it no moral or legal sanctions, although within the tribe his rights to his wife or other property would be respected. But if a man from another tribe seduced a married woman, he committed no unlawful or dishonourable act, and poets constantly boasted of their conquests. Seducers, however, were fair game for the vengeance of both the husband's and the wife's kinsmen.

In addition to marriage by capture there existed, before Mohammed's day, marriage by contract. This made no difference to the status of women, as the suitor paid a sum of money to the woman he wished to marry, and sometimes to the father also. This payment gave the husband exclusive rights to the services of his wife.

---

1. Inheritance only became a problem when there was a significant amount of property to inherit. In the harsh nomadic life of the desert, inheritance was largely irrelevant. Apart from a few personal possessions, the only significant property was the camel herds on which the survival of the group depended. Settlement based on agriculture was very limited in scope, but the establishment of the caravan trade made settlement in towns both possible and necessary, and led to the accumulation of wealth in the hands of individuals. This shift of emphasis reflects the attitude of a society moving from a communal basis to an individualistic one.

Property Rights

Payments such as those made in a marriage by contract have a bearing on whether women in pre-Islamic times could own property. Although there is contradictory evidence, direct payments to women suggest that they could. This view is also supported by the position of Mohammed's first wife, Khadija, who all sources agree was a wealthy widow in her own right. Indeed, according to tradition, Mohammed encountered considerable financial hardship when she died, which suggests that, instead of her husband and daughters inheriting on her death, her assets reverted to her nearest male kin as custom demanded.

In the matter of inheritance the Koran made important social reforms. No doubt some of the principles involved in the revised laws were brought about by the circumstances of the times. Tradition relates that after the battle of Uhud a widow of one of the fallen complained to Mohammed that she and her three children were left destitute because her husband's inheritance had reverted to his kinsmen, perhaps because the husband's family was hostile to Mohammed's cause. The Prophet received the revelation:

> To the men a share of what parents and kinsmen
> leave, and to the women a share of what
> parents and kinsmen leave, whether it be
> little or much, a share apportioned.

> (Koran 4:7)

Later in the same *sura* more detailed instructions were given concerning what proportions of a man's inheritance were to be given to his family and relations. Equality was not the purpose, because sons inherited twice as much as daughters, but strict provision was made for wives, mothers and daughters depending upon the numbers involved and the numbers of male relatives entitled to a share. There was also a clear statement that husband and wife should retain control over their own property; there was no provision for common ownership, and a woman retained her complete freedom of dealing. A woman also had exclusive rights over her wedding dower, which probably confirmed existing practice. The Koran forbids any coercion of women in respect of their property and it is illegal for a husband to withhold divorce from a woman who is entitled to it if his motive is to retain her possessions within the family. It is also illegal to divorce a wife on a false charge so that a husband may retain some of the property lawfully belonging to her.

In matters of property, therefore, women have been guaranteed by law a share in inheritance since the seventh century. In this respect they were ahead of some of their sisters in the West. This long tradition of the right to property has encouraged women who are so minded to conduct business in their own right.

In certain of the more conservative countries it is necessary for them to do this through the services of a *wakil*, or commissionaire, who deals with all the necessary face to face business. This cumbersome arrangement naturally does not encourage women to participate in commerce, but in countries where constitutional changes have been made, Muslim women participate openly in business affairs. Although it is the common Muslim view that women are unsuited to working in public and holding public office, there is no edict to this effect in the Koran.

Marriage

In Islam marriage is a contract and not a religious ceremony. The taking of more than one wife, which to many outsiders appears to be a licence, was in fact, at the time, a limitation. Before Mohammed there was no limit to the number of wives a man might have, except that dictated by his means. The Koran limits the number to four and at the same time recognizes that there might be difficulty in treating wives with impartiality. In modern times, it is comparatively rare in most Muslim countries for a man to have more than one wife at a time. Apart from Western influences on relationships there are few men who can afford the separate establishments required by law, custom and expediency. The Koran provides that polygamy for women is forbidden, and they are always restricted to one husband.

There are many *hadiths* on the subject of marriage and one in particular deserves notice here. That is, that no woman can be married without her consent. It is a popular misconception that arranged marriages are part of the Islamic faith; it is, more accurately, an Eastern custom which is not confined to Muslims. It is true that the practice is firmly established in almost all Islamic countries, but it is not a religious requirement, and the Koran says nothing about it.

Moreover, an arranged marriage is not the same as a forced marriage, and, while custom encourages the first, it does not sanction the second. Marriage in the East is seen as uniting two families rather than two individuals. (Mohammed himself used marriage with several of his wives to strengthen alliances with neighbouring tribes.) As such the choice of a suitable partner is the concern and business of the whole family. Nor is an arranged marriage a marriage of convenience. It is usual, rather than exceptional, for family relationships to be very close, and it is against a background of love and trust that parents will select what they judge to be suitable matches for their children. This is not to say that there is no family pressure, but, as in the West, this is usually reserved for what parents consider an unsuitable match. Pressure usually concerns a father's relationship with his son. If a father wishes to be united with a certain family, he will make it known to his son that he would particularly like him to marry a particular girl and more often than not the son will comply with his father's wish. Marriage is thus seen not as a way of achieving individual satisfaction or happiness but as a way of caring for needs, ensuring the survival of the family unit, and providing an environment in which religious precepts and obligations may be fulfilled.

Koranic law and custom both lay down specifications as to whom a man may marry. In general the Koran makes it lawful to marry any woman except an idolatress. Chaste women who have received revealed scriptures (that is, Jews and Christians) are approved. The Shafi'ites make it almost impossible to wed non-Muslim women, although the Prophet did not confine his marriages to believing women. On the other hand, by Koranic law, a Muslim woman may marry no-one but a believer, although this custom has been modified in certain countries.

Islamic law made sweeping changes to pagan custom as regards marriages which were prohibited as incestuous. It is not lawful for a man to marry either the widow or the divorced wife of his father, nor is he allowed to marry the sister of a woman to whom he has been married. Such marriages were allowed in pre-Islamic times. It is also prohibited for a man to marry his daughters, his sisters, his aunts on either side of the family, his brother's and his sister's daughters, his son's wives, a woman and her daughter, or a woman who is already lawfully married. A law peculiar to Islam is that forbidding marriage between two people suckled by the same foster mother, or between the foster mother and the person who has been suckled. The law also prohibits a man from marrying his grandmother or granddaughter, or a woman and her niece at one time.

Islam has no fixed age limits for marriage, and quite young children may be married legally; one of Mohammed's wives was betrothed to him at the age of six. A bride is not handed over to her husband, however, until she is fit for marital congress. Betrothal may take place at any age. In practice, either the age limit for marriage is laid down by the State, as in the USSR,[1] or judicial obstacles are put in the way of child marriage without actually making it illegal, as in Egypt where marriages cannot be registered unless the parties have reached a specified minimum age. Nevertheless, in Egypt not many girls remain unmarried after 16, but here, as elsewhere, there is a tendency for the marriageable age to increase.

The preliminaries to a first marriage are, with some exceptions,

1. USSR here refers to the Muslim Republics in the South which are subject to Soviet law.

similar in most Muslim communities. Traditionally, whether the family or the bridegroom selects a prospective wife, it is the bride-groom's mother or near female relative who calls on the mother of the girl and asks her to put the matter to her husband. If the suitor's mother receives an evasive reply, the matter normally ends there. If the girl being married is a virgin she may be ignorant of negotiations that are proceeding, and in theory she may be promised to a man she has never seen.

On an appointed day the *imam* (prayer leader) goes with the prospective bridegroom and his friends to ask the girl's father formally for his daughter's hand. The amount of the *mahr* (marriage dower) is then settled. Next, the *imam* recites prayers and sends to a *qadi* to ask him to grant the necessary permission to marry, after which the two people are considered betrothed.

There are variations on this arrangement, notably among the Bedu of the North African desert, where direct courtship takes place, and in Chinese Turkestan where children are not segregated. Among the Tuareg of the Sahara women choose their own husbands.

Although the wedding ceremony itself is simple, great importance is attached to it. The wedding normally takes place in the house of the bride's father where the guests assemble. An *imam* invites a represen-tative from both families to act as the two witnesses, whose presence are essential to the wedding. It is the witnesses, not the bride and groom or the *imam*, who sign the wedding contract. They must be adult males of sound mind and Muslims. If two suitable men are not available, two Muslim women may take the place of one of them. At least two witnesses are required and they must possess the legal quali-fications for a witness. Their presence is required not simply for evidence, but as essential to the validity of the marriage.

When the contract is signed, the *imam* formally asks the two families' representatives if they consent to the terms of the marriage; he then puts the hands of the bride and bridegroom together, so that their thumbs touch. He holds them in this position and recites a prayer after which all present recite the opening chapter of the Koran. The formal wedding is then over. A feast invariably follows and the host provides the best entertainment he can. It is, of course, his business to see that all the food, drink and vessels are ritually lawful.

The *wali* can only give a bride in marriage with her consent, but in the case of a virgin silent consent is sufficient. Only the father or grand-father has the right to marry his daughter or granddaughter against her will so long as she is a virgin. As minors are not in a position to make a declaration of their wishes which is valid in law, they can only be married at all by a *wali*.

The man can demand from his wife readiness for sexual intercourse and general obedience; if she is continually disobedient she loses her claim to support and may be chastised by the man. The latter in his turn is expressly forbidden to take upon himself the vows of continence. The prescriptions of the law regarding the rights and duties of husband and wife cannot be modified by the parties in the contract.

An important feature of the marriage contract is the *mahr*, the value of which must be specified although there are no prescribed limits. The *mahr* is paid to the bride, probably in two instalments, and until the first agreed instalment is paid the bride is within her rights to refuse to comply with any of her husband's wishes. The second instalment might be held in reserve in case her husband should die, or she is divorced. The actual position of the married woman is in all Muslim countries dependent on local conditions and on many special circumstances. Yet it is not a contradiction of this to say that the legal prescriptions regarding marriage are as a rule most carefully observed.

Apart from the modern tendency of Muslims to limit themselves to one wife by choice, legislation in various countries has added to the decline of polygamy. It is illegal in the USSR and China, and it was abolished in Turkey in 1926 with the introduction of the Swiss Civil Code. It has become more difficult in Egypt and other countries in recent years.

Modern Egyptian legislation illustrates the tendency towards bringing marriage under closer control by the State and towards adopting, with orthodox Muslim arguments, some of the leading Western ideas on this subject. Nevertheless, marriage, at least between Muslims, remains governed here, as elsewhere, by *sharia* law. Turkey and Albania are so far the only Muslim countries which have regulated this institution, together with the whole of family law, by the wholesale adoption of modern codes.

In pre-Islamic Arabia a form of temporary marriage (*mut'a*) was known and it persisted until after the Prophet's death. The Caliph Umar attempted to abolish the practice which is regarded as illegal by the Sunnis. It is permitted in Shi'ite countries where justification is found for it in the Koran (4:24). The object of a *mut'a* marriage is not to establish a home or beget children. It is a personal arrangement between two parties as a means of providing a man with a wife for a specified period, at the end of which both parties are free to part, providing the woman has received the fee due to her. Families are not involved, and no ceremony is necessary. One tradition declares that Mohammed made it unlawful because it differed little from prostitution, but other traditions appear to sanction the practice. Consequently, in Shi'ite countries, the Muslim may take a Christian, Jewish or Muslim woman for a fixed period of time varying between hours and years. There has to be a contract drawn up by the officiating *mulla* [1] in which the payment and the term must be specified. The contract binds the parties to each other for a specified period unless they agree to divorce by mutual consent. The children of such a marriage are legitimate and have the right to share inheritance, but the two parties to the contract do not inherit from each other.

It is almost certain from tradition that the Prophet permitted *mut'a* amongst his followers, especially on the longer campaigns. Even the Sunnis have practically the same arrangement; those who wish to live as husband and wife for a certain period simply agree to do so, without stipulating it in the marriage contract. Irregular unions regarded by the *sharia* as unlawful have been permitted by local custom in various parts of Islam at different times. Although the *mut'a* marriage is generally regarded as forbidden to Sunnis, in recent times it has been unofficially acknowledged as valid by certain people in the sacred city of Mecca. Even the prohibition against the marriage of sisters to the same husband has not always been obeyed. Up to the time of the Wahhabis in the mid 18th century a husband of the Asir tribe might lend his wife to a guest [2], and there was a time when a man might enter into a partnership of conjugal rights with another man in return for his services as a shepherd. In some parts of Baluchistan a host might provide an unmarried, but nubile girl, for the better entertainment of the guest. All modern authorities agree, however, that such practices, outside the contract of *mut'a*, are tribal rather than Islamic.

The position regarding concubinage is now academic as only slaves may be held as concubines. Slavery has now been abolished in all Muslim countries.

Prostitution

There is no doubt that prostitution existed before the days of the Prophet and it seems that there was no stigma attached to those who patronized prostitutes. Islam brought about a change, but in spite of official disapproval most Muslim countries have not succeeded in suppressing prostitution completely.

Unlawful Intercourse

There is no concept of adultery in Islamic law. Sexual intercourse is either lawful or unlawful, and unlawful intercourse is not a transgression against a marriage partner, but a crime against God.

1 Persian form of Arabic *ulama*, learned man, scholar in the widest sense.
2. According to some recent accounts this custom is still to be found among the Bedu.

Unlawful intercourse is a serious crime, but the evidence required by the Koran makes it practically impossible to prove. A confession must be repeated three times, and the evidence of four witnesses is required who must actually have seen the act take place. Tradition has passed down a story of A'isha, one of Mohammed's wives being suspected of unlawful intercourse. The case was resolved only by a Koranic revelation which not only exonerated A'isha, but also laid down that in future four witnesses must be produced to prove such accusations. If, however, the case is proved, the Koran demands a harsh punishment, but there are two versions of what this should be.

> The fornicatress and the fornicator –
> scourge each one of them a hundred stripes,
> and in the matter of God's religion
> let no tenderness for them seize you.

(Koran 24:2)

Alternatively:

> Such of your women as commit indecency,
> call four of you to witness against them;
> and if they witness, then detain them
> in their houses until death takes them
> or God appoints for them a way.

(Koran 4:19)

It is generally assumed that the first of these is an earlier passage, and there is a provision that if the accuser cannot substantiate his case he will receive 80 lashes for casting imputations on chaste women.

The second punishment is more ambiguous, and it is believed that in the early days of Islam guilty women were simply locked up. At some stage, however, the punishment seems to have been changed to stoning to death, although it is difficult to see how the text of the Koran can be used to justify this.

To rationalize different punishments for the same offence, subsequent jurists have divided offenders into two classes – those who are *muhsan* and those who are not. The former are free men or women, sane and mature, who are in a position to enjoy lawful marriage. The penalty for these is death by stoning. The penalty for people who are not *muhsan* is 100 lashes if they are free men or women (and half that number if they are slaves).

A husband who accuses his wife of illegal intercourse but is not able to bring the necessary evidence, must testify four times by God that he speaks the truth, and a fifth time that the curse of God shall be on him if he lies. A wife can defend herself and escape punishment, by testifying to similar oaths, but in any event the marriage is annulled, and under no circumstances may the husband resume cohabitation.

Divorce

The Koran has much to say about the circumstances and provisions of divorce, but it has nothing to say about the grounds for divorce. It has been assumed that a husband needs no grounds to divorce his wife, and the *sharia* law is structured accordingly. A wife does not have a similar right. In some respects the right of the husband is derived from pre-Islamic practice where a man only needed to repeat the dismissal notice three times to be clear of all obligations to his wife. The difference in Islamic practice is that after the first and second repudiations (*talak*) a man may take back his wife without her permission, providing he does so before the end of the period of waiting required by law before she might marry another man. But if he pronounces the formula for the third and final time, he loses all further right to her and cannot resume a relationship until she has first been married and divorced by another man. A *talak* pronounced in jest is considered legal and binding.

The circumstances under which a woman may claim divorce are restricted. If two non-Muslims are married and the woman then adopts the faith but her husband does not, she may claim divorce. If it is the husband who is converted but not the wife, the *qadi* decides between them.

In general the other grounds on which a woman can seek divorce are few and often difficult to prove. They are:

- Grave chronic diseases and physical defects (including impotence) which prevent marital intercourse.
- Non-payment of the *mahr* before completion of the marriage.
- Inability of the man to provide support (this separation is not final as long as the woman's *idda* runs).
- Non-fulfilment of special conditions and obligations of the marriage contract.
- Ill-treatment of the wife by the husband, but only if repeatedly and seriously done – this separation may be either revocable or final.

Another ground on which divorce can be sought is rebelliousness in the woman or incompatibility in the man, and general discord between husband and wife; this case has special rules based on *sura* 4:35. The *qadi* appoints two referees, one from the family of each consort, who first attempt a reconciliation. If their efforts fail they decide the question of guilt; if the fault is on the woman's side the husband is empowered to use the Koranic means of compulsion (admonishment, confinement, beating). If it is on the side of the man it is annulled by the referees. If the fault is on both sides the marriage is annulled and the referees decide about the payment or return of the *mahr*. The verdict of the referees is confirmed by the *qadi*.

In many places custom is stronger than the strict provisions of the *sharia* law. For example, in some communities where virginity is considered to be of paramount importance, a bride claiming to be a virgin can be divorced if she turns out not to be, notwithstanding the fact that neither the Koran nor the Prophet attached any importance to it. Similarly, although divorce is specifically condoned by the Koran, in the United Provinces of India it is considered shameful because it brings shame on the family.

The *khul* is a special form of divorce by which the wife purchases her freedom. Under the arrangement separation is legal after the partners have made a bona fide agreement in return for compensation. Some sects allow the possibility of a divorce by agreement without compensation. Modern practice varies in different countries according to the strength of secular constitutions. In the USSR, China, Turkey and Albania women are on a par with men for marriage and divorce. In other areas, notably Saudi Arabia and the Gulf States, the original word of Islam stands virtually intact.

Before a woman may remarry, she must wait a period of three menstrual cycles. She continues to be regarded as a wife during this time until it is established that she is not pregnant. If she is, the husband is encouraged by custom to take her back until the child is born, for it belongs to him if conceived legitimately. The woman is forbidden to marry anybody else until the child is delivered. During the period of suspended divorce (*idda*) a husband may take back his wife and resume cohabitation. In unscrupulous hands this divorce procedure can be used to keep a woman in a perpetual state of being neither divorced nor married and can be used to extort property or payment from unwilling wives. The Prophet expressly forbade this practice, and the Koran seeks to restrict the practice of a woman ransoming herself from marriage. This was apparently a common procedure before Mohammed's time and Islam has modified the worst excesses.

Seclusion of Women

The seclusion and veiling of women is a subject peppered with ambiguities and contradictions. It has been suggested that in ancient Arabia the Bedu women of the desert went unveiled and associated freely with men, whilst women in the towns were veiled. One source says that in the Prophet's own tribe, the Quraysh, veiling was generally observed. Another authority has it that in ancient Mecca unmarried daughters and female slaves were dressed in their finery and paraded to attract possible suitors and buyers. If this was successful the women were said to have resumed their veils once and for all.

Wives of the Prophet, you are not as other
women ... speak
  honourable words.
Remain in your houses; and display not
your finery, as did the pagans of old.

(Koran 33:32)

And:

O Prophet, say to thy wives and daughters
and the believing women, that they draw
their veils close to them; so it is likelier
they will be known, and not hurt.

(Koran 33:59)

The suggestion here is that this command came in the early days when
the believers and their wives were likely to be molested and harassed by
a hostile public. But it also indicates that veils were then common,
otherwise they would simply have drawn attention to themselves.

There were special rules for Mohammed's own wives in terms of
veiling and seclusion. The Koran specifically asks the followers not to
enter his house without permission, and to address his wives 'from
behind a veil'. The intention of these commands is open to different
interpretations. The first is that the wives of the Prophet were entitled
to special consideration and that they should act as an example of how
women should be treated and behave, implying that all women should
be secluded and veiled. But it may also relate to the physical conditions
under which Mohammed and his wives were living. Mohammed's
establishment in Medina consisted of a walled courtyard, inside which
each of his wives had a hut reserved for her use. Mohammed had no
apartment of his own, and he would spend one day with each wife in
turn. But the courtyard was also used as a common meeting place for
his followers, as a place of prayer, and as the general focus for many
activities of the new movement. As the Message spread and the ranks
of the faithful grew, the pressure of numbers on the Prophet's household must have been suffocating, so it is possible that neither he nor his
wives would have had any privacy without such special protection.
Subsequent generations of Muslim jurists have interpreted the Koran
very much in line with the first option, although there is no clear command that all women should be veiled and secluded. The general tenor
of the text in terms of modesty and chastity, combined with the
revelations placing men in charge of the affairs of women, has resulted
in seclusion sometimes taking an extreme form.

The evidence suggests that, so far as the Prophet's own family was
concerned, he wished to follow the ordinary conservative custom of
his tribe. But it is hard to see how the events of the time taken as a

whole can be interpreted to exclude women completely from public life. The Prophet himself had no objection to praying in the presence of women. Until at least 300 years after the *Hijra*, women enjoyed the right to pray in the mosque, and the Caliph Omar is said to have appointed a Koran reader especially for them at public worship.

It seems that the rigid seclusion of women grew up over generations, although it is not possible to say when the *harem* system began to be general. It has been suggested that the early interpreters of the Koran were men of Persian origin amongst whom such seclusion was traditional. At all events the system was firmly established by the Middle Ages, particularly among the town dwellers, where settled prosperity resulted in special buildings staffed by eunuchs. The practice was not nearly so widespread among the peasants of the field and the Bedu of the desert, and there are records of travellers among these people who were shocked by the lack of modesty shown by women in the presence of men, and by the open friendship between unrelated men and women in public. It is impossible for a man to shut his wife up if he is living in a tent and requires her to work, fetch water and firewood and herd the goats.

It seems likely, then, that in the early days of Islam, when the new religion was coming to terms with established tribal custom, there was a much more flexible and open attitude towards the status of women. By the Middle Ages religious authority had passed to the centres of learning in Turkey and Persia, who imposed their own more rigid codes of behaviour.

Interpretations differ as to the meaning of 'letting down the veil'. Some say it means that women must cover their faces and heads, some say that the eyes need not be covered, and yet others insist that the face may be uncovered but the forehead and hair must not be shown. Thus various traditions and customs have been established and the present day situation varies from place to place.

In Saudi Arabia, all women still go fully veiled in public. Both the veil and the *abba*, an over-garment stretching to the ground, are black. But there are some subtle distinctions to be seen. Generally, the older women wear veils so thick that even in the brightest sunlight it is impossible to see an outline of the face, while young girls often wear thin veils through which their features can be seen quite clearly, and which are little more than a token. Fashions clearly change, as in 1853 Sir Richard Burton described the women of Yanbu, in Arabia, as having veils covering only the lower part of their faces.

In the Gulf States, the women also wear the *abba* which is used to cover their heads, but the lower part of the face is covered by a *petula*, leaving the eyes visible. A *petula* is a leather or fabric mask covering the nose and mouth, tied at the back of the head. In all these countries the over-garments are worn only in public. What is worn underneath seems to be a matter for personal choice, providing it is modestly tailored to the wrists and neck and reaches the ankles.

In Iran the over-garment is the *chador* which is similar in style to the *abba*. The custom in respect of veiling varies from place to place depending upon the strength of religious community or Western influence. In some religious centres, the women are veiled, and in the cities many women go in Western dress.

Wherever it is the custom, women must cover their faces in the presence of all men, except close relatives. They will certainly do so in the presence of a strange man, but will not bother in the presence of a boy.

In modern times, especially among the younger families of the Arabian peninsula, it is possible to see how custom rather than religious dogma decides on the degree to which women are secluded in various circumstances. In Saudi Arabia, for example, although it is unheard of for a Saudi woman to attend any mixed gathering or company unaccompanied, Saudi couples do attend mixed parties both in their own country and abroad. The more usual arrangement, however, is for the woman to adhere strictly to Saudi custom whilst at home, and to adopt a different style of dress and behaviour whilst abroad. It is not therefore unusual to find a young Saudi wife not permitted even to go shopping by herself in Riyadh (in which case the husband does the shopping), but whilst in London and Paris to be out in the city from dawn till dusk alone, dressed in the latest Western fashion. This seems to be an increasingly common arrangement which is tailored to suit the situation, particularly when the woman has been educated abroad.[1]

Sex

The Arabic word for marriage and sexual intercourse is the same: *nikah*.

Islam has never placed any restriction on the gratification of sexual pleasure and enjoyment, providing it is within the limits prescribed by the law. This is an unbroken tradition which stretches back to the Prophet himself, and at no time has there been any of the guilt or inhibitions which Christians have placed on sensual pleasures over the ages. Mohammed is known for certain to have had 10 wives and at least three concubines, and from that time the idea that sex is enjoyable has been taken for granted by Muslims. Sexual intercourse is regarded as no different from any other natural function of the body. It is discussed

1. There is justification in the *sharia* for differing behaviour in Islamic territory and elsewhere.

freely even when children are present, and sexual satisfaction is positively encouraged. One *hadith* goes so far as to suggest that the best in a Muslim community is he who contracts most marriages. Celibacy is against the *Sunna*, is positively discouraged and appears to be unknown except among Sufis. The Bedu of the desert, when on journeys, can be celibate for months on end, yet not one of them, even the most austere, would regard celibacy as a virtue. They want sons, and consider that women are provided by God for the satisfaction of men. Deliberately to refrain from using them would be not only unnatural, but also ridiculous, and the Bedu, like most Arabs, are very susceptible to ridicule. Sexual satisfaction is allowed to be mentioned as a blessing in prayer or thanksgiving.

Homosexuality is condemned in the Koran:

> What, do you come to male beings,
> leaving your wives that your Lord created
> for you? Nay, but you are a people
> of transgressors.

(Koran 26:165)

However, it does not appear to be uncommon, or condemned by popular opinion.

The Muslim attitude towards virginity is inconsistent. To the Prophet it seemed quite unimportant, as only one of his wives was a virgin when he married her. Although many of his marriages can be considered as political alliances, this was not true of all of them, and his overriding consideration seemed to be that widows and divorced women should be included in the community through remarriage. Yet in some Muslim countries, particularly in North Africa, the importance attached to virginity in a bride can be obsessive. However, such attitudes could be more properly described as tribal rather than Islamic.

Attitudes towards chastity are also not entirely straightforward. Apart from the legal aspect, unchaste or immodest conduct is seen as bringing dishonour not only upon the girl herself, but on the whole family, and to a lesser extent, on her tribe. It is the inescapable responsibility of the near male relatives to protect not only the honour of their women, but to demonstrate publicly that the honour of the family is encapsulated in the chastity of their women. It is therefore the clear duty of men to redeem the family honour if it has been violated. What constitutes violation and the action taken in redemption can both take an extreme form. A woman does not actually have to do anything to bring disgrace. It can be enough that she is talked about, and that people believe she has been unchaste, or is capable of unchaste conduct. There are many examples of a brother killing his sister in such circumstances, and everyone concerned thinking he is completely justified in his action. Compared with the honour of a family, one life is of little importance. Yet an Arab will use his sister's name as a battle cry, and go to any lengths to help and protect her. Dishonour has to do with losing face, and this is not necessarily related to anything that has happened; it is more a matter of what people believe has happened. It is therefore the collective responsibility of a family to see to it that they are respected. It is possible for a man who knows that his wife has been unfaithful to him to do nothing if discretion has been shown and no public attention is aroused.

Not all Muslims react in the same way, however. Some of the Bedu tribes regard it as barbarous to kill a girl even if she has been immoral. But as usual the Bedu are a case apart; Thesiger was once advised by one of them that if he wanted to try his luck: 'next time you see a girl who pleases you, sit down next to her in the dark, push your camel stick through the sand until it is underneath her, then turn it over until the crook presses against her. If she gets up, gives you an indignant look, and marches off, you will know that you are wasting your time. If she stays where she is, you can meet her next day when she is herding the goats.'

Employment and Public Life

Among the states of the Arabian peninsula there are significant differences in attitude towards the public status of women, notwithstanding that each sees itself cast strictly in the mould of Islam. In Saudi Arabia women are not allowed to take any employment, except in institutions and organizations run exclusively for their own sex, where it is obligatory that all staff should be female. This applies not only to schools, colleges and hospital departments, but also to shops selling exclusively women's clothes. This general rule applies also to foreign Muslims and to Western women, who are generally allowed into the country only if accompanying a near male relative. There are very few exceptions to the rule. Television broadcasts, films from other countries with women taking part, and airlines employ foreign stewardesses as a matter of course, presumably to look after the women passengers. Apart from jobs, women are expected to play no part in public life, including not being allowed to drive motor cars. All women, including Westerners, are expected to dress modestly in public, although foreigners, including Muslims, are not expected to adhere to the strict Saudi standards of seclusion. It is still to be expected that both Saudi and foreign women not properly dressed, especially during Ramadan, could receive from the Morals Police (controlled by the *ulema* – the religious authority in Islam) a few sharp cracks with a stick or a dab of green paint on exposed ankles and arms. In the Gulf states by contrast, foreign women are allowed to take jobs, conduct business openly and drive cars, and are allowed considerable latitude in the way they conduct their private lives and dress in public.

The seclusion of women, and the denial of any kind of public role, has emphasized the special problems of developing countries. It is apparent from all the development programmes published by Saudi Arabia and the Gulf States in recent years, that the one commodity they are notably short of is human resources. They must import not only unskilled labour, but also managerial and technical resources. A great self-imposed handicap is being felt by excluding half of the population from the process. In addition, many of the facilities necessary for development must be duplicated: lecture rooms, laboratories, medical facilities, recreation projects, restaurants and even mosques are provided for each sex. Yet women are encouraged to take up the educational opportunities open to them. They may study abroad, and are given generous state assistance to obtain degrees and qualifications in foreign colleges and universities. At present the numbers involved are small: those who have attained the necessary standards are few, and to study abroad women normally have to be accompanied by their husbands.

In Egypt, by contrast, since the Revolution of 1952, there are no laws that discriminate between the sexes in relation to education and employment. There are women members of Parliament (though only six) and for some years there has been a woman in the Cabinet. But some contradictions remain. So far no woman has been appointed a judge, and women are not allowed to hold public office of an executive nature, such as Governor of a province, or Mayor. Women employed in the public sector receive wages equal to those of men, although many complain that opportunities for training and promotion are not equal. Even so, when women take the equal place in work that the law provides, the right that Islam has given women to control their own possessions and money could put them in a more advantageous position than their sisters in the West.

Yet in many Muslim countries one area of the law seems at odds with another. The labour laws in places like Egypt, Syria and Iraq allow women to be employed outside the home. Yet marriage regulations and family law give a husband an uncontested right to refuse his wife permission to leave the house, go to work, or travel.

It is a curious paradox in Islamic law that a woman may execute the office of *qadi*, except in cases of *hadd* and *kisas* in conformity with the rule that she may not give evidence in these cases. There is no prohibition against a woman assuming the government or head of state. Rulers of the Muslim state of Bhobal in central India were women for several generations in the 19th century.

Women Saints

Strict Islamic authorities do not approve of canonization. Nevertheless, Islamic sects and movements, notably the Sufis, through their mystical interpretations of the Message, have not only saints, but women saints; this comes about because the Sufis are preoccupied with the importance of the spiritual Message to be received through the mystical experience, so that outward form and sex simply is not important. (It is remarkable that in the oldest Turkish mystical order (Yesviya) women took part in the ceremony (*dhikr*) unveiled.) This is consistent in that Mohammed taught that the attainment of the divine lies not in appearance, but in purpose. On this basis scholars have admitted women into the ceremonies of Islam.

However, when it comes to considering women taking a lead in religious matters, the compliments become somewhat backhanded. 'If it is possible to have learnt two thirds of the faith from A'isha (one of Mohammed's wives), then it is possible to learn some of the truth of religion from one of her handmaidens . . . A woman on the path of God becomes a man, she cannot be called a woman' said Al-Din Attar writing of Rabi'a, a female Sufic saint. Perhaps the depth of Muslim feeling on the subject of women could not be better summarized.

Swiss Civil Code in Turkey

The most important change to the status of women in Islam came with Turkey's adoption of the Swiss Civil Code in 1926 which replaced the religious law – the *seriat* (Arabic: *sharia*) – governing marriage. Among other features, the new code retained the Muslim practice of separating the property of the spouses. It permitted abandonment by the husband as grounds for divorce, and for the first time allowed marriage between Muslim women and non-Muslim men. Perhaps the most important feature of the 1926 Civil Code is the complete revision of the procedures for contracting marriage. Instead of the traditional contract between families, the new code recognized only a contract between individuals established at a civil ceremony. Thenceforth unregistered unions were considered illegal, their offspring illegitimate, and both parents and children ineligible for certain government assistance.

However the new Civil Code had only a limited effect in the countryside, and illegal traditional marriage continued to produce illegitimate children. This became so common that the government enacted several bills to legitimize millions of children. In the half century since the Republican reforms, civil marriage is now much more widely accepted, but whether there has been any basic change in the relationship between the sexes is less clear.

To a considerable extent the outward signs of sexual segregation are disappearing. Women no longer occupy special sections of buses and trains, and do not have special areas in cinemas. Although, especially in the cities, women move about with apparent freedom, it is still a mistake to think in terms of the social relationships that exist in Northern Europe or the United States. Women enjoy the right to vote and have legal equality. They commonly take all kinds of jobs at all levels, and form an increasing proportion of students. But many old ways remain. Men generally do not take their wives to public entertainments nor introduce them to friends. The basic social institutions of the coffee house and the guest room are still exclusively male preserves.

* * *

Although it is outside the scope of this book to relate the Women's Movement to Islam, it is nonetheless worth noting that criticism of Islam is much more likely to be levelled from the Western, rather than the Muslim, wing of the movement. The general role played by women in the Iranian Revolution is remarkable, and it is noticeable that even the most strident Muslim feminist and political revolutionary is unlikely to attack Islam as such. Nawal El Saadawi[1], for example, whilst making the most virulent attack on the structure and nature of Arab society in general and the position of women in particular, describes Islam as 'one of the most tolerant and least rigid of religions, rational in many of its aspects, adaptable and leaving scope for change'. At another point she remarks on 'the broadmindedness and tolerance of Mohammed the Prophet of Allah, when compared with other prophets and religious leaders'. She considers that the Christian Church has exercised an even more ferocious oppression of women than the Islamic, Arab or Eastern cultures. Furthermore, the first blow for women's liberation can be said to have been struck at the very beginning of Islam. 14 centuries ago Muslim women succeeded in changing the exclusive use of the male gender in the Koran itself. They said: 'We have proclaimed our belief in Islam, and have done as you have done. How is it then that you men should be mentioned in the Koran and we ignored?' Until then the only reference in the holy book was to Muslims, but from then on the Koran speaks of 'the Muslims, men and women, and the believers, men and women'.

1. *The Hidden Face of Eve*, Zed Press, 1980.

Chapter 8
Commerce and Trade

This chapter does not offer any advice on how to do business in Islamic countries. It seeks to outline the attitudes and qualities of the Muslim mind which affect, consciously or otherwise, modern practices and methods.

The Traditional Role of Commerce

The language and ideas of the Koran reflect the fact that it was first addressed to people engaged in commerce. The Prophet was a successful merchant. The Meccan caravan trade was central to the life of the community, and the commercial terms used in the Koran are seen by scholars as expressing fundamental points of doctrine, and not simply as illustrating ideas. The Koran states that the deeds of a man are reckoned in the book; the Last Judgement is a reckoning; each person receives his account; the balance is set up and a man's deeds are weighed; each soul is held in pledge for the deeds committed; if a man's actions are approved he receives his reward; and to support the Prophet's cause is to lend a loan to God. It is not surprising therefore, bearing in mind the literal nature of the Koran, that commerce has always had a significant place in the minds of Muslims.

In the 14th century Ibn Khaldun said:

> It should be known that commerce means the attempt to make a profit by increasing capital, through buying goods at a low price then selling them at a high price, whether these goods consist of slaves, grain, animals, weapons, or clothing material. The accrued amount is called profit. The attempt to make such a profit may be undertaken by storing goods and holding them until the market has fluctuated from low prices to high prices. Or the merchant may transport his goods to another country where they are more in demand than in his own. Therefore, an old merchant said to a person who wanted to find out the truth about commerce: 'I shall give it to you in two words: buy cheap and sell dear.' [1]

1. Maxime Rodinson, *Islam and Capitalism*, Allen Lane, 1974

It is true that the Koran emphasizes the uselessness of wealth in the face of God's judgement and warns against the temptation to neglect religion that wealth brings, but it has nothing to say against the accumulation of private property, or inequality in terms of wealth and possessions. It looks with favour upon commercial activity, and confines its criticism to condemning fraudulent practices, and requiring abstention from trade during certain religious festivals. The Prophet is believed to have said that 'the trustworthy merchant will sit in the shade of God's throne at the day of Judgement'. According to holy tradition, trade is a superior way of earning one's livelihood, and 'a *dirham* lawfully gained from trade is worth more than 10 *dirhams* gained in any other way'.

Nevertheless strict Islamic law and custom restrict an individual's right to hold property in certain basic respects. It is not permissible, for example, to make a charge for such primary products as water and grass. The right of ownership is also subsidiary to the right of everyone to life. A man dying of hunger is justified in taking the minimum of food he needs to keep alive at the expense of the legitimate owner, and is permitted to use force if he can do it in no other way. Indeed, according to the Shi'ites, refusal to give food to a starving man amounts, in effect, to complicity in killing him.

There are no more restrictions placed upon a Muslim business man or trader than are placed upon his counterpart in the West, but restrictions can occasionally have important consequences. For example, the Koran emphasizes the prohibition of a certain game of chance (*maysir*). As a result, any gain accruing from chance or undetermined causes is prohibited. It would not be allowed, for example, to promise a workman a fleece for skinning six sheep, because it is not possible to know for certain whether the skin may not be damaged during the course of the work.

Certain commercial practices are forbidden by the *Sunna*: those which are either fraudulent, involve trade in impure goods (wine, pigs, animals that have died by means other than by ritual slaughter) or in goods that are common to everyone (water, grass and fire). Speculation in food, especially with a view to cornering the market, is forbidden. Above all, the selling of any commodity where there is an element of uncertainty is prohibited. This includes, for example, sale by auction, since the seller does not know what price he will get for his object; or any sale in which the merchandise is not precisely numerically defined.

Although Islam has never raised any objection in principle to the capitalist mode of production, at times religious opinion has condemned the making of certain goods, or certain forms of exploitation which conflicted, not so much with the scriptures, as with a tradition which had acquired religious validity after centuries of stagnation. This applies, for example, to the making of alcoholic drinks, or the employment of women as productive workers. Attitudes in Islam have changed over the centuries; in particular, the habit of condemning any practice that did not go back to the time of the Prophet has been abandoned. At one stage, innovation (*bid'ah*) of any kind was condemned out of hand, and this applied, for example, to the use of coffee and tobacco when they were first introduced. More recently, a distinction has been drawn between innovations which are praiseworthy, and those which are not. Thus many innovations that were condemned in their time were subsequently endorsed by religious leaders, whose predecessors had taken an opposite point of view. Opponents and supporters of the new ways were never short of texts or arguments to back up their mutually contradictory opinions.

The situation in Saudi Arabia, the most orthodox Islamic state, illustrates the point. The strictly orthodox Wahhabi sect controls all religious matters, and its religious scholars were initially opposed to many modern innovations. But its political leaders, notably King Abdul Aziz ibn Saud, himself a sincere Wahhabite, were able to overcome opposition to, for example, the telegraph, the telephone and broadcasting.

Islam modified only marginally the attitude of ancient Arabia towards accumulated material wealth. As we have seen, it introduced *zakat* (alms) to provide for the needy, and also revised the laws of inheritance to give a fairer distribution within the family. But it has no objection at all to individuals or groups acquiring vast wealth, providing the guidelines laid down by the Koran are observed. The Christian idea that it is easier for a camel to pass through the eye of a needle [1] than for a rich man to enter the Kingdom of Heaven is quite alien to Muslims.

The Example of the Prophet

Because of the Prophet's responsibilities to the community, there was no distinction between the public exchequer and his personal possessions. Shortly before his death, he compelled newly conquered groups by formal treaty to hand over a fixed proportion of their income or property each year. A special tax was imposed upon Christian Arabs, but this was no higher than the contributions required from Muslims. The Prophet was also not averse to accepting private gifts and legacies. Besides these, Mohammed received a fifth of all spoils taken from the enemy, as compared with the quarter required by tradition by Arab

---

1. This image is reserved for sinners: 'nor shall they enter Paradise until the camel passes through the eye of the needle' (Koran 7:39).

chiefs. In addition, the Prophet had the right to share equally the thing or person he liked best before the general distribution. If the plunder were won by negotiation, rather than battle, Mohammed took it all.

After the capture of Khaybar, the owners were left in possession, but Mohammed sequestered half the produce on behalf of the Muslims. His position imposed a number of heavy financial obligations. As he was engaged full-time in public and religious affairs, he could not earn his living as others around him did. As the *Sayyid*[1], he was necessarily engaged in extensive hospitality, and gave generous gifts to those around him. The Koran commanded him, like other men, to give generously to his relatives, to orphans, beggars and travellers. He had also to contribute towards ransoming captives.

From the very beginning, therefore, business and financial affairs have occupied an important place in the administration and functioning of the religious community, and there is certainly no contradiction between the rich and the pious in Islam. Nevertheless, the rich are urged to do good works, and the love of wealth for its own sake is condemned. Damnation and hell-fire are promised the sinner who thinks he can ransom himself on the Day of Judgement:

> Nay, verily it is a furnace
> snatching away the scalp,
> calling him who drew back
>   and turned away,
> who amassed and hoarded.

> (Koran 70:15)

Associations and Combinations

Religious authority condemns practices that interfere with the free play of supply and demand. A tradition is said to have come from the Prophet himself condemning obligatory price fixing or the laying down and fixing of price levels. This general edict, together with the Koranic prohibition on conclaves in general, has had far reaching effects on the organization of people in work situations in strict Islamic countries. It effectively prohibits, in theory, the organization of any trade union, trade association, chamber of commerce, guild, professional association or institute, learned society, academic association, charitable organization or political party. In addition it could be taken to mean that no prices, wages, salaries, or fee scales can be laid down. But in practice these principles are applied selectively. The most obvious example is the strenuous effort of some OPEC countries to control oil prices, but other more parochial examples can be found. In most countries the government controls hotel prices, air fares and

1. A term now used as a mark of respect.

some food prices, and has a set salary structure for government employees. In those same countries combinations of workers to fix wage rates, or associations of professionals to fix fee scales, are illegal.

One important result of this is that professionalism is almost unknown in most Muslim countries and poorly understood in the rest. Professional firms and consultants are treated like traders or contractors when it comes to price, but are expected to behave differently from contractors when it comes to performance.

Customs in Business

There are general rules for conducting business affairs, and naturally these are best understood by Muslims. There is a very strong tradition for conducting business and concluding agreements on a verbal basis. Such agreements are as binding as any other kind. It is essential to a man's honour that, having reached an agreement, it should be fulfilled. Probably for this reason, there is rarely any pressure for an agreement to be concluded. Discussions might range over a long period, whilst all aspects of a deal are considered. One can be quite sure that however long and detailed the discussion, an Arab will remember precisely what was said and the terms of any agreement reached.

It is an extraordinary characteristic that, however long or involved or complicated negotiations might be, it is very rare for an Arab to take notes of a meeting, a result, perhaps, of the immensely strong oral tradition which stretches back centuries. It began with committing to memory the epic poems of the desert, and continued with learning the whole of the Koran by heart. Modern education in many places consists of committing all school books to memory, and it is not surprising therefore that the average Arab has a prodigious capacity for remembering detail. The Bedu seem to be positively suspicious of the European habit of committing everything to paper, and in a traditional *sharia* court only oral evidence is accepted; written evidence is not generally allowed.

A Muslim, both by his religion and ancient tradition, is honour bound to stand by the terms of an agreement. Westerners sometimes get into difficulties when they expect not only the terms, but also what they consider to be the spirit of an agreement, to be implemented. An Arab may insist on the letter of an agreement which could seem to contradict the spirit. This is not a devious conspiracy; rather is it a mistake to consider that any agreement or contract has a spirit. This tradition goes back a very long way and is illustrated in an incident involving the Prophet Mohammed. While Mohammed was living in Medina, he concluded a treaty with his enemies in Mecca, which provided, among other things, that tribes and individuals were free to enter into alliance with the Muslims or the Meccans as they desired. However, minors under the protection of either side were not allowed to defect, and had to be handed back to their parents. One youth from a Meccan clan was a Muslim sympathizer, and attempted to join Mohammed in Medina. Mohammed sent the young man back under guard. The youth killed one of his guards and returned undaunted to Medina, but Mohammed again attempted to return him, thus fulfilling his treaty obligations and at the same time demonstrating that the youth was not under the protection of the Muslim community. The youth, however, left Medina and set up camp on a coast road nearby. Here he gathered around himself 70 or so sympathetic Meccan Muslims and set about raiding the Meccan caravans that passed their way. Now another provision of the treaty was that Mohammed's supporters would stop attacking Meccan caravans, but as the youth and his followers were operating outside Mohammed's technical control, Mohammed could not be considered in breach of the treaty. On the other hand, the Meccans, if they wished to do so, were free to use violence on the raiders without provoking Mohammed and his community. In the end, the raiders became such a thorn in the side of the Meccans that they asked Mohammed to take them into his community, thereby waiving their rights under the treaty. By Arab standards Mohammed's conduct was formally correct, and was never challenged by the Meccans.

According to *hadith* the intent of the believer is more important than his action, and this has to be considered in relation to the object to be attained. In other words, the end does not justify the means; it would be an evil act to build a mosque with extorted money, whether the builder was conscious of the source of the money or not. Business must therefore be transacted according to certain rules. A Muslim has to be careful that an act valid in law does not leave opportunity for injustice to be done which will provoke the anger of God; morality must take precedence over a legal contract. If a man purchases food in a time of famine in order to hoard it and sell it at high prices, it is wrong according to the *sharia* because it is against the interests of the community, regardless of whether the contract is commercially valid.

All actions must be based upon sound knowledge and it is the duty of a trader to acquire the necessary knowledge. If, for example, counterfeit money or faulty goods are put into circulation, the man first dealing in them must take the burden of ascertaining their true value. Having done so, he must dispose of them or put them out of circulation. If he does not they might be passed on to another who does not know, and who might become a transgressor through no fault of the first merchant. The danger here is one of general distribution to the public harm. Likewise, transactions that harm individuals are forbidden. It is a general principle that a Muslim should desire for fellow Muslims that which he desires for himself and reject for them what he rejects for himself. This means that he shall not praise a commodity for qualities it does not possess, nor conceal its faults or any fact concerning weight or quality which would prevent the sale.

However, a foreigner should be aware that, as in most aspects of moral and social behaviour, there is a sliding scale; all men are not dealt with equally. A brother has many special claims, a more distant member of the family fewer and a non-related fellow Muslim fewer still. Lastly come *jar* (protected foreigners). A non-Arab Muslim is to be treated with favour rather than cold justice. Christians and Jews, and others by and large, should reckon to have the strict letter of the contract enforced.

The three worst vices are folly, meanness and falsehood. Lies which avert harm and bring benefit may be justified, but they are still vile. A man who boasts of his possessions, although he is telling the truth, is nevertheless vile. The vilest of all men is he who boasts of what he has not.

Yet a great gap exists between theory and practice in business. The *sharia* entirely forbids the sale of certain things because they are ritually unclean, such as dogs, pigs, wine, dung, or unclean olives, yet it is lawful, though disapproved, to buy grape juice from one who has extracted wine, weapons from one who has used them against God, or any goods from a man whose property is illicitly acquired. It is illegal to sell anything for which no use can be found: vermin, wild animals not used for hunting, or things not actually in existence – for example, fruit not yet on the tree, or goods not manufactured. It is illegal to sell that which cannot be delivered or that which would cause harm in delivery. A sale is illegal in which the exact quantity or quality of the goods is unknown. A sale must take place and delivery must be completed within three days of the contract being settled, and a purchaser cannot claim possession of goods until they are actually delivered. Until then the seller is responsible for them: if the buyer dies before delivery the sale is void.

There are two views about the sale of commodities which the purchaser has not seen. The first is that it is illegal. The second is that it is legal if a description of the thing is given and the buyer has the option of purchasing, if the goods, when seen, comply with the descriptions.

Conditions in general, except where they are of essence to the contract, nullify sale. Thus a contract cannot be made where one side sells a barrel of oil for $10, if the other side reciprocates by selling a rifle for $5. However, it is lawful to sell goods for a profit if the costs and the amount of the profit are disclosed. In this way one commodity can be bartered for another.

Making Contracts

The requirements of the *sharia* that a contract has to be completed within three days is clearly impracticable in many cases. One way round this is to make an advanced payment (*salam*) in order to secure an option on the goods which may be rejected if they do not conform to the specification. Alternatively, it is possible to arrange a contract with a skilled workman (under *istisna*) to make an article, so that an advanced payment does not have to be made, nor a period stipulated.

Some commercial dealings between Muslims go back further than Islam itself. The conditions and arrangements are dictated by custom, and it is seldom that details are specified in commercial contracts. Much is left to the pedigrees of the parties concerned, and everything customary is deemed to be included.

It is in the nature of a Muslim's belief and way of life to take all things literally, and consequently to offer nothing superfluous to a situation. In recent times more than one Western contractor, when handing over a completed building, has been startled to be asked by his Arab client for the motor car shown on the artist's sketches in the early days when the design was being discussed.

The concluding of an agreement is not to be confused with the bargaining process that precedes it. For the average Westerner, if he takes part in it at all, this is normally considered a tedious, if not embarrassing, process, a simple game of numbers played to arrive at an eventual price. For an Arab, it is the stuff of life, in which personality and imagination is given full play. In essence it is the art of compromise without backing down or losing face, and at each stage, a reason must be given for changing one's position, however implausible the reason might logically appear. Whether the bargain is being struck in the verbal violence of the camel market, or in the dusty quiet of a government office, the underlying procedure is essentially the same, and if the bargain is well made, the pleasure expressed by both parties at the end will be genuinely enjoyed.

Another pitfall for the unwary Westerner is the way in which details of negotiations are or are not connected. If, for example, a development project was being discussed in London or New York, it might be agreed at an early stage that one party would provide the land, another the finance, and a third the contracting services. As the discussions progressed, however, the general strategy could be modified if a better one emerged. Not so in Riyadh or Cairo; once a verbal agreement has been made, even though it does not cover the whole situation, and even if a better strategy can be found, it is inviolate. Any attempt by one of the parties to modify an aspect of the agreement, especially if in doing so he appears to be delivering less than originally promised, will be seen as dishonourable and unbusinesslike.

Usury

The Koran specifically forbids usury (*riba*) on no less than four occasions. In a commercial centre like Mecca in Mohammed's day, the taking of interest was probably commonplace. The Koranic disapproval of interest dates from the period after the *Hijra*, and it has been suggested that it appears to be directed against the Jews rather than against the Meccans. In the Koran the Jews are accused of practising usury though forbidden to do so. It is possible that when Mohammed and his followers first settled in Medina and appealed for material support, the Jews refused a contribution but offered to lend money at interest. By adopting this position they were in a way refusing to accept Mohammed's claim to Prophethood, and this may explain the Koranic insistence that usury is wrong. It has also been suggested, however, that the idea underlying the prohibition of usury was that all believers are brothers and therefore ought to help one another financially as well as in other ways.

In present day Muslim countries the situation regarding usury varies from place to place. From the beginning of the 19th century pressure has been brought to bear on traditional Islamic values by the colonial expansion of the European powers, and the financial institutions exported from the West. When the Ottoman Civil Code was promulgated in the 1870s there was no mention of loans at interest. This made it possible in 1888 to establish the Agricultural Bank, whose written constitution allowed it openly to lend and borrow money at interest. The present day situation varies, therefore, from a country like Turkey, which places no religious restrictions on its financial and economic institutions, to a country like Saudi Arabia, whose law quite specifically forbids the charging of interest. Even in Saudi Arabia, however, not all business transactions are free from interest charges; for example, the Saudi Industrial Development Fund (owned by the government) grants loans to licenced projects at an annual interest rate of two per cent. On the other hand, the loan granted by Saudi Arabia to Syria in 1950 was expressly defined as being free of interest. In between these two examples is a country like Pakistan, which has made great efforts to introduce Koranic legislation into its law. Its draft constitution provided for the elimination of interest as one of the most important principles underpinning the new state. However, the final text in 1956 referred simply to the rapid elimination of *riba* as one of the aims to be strenuously pursued, along with, for example, the welfare of the people. In the meantime, its banks raise and lower their interest rates like any others.

This situation is possible because there are those who believe that all forms of usury are forbidden, and those who distinguish between usurious interest, which is to be condemned, and participation in the profits of the business, which is legitimate. Some believe that a second category is that of interest paid by banks.

The prohibition on usury presents considerable problems for modern Muslim banks. In a fundamental sense a Muslim bank is a contradiction in terms, since in essence the business of the bank is characterized by the creation of profit through charging interest. Recently, one Arab bank based in the Lebanon has been formed to conduct its business strictly in accordance with Koranic practice. Essentially its business is to lend money and thereby derive profit, but instead of charging interest it takes a share in the equity of the project or enterprise. This makes it similar in character to a European merchant bank, and presumably restricts the nature of its business. It represents an interesting attitude towards economics, as only enterprises that are productive and potentially profitable would attract loans. Loans for the purposes of consumption are virtually ruled out. As a result of religious ideology a new way of recirculating money has come into existence, and one of the cornerstones of society, the banking system, has been transformed. Instead of banks being institutions for the manipulation of money as a commodity, they are forced into a constructive and creative role, and take a share in the social success or failure of private or public enterprise.

However, these restrictions on normal commerce have been either ignored or, in many cases, observed to the letter of the law so as to make nonsense of them. Interest might be allowed to accumulate in a bank account without the beneficiary withdrawing any of it. A money lender might take interest indirectly through payment in kind. A common way of evading the law is for a loan to be made and the recipient to hand over some property. The property is then bought back at an inflated value.

However usury is interpreted, it seems to be generally agreed that the total amount of interest charged must never exceed the principal of the debt:

> O believers, devour not usury, doubled
> and redoubled, and fear you God; haply so
>   you will prosper.

> (Koran 3:125)

By the same token the charging of compound interest is expressly forbidden.

There are those pious Muslims who believe that the sin of *riba* is not only endangering the structure of Islam, but has already undermined and corrupted the institutions of the West. What is more, they point out, usury is specifically forbidden to both Christians and Jews as well as Muslims. But these other religions have failed, and, in the clash between Islam and the Christian world, the latter is in the wrong, and must be the one to yield. Examples have been given of cooperative loan societies being set up in Muslim India since the end of the last century. These were influenced to some extent by the cooperative movement in Europe, but they represent a successful, if modest attempt to fulfil the financial needs of the community within the Muslim ideology.

Debt

The teachings of the Koran are in the mainstream of the oral tradition of the Arabs. The rules and directions it gives to the faithful for living their lives, even in such contracts as marriage, divorce and inheritance, are to be observed orally through ceremonies and rituals. It is only debt that should be recorded in writing and witnessed:

> O believers, when you contract a debt
> one upon another for a stated term,
> write it down, and let a writer
> write it down between you justly.
>
> (Koran 2:281)

The result of forbidding usury is that a debtor cannot make his situation worse by postponing repayment: the debt cannot increase by the accumulation of interest. Yet clearly a debt is to be viewed as a serious matter.

Insurance

Insurance represents another example of changing attitudes. Until recent years orthodox opinion frowned upon insurance so that it was almost unknown in Muslim countries. This was a result partly of resistance to innovation, and partly of the fact that conservative opinion held insurance to be an attempt by man to frustrate the will of God. If it is God's will that a man should suffer loss, misfortune, or disaster, it is a Muslim's duty to submit, not to seek compensation. It has taken the huge capital investments made possible by oil revenues in Saudi Arabia and other Middle Eastern states to change this attitude. The risks involved in leaving such large investments uninsured have proved too much for any responsible government. Although in many Muslim countries certain restrictions and rules are laid down for insuring property, it is now a common practice.

Decision Making

It is part of the faith that there are no intermediaries between God and man. One result of this is that in Muslim countries the head of any organization, ministry, or department, will not generally delegate decisions. This nearly always makes the concluding of any business, however trivial, a time-consuming matter. It is usually easy enough, even for an outsider, to find the right man to see, and, in principle, direct access to very important and busy people is usually easy enough to arrange. But at this point practical difficulties often arise. First, it is difficult to find people in their offices; one consequence of decisions being taken personally is the mobility required of all businessmen and officials. The alacrity with which the modern Arab leaps on and off aeroplanes is remarkable and he is inclined to treat continents like adjoining parishes[1]. Having run your man to ground, the second problem is conducting a private interview. The *majlis* tradition has spilled over into all but the most modern business practice and government administrations. Most offices are physically fairly large with comfortable chairs arranged continuously around the walls. The chairs are occupied by people who have some business to conduct, or some enquiry to make, or are visiting a business acquaintance to pass the time of day, or by friends and relatives paying a social call, or, in the case of public offices, by people off the street wanting somewhere to sit down out of the sun. The host sits behind his desk which has on his left and right one or two additional chairs. In a busy office there might well be three or four different meetings or discussions going on with the occupant at the same time. The other people in the room might join in with one or more of the discussions, or be having conversations between themselves, or simply adopt the role of onlookers. This is not nearly so chaotic as it at first appears, and, as in most things Islamic, there is an underlying structure. The seat of honour is to the left of the host. In most cases this will be given as a matter of courtesy to a foreigner, but its occupant is expected to know when a more important visitor arrives, and be prepared to relinquish it. When this happens all discussions stop until the formalities have been completed with the new visitor and the nature of his business ascertained; at a suitable moment the host might revive the previous discussion and continue to conduct two or three meetings at once. When this happens it can be assumed that no serious business can be concluded. At no time will anybody be made to feel that he ought to leave, or that he has outstayed his welcome. The arrival of a senior member of the host's family or tribe will immediately take precedence over any business discussion. Another facet of the principle of instant availability is that the host

1. In 1977 Saudi Arabia ran out of passports!

himself, unless he is the king, ruler or president, is a subject of the system. If his superior requests his attendance, he departs immediately, leaving a roomful of unfinished business to be dealt with at a later date.

For Arabs business is never carried on at the expense of social ritual. The most refreshing experience for the outsider is the willingness with which people make themselves available, and with a little patience almost anyone can be seen without secretaries or assistants acting as intermediaries. Naturally, an introduction helps a good deal, and much importance is attached to being 'known', that is, being passed on as a suitable person by friends, relatives, or business acquaintances. In any event, a visitor can be almost certain of a courteous, even friendly reception, and of receiving a hearing which varies from polite interest to real enthusiasm. This should not be taken as encouragement, let alone agreement to any proposal. Everyone gets a similar hearing, and this gives time an unstructured appearance, which partly explains the apparent chaos of many establishments.[1]

It is a Muslim characteristic that business is not separate from the rest of life, and there is therefore no reason why it should operate under different rules and conditions. As with other aspects of life the day to day objective is not to get things done, or even to acquire riches, it is the ancient desire to win prestige in other men's eyes, and to win a respected and important place in society. In Islam it is people who regulate and dominate business, not business that dominates them.

But, finally, it must be remembered that, in business as well as in all other matters, it is not man that ultimately orders events, but God. Awareness of the divine will runs parallel with all human decisions, and can override them at any turn. God's will is everywhere, and nothing is too trivial for his attention. A visa will be granted or a contract made *inshallah* (God willing), a building will be completed if *maktoob* (it is written), and some extraordinary human achievement like a moon landing will be greeted with *La illah il-Allah* (There is no God but God).

---

1. It is noticeable that some of the younger executives in rapidly developing countries like Saudi Arabia have chosen to occupy very small offices with room for only the minimum of furniture and only two or three visitors' chairs. This does nothing to relieve bottlenecks, but it does create a certain order, and enables work to be processed.

Conclusion: The Oil Factor

For Muslims in general and Arabs in particular it is no coincidence that the richest oil deposits in the world are to be found under the cradle of Islam. For them it is surely part of the divine will that Islam should take its rightful place at the centre of world events, having suffered the injustice and indignity of domination and exploitation by foreigners for generations.

At a critical point in history, when the Arabs were ready to receive the Message, God sent his Prophet. Shortly afterwards the rest of the world felt the effects in spectacular fashion. Similarly now, just at the moment when the whole industrial world becomes critically dependent on oil for survival the Islamic world finds itself not only awash with it, but needing comparatively little for its own use. Things could hardly have been better arranged. Furthermore, it could well happen that, within a few years, the positions of Islam and the rich nations could be dramatically reversed. Oil could provide enough wealth for the Middle East not only to dominate the economy of the western world, but to gain a major, if not controlling, interest in it. The thing most likely to stop this happening is not the ability of the West to prevent it, but Islam's inability to resolve its own internal political conflicts. As if this possibility was not dramatic enough, oil is also high on the list of strategic subjects important enough to trigger off a war involving the major powers. In either event the rise of Islam in the 20th century based on oil is hardly less important than its rise in the seventh, based on the Message.

The story began at the turn of the century, when the British Admiralty decided to convert its fleet, by far the largest in the world, from coal to oil fuel. This led to Britain financing the first successful oil exploration in the Middle East, and in 1908 large deposits of oil were proved to exist in Persia.

Serious competition between the Western powers began in the Middle East after the First World War, stimulated by the dramatic increase in industrial production and the manufacture of motor vehicles. On the face of it Britain was well placed at the end of the war.

Besides her Persian concession she controlled Iraq and the eastern shore of the Persian Gulf, where the richest deposits were found. However, when the Pan-Arab state which Britain had promised failed to materialize, the various Arab Amirs (rulers) let it be known that they were open to offers for oil concessions. The next 10 years saw the most intense competition between oil companies, at the end of which the United States came out best with the concessions of Saudi Arabia and Bahrain; Britain was second best with Persia, Qatar and half of Kuwait. The oil fields of Iraq were controlled by a British-Dutch and American consortium.

After the Second World War the major international oil companies expanded their operation in the nations of the Middle East until by the early 1950s they were virtually states within states, dictating not only oil prices but domestic and foreign policies. They maintained peace by paying the ruling families and governments enough to keep their personal exchequers filled, under royalty contracts initiated and executed between the wars.

Perhaps significantly, the first reaction to these arrangements came from Iran in 1951 against the British controlled Anglo-Iranian oil company. Buoyed up on a wave of anti-imperialism, the nationalist movement set out to reject British influence by nationalizing Anglo-Iranian, undaunted by the knowledge that Iran had little of the technical or management expertise to run the company assets.

The only other oil producer in the region was motivated not by political but by financial ends. There was no interest in revolutionary nationalism in the entrenched and deeply conservative monarchy of the Saud family, but when King Saud and the generation of Saudis learnt that Aramco, the American consortium, was paying more to the United States treasury in income tax than it was to Saudi Arabia in royalties, pressure mounted for revisions to treaties negotiated before the war. The problem for Aramco was how to meet the Saudi point that a foreign government was receiving more from the exploitation of their own mineral wealth than they were. To ignore the demands and rely upon the terms of properly negotiated treaties would risk spreading unrest, and undermine their extremely profitable position. But to increase royalties out of company earnings would, of course, decrease the profits. With the approval of the United States government Aramco proposed that the concession treaties should be left as they were, but that Saudi Arabia itself should impose an income tax on oil. As a royalty as well as a tax was paid on each barrel, this would effectively double the Saudi revenue. The consortium profit would not be affected because it could write off taxes levied in Saudi Arabia against the taxes due in the United States. Both Aramco shareholders and the Saudi government were suitably pleased with the solution; so much so that Aramco's lawyers were invited to draft the Saudi income tax legislation. The US government was not so pleased when it realized later the huge tax revenues it had lost through this arrangement.

The tension in the Gulf was largely eased in 1954 when the Iranian nationalist government was overthrown by the American CIA, and a consortium of British, French, Dutch and American companies was given access to Iran's oil.

Stability had been restored to the region, at least on the surface, but it was not to last very long. In 1956 Britain, France and Israel invaded Egypt in a last desperate attempt to stem the tide of Arab nationalism, and re-establish their imperial interests by military means. This triggered a violently anti-Western reaction throughout the Middle East, including riots in Kuwait among the large immigrant worker population of Egyptians and Palestinians. Although the Suez invasion was a military defeat for Egypt, it paradoxically rallied the forces of Pan-Arab nationalism solidly behind President Nasser, and accelerated the pace of declining Western influence.

But the decade of the 1950s was not merely important for development of nationalism, it was also the decade in which the owner countries became aware of the economic power residing in their oil sources. Once more the first significant move came in Iran. The overthrow of the Iranian nationalist government in 1954, orchestrated by the United States, had restored to power the Shah Pahlevi. This apparently dependent and easily led young man learned quickly from his American tutors, and in 1957 enacted a law which was to revolutionize the oil industry. This was to be called the Joint Venture law, and it provided that in future international oil companies would not only pay for concessions and pay royalties and taxes but in addition they would pay half the residual profit to Iran. This included profits not only from the production of oil, but from all its various by-products. In effect the future profits of all foreign oil companies would be halved.

The Arabs on the other side of the Gulf were not slow to follow suit. The tiny sheikhdoms along the coast, which with the help of the British had remained independent from Saudi Arabia, embraced the idea with considerable enthusiasm. From then on joint venture was a standard procedure in the exploitation of the rich oil fields on the Arabian coast. The oil companies were quick to appreciate the significance of this turn of events and began to sound warning signals to the political forces at home of possible future crises in oil supplies. Both sides began to focus on the issue of oil as the crucial factor in their future relationship with each other: the West because of its vital importance to its industrial base, and the East because of the potential economic development it offered. Once the basic message had sunk in, nationalism took a decisive turn. It was no longer good enough to reject foreign troops and the colonial administration that went with them, it was now necessary to overcome the economic imperialism, headed by oil companies, which, to an increasing number of Arabs and Iranians alike, was even more insidious. This mood came to a head in Iraq in 1958 when an anti-Western government was established by revolution and openly threatened Britain's control of its considerable oil reserves.

Shortly afterwards matters reached a crisis point in Saudi Arabia. Crown Prince Faisal had been appointed by the Saudi royal family to replace his brother, King Saud, in order to bring the country's finances under control. In spite of the Kingdom's considerable income through taxes and royalties, it was on the verge of bankruptcy with debts close to $500 million. Just at the time when Faisal had contained the situation by fiscal controls based on future oil revenues, the oil companies slashed the price of oil and reduced Saudi Arabia's income by $30 million for the following year.

The Saudi response was swift and devastating. First they negotiated a new kind of contract with a Japanese company for offshore exploration. It gave Saudi Arabia 56 per cent of all profits made, no matter where and in what form. For the first time a condition was imposed that the oil must not be sold to 'enemies of the Arabs'. From the point of view of the Saudis the contract was better than a joint venture agreement because it released them from any capital participation or risk.

Secondly, in 1960 the Saudis organized the Organization of Petroleum Exporting Countries (OPEC), an alliance that was ultimately to alter the balance of economic power in the world. The basic purpose of OPEC was to present a united front to the oil companies, and to negotiate standard terms and prices. The first real test for the organization came from an unexpected source: the Arab-Israeli six-day war in 1967. Although its member countries had agreed not to allow their different politics to interfere with united action, the war divided them along predictable political lines. The Arab countries of the Gulf embargoed the oil supplies to Israel's supporters in Europe and the United States, whereas Iran, Venezuela and Libya did practically the opposite and stepped up production to make good this shortfall. Although the Arab embargo remained in force for only one week, the cash-flow situation in Saudi Arabia was so critical that at the end of the week the treasury was empty. The first time that the oil weapon was openly used as a political instrument by an almost exclusively Muslim body it ended in failure.

But even this failure was not without its positive side. The Arabs, although dismayed by their inability to hold OPEC together in a crisis, were furious at the treachery displayed by Libya under the leadership of

King Idris. Nor was this disapproval restricted to the Arab countries which felt betrayed, it found expression also in Libya itself, notably among a group of disgusted and pious army officers, led by Lieutenant Qadhafi. This internal unrest and disapproval of the Libyan régime was compounded by the spiralling corruption which took place after the 1967 war. The war had closed the Suez Canal and the rich and accessible oil fields of Libya were suddenly in a highly favoured position, and their products in greater demand than ever. At the end of 1969 Qadhafi made his move and staged a totally unexpected *coup d'état*. The new régime not only quickly purged Libya of its most pernicious foreign influences, it also instituted a vitally new element in dealing with foreign oil companies. Qadhafi's first instinct was to nationalize the entire Libyan oil industry at a stroke, but he was dissuaded from this by the voices in the revolutionary Council who argued that there would be enough trained Libyans to run the facilities. Instead Qadhafi selected one operator, Occidental, which had no other source of supply, and put pressure on it to renegotiate existing contracts, giving substantial increases in taxes, royalties and prices. Rather than close down its business, Occidental agreed, and from then on contracts on existing concessions which had to date been fixed and sacrosanct were renegotiable.

The significance of the exercise was not lost on the other oil producers. The following year they called an OPEC meeting in Tehran, and confronted the major oil companies with demands for huge increases in revenues. Rather than face the threat of nationalization, the companies acceded to the demands, and agreements concluded effectively doubled the income of the producers. The companies passed on these costs to their consumers.

The real significance of Qadhafi's breakthrough was not so much the increase in wealth derived by the producers, as the realization that the political initiative was passing into their hands. Oil minister Sheikh Yamani of Saudi Arabia took up the initiative. He demanded participation in all phases of the companies' existing operations, with an ever increasing share in the ownership, culminating in 100 per cent ownership and control of all foreign oil companies. Aramco, the first target, resisted selling any of its equity as long as possible, but in the end was forced to agree under the threat of legislation which would compel it to do so. Oil companies in other countries were forced to follow suit, and the Western domination of the Middle Eastern oil resources ended.

By the time of the 1973 Arab-Israeli war, the Muslims were able to impose a second but effective oil boycott, which not only provoked an energy crisis in the West but also caused a quadrupling of price, taking the Western economy to the edge of an economic crisis, and a dazzling increase in the oil revenues of the producing states.

Although the producing countries have had control of their oil industries for less than a decade, there has already been a massive transfer of wealth from the Western industrialized world into the coffers of Islam. Nor is the process complete, as each year the acquisition of capital grows. This represents an historically unique situation, for up until now wealth has flowed inexorably from the less developed to the more developed regions of the world. The events in the last few years have dramatically reversed this process, and for the first time the world has seen a region which is both under-developed and rich. Yet even the basic economic and political implications of the oil factor have not yet penetrated the Western consciousness to any depth.[1]

Nor has the massive scale of the dramatic transfer of revenues, and ultimately wealth, been appreciated. The monetary figures are so astronomical that, for all except bankers and treasury officials, they border on abstractions. As figures and estimates vary according to source, and statistics fluctuate from year to year, we shall use a comparative rather than a statistical method to gauge the scale of this shift in wealth, at the risk of oversimplifying the matter.

The United States is by far the richest nation in the world, with a gross national product of $1000 billion dollars. It has a total money supply of just over one quarter of that amount. Most economic experts agree that this is the sum that will pour into the Treasury of Saudi Arabia alone, in the form of oil revenues, in a period of five consecutive years.

If these figures are going to vary relative to each other in the foreseeable future they are likely to favour the Saudis. All sources agree that at the present rate of production Saudi Arabia has oil reserves for at least another 150 years, and possibly twice that long. Clearly, Saudi Arabia, with a population of only some eight million, cannot absorb such vast sums into its economy, even if it wanted to. Most, but not all, is recycled in the form of investments in the Western economy in general, but the only financial medium large enough to absorb the surplus is the dollar market, and the vast majority of Saudi Arabian assets are held in the United States.

In 1976 the Saudi oil industry earned about $37.8 billion, or just over $100 million a day. At that rate of oil production Saudi Arabia would be able to buy all shares listed on the US Stock Exchange in 26 years, all the gold bullion in US central banks (including the IMF) in four years at $145 per ounce, all real estate in Manhattan in five months, and the whole US communications industry (all TV stations,

---

1. A CBS News-New York Times public opinion poll taken in 1978 indicated that 48 per cent of Americans did not believe that the United States imports oil.

radio stations, newspapers and magazines) in approximately four weeks.

But Saudi Arabia is not the only Muslim country with huge surplus revenues derived from oil. If the demand for Middle East oil continues at the present rate, in 10 years the total Arab accumulation of monetary reserves could amount to $600 billion, enough, in theory, for the Arab world to buy the majority interest in the publicly owned American business and industrial complex: in other words into majority owner-ship of the United States. It is not only the scale of this change which is difficult to grasp, but also the pace. It was only a generation ago that the power station at Jeddah was powered by coal imported from Britain, and hardly longer when the wheel was introduced to Saudi Arabia fixed on the axle of a motor car.

The oil factor has shifted Islam back dramatically into the centre of world politics. Of all the OPEC members, it is only the Muslims in general, and the Arabs in particular, that have budget surpluses; the remainder have overall deficits. Furthermore, there is an increasingly deeply held conviction among Arabs that oil will solve their political problems, and that the Arab nation, and with it Islam, will be restored to its former dominant position in the world. This is a view held not just by a few immature students, but by the majority of Arab leaders, politicians, economists, bankers and academics, as well as by political zealots throughout the Arab world. The oil under the sea and sand of the Middle East is not seen as Saudi, Kuwaiti, or Qatari oil, even by its owners. Throughout the entire Arab world it is universally regarded as Arab oil, to be used to further the interests of the Arab people, and to finance the rise of the Arab nation. It is to be used as an instrument of ideology and political will, and was placed there by God for this reason.

The Islamic Calendar

The Islamic calendar starts from the Christian year AD 622 when the Prophet and his small band of followers emigrated from Mecca to the sanctuary of Medina. Known as the *Hijra*, the emigration was the first united act of the Muslim community and demonstrated its determination to survive at all costs; this was subsequently designated the Muslim year AH1. But the difference between the Islamic and the Christian Gregorian calendar is not simply the date of its inception; Islam officially uses a lunar calendar of 12 lunar months, giving the year 354 days. This means that all the months, including those of the pilgrimage and fast, come about 11 days earlier each year by solar reckoning. The Arabs in pre-Islamic times also used a lunar calendar but they kept it in sequence with the solar year by inserting an extra month where necessary. This practice was forbidden by the Koran, although no-one has provided a logical explanation for the change.

It has been pointed out that the Muslim adoption of the lunar year shows the non-agrarian character of Islam; Islam is often said to mould or influence every aspect of life, but it has not penetrated the agricultural life of the million Muslim peasants. Their farming methods, and some of the religious ideas connected with them, continue to observe the solar seasons.

Modern Islamic States

Apart from Saudi Arabia and Iran, whose constitutions have been
outlined in Chapter 4, modern Islamic States have adopted a wide
variety of political structures and state legislatures. There follow brief
descriptions of some of these. There are, of course, many other states
with Islamic populations, but the following examples are chosen to
highlight the variety of structures that can be accommodated within
Islam.

Algeria
State religion: Islam (with provision for other beliefs).
Form of government: 1976 Constitution provides for single party
socialist state.
Power of head of state: Executive powers for 6 year renewable term.
President of Council of Ministers, High Security Council and
Supreme Court, and head of Armed Forces. Appoints ministers,
initiates legislations, and can dissolve legislature.
Type of legislature: National People's Assembly elected by universal
suffrage for 5 years. Meets for 6 months a year and can legislate on
all issues except national defence. Referanda widely used.
Distribution of seats: 261 members elected to NPA from list drawn
up by FLN (Front de Libération Nationale).
Legal system: Criminal justice system as in France.
Date of independence: 1962.

Arab Republic of Egypt
State religion: Islam.
Form of government: Republic:Democratic Socialist State.
Power of head of state: President nominated by Assembly and
confirmed by plebiscite for 6 year term.
Type of legislature: Governed by People's Assembly, single chamber
legislature with 5 year term. Has 372 elected members and 20

nominated by President. Universal suffrage: compulsory voting by men.

Distribution of seats: 1979 election returned: National Democratic Party (Sadat) 330; Socialist Labour Party 29; Liberal Socialist Party 3; Independents 10.

Legal system: National Courts system established 1883 and amended 1931 and 1946. No religious courts, but *sharia* law still governs some family affairs.

Date of independence: 1946.

Jordan

State religion: Islam (the King can trace an unbroken descent from Mohammed).

Form of government: Constitutional monarchy.

Power of head of state: King has executive power, appoints PM and cabinet, orders general elections and approves and promulgates laws through Assembly in joint session. Has power to override veto and must approve treaties.

Type of legislature: National Assembly comprising: 1. Council of Notables – members appointed. 2. Council of Deputies – by general election.

Distribution of seats: Council of Notables – 30 members, 15 from East and 15 from West Bank. Council of Deputies – 60 members, 30 from East and 30 from West Bank. Traditional composition: 48 Arab Muslims, 10 Christians, 2 Circassians.

(Political parties outlawed in 1963. Last election held in 1967. In 1976 Assembly met and agreed to indefinite postponement of elections and dissolution, as it was no longer possible to hold elections on West Bank. National Consultative Council appointed by King's decree in 1978 to advise King and cabinet on legislation. 60 appointed members.)

Legal system: Law based on Islamic law for both civil and criminal matters, except for personal matters concerning non-Muslims. System of High Courts and Magistrates Courts, and religious courts for both Muslims and Christians.

Date of independence: 1946.

Lebanon

State religion: Population almost equally divided between Muslims and Christians.

Form of government: State offices divided according to religion in accordance with National Pact 1943. 1926 Constitution with frequent amendments.

Power of head of state: President must be a Maronite Christian elected by two thirds majority of Chamber of Deputies. Has power to initiate laws. In exceptional circumstances can dissolve the Chamber and force an election.

Type of legislature: Chamber of Deputies seats allocated by a system of proportional representation based on religious groupings. Election by universal suffrage for 4 year term.[1] President of Chamber is a Shi'ite Muslim. The Prime Minister must be a Sunni Muslim.

Distribution of seats: Maronites 30; Sunnis 20; Shi'ites 19; Greek Orthodox 11; Greek Catholic 6; Druse 6; Armenian Orthodox 4; Armenian Catholic 1; Protestant 1; Other 1 – (ie 53 Christian, 45 Muslim): Total 99.

Legal system: Law and justice based on codes derived from modern theories of civil and criminal legislation. Higher, lower and appeal courts. Islamic, Christian and Jewish religious courts deal with affairs of personal status.

Date of independence: 1946.

Socialist People's Libyan Arab Jamahiriyah

State religion: Islam (the Holy Koran is the country's social code).

Form of government: Since 1977 the Jamahiriyah (State of the Masses) was promulgated and the official name of the country changed.

Power of head of state: The Secretary of the General People's Committee has functions similar to those of Prime Minister.[2]

Type of legislature: The constitution provides for 'Direct people's authority as the basis for political order. The people shall practice its authority through people's congresses, popular committees, trade unions, vocational syndicates and the General People's Congress, in the presence of the law'.

Distribution of seats: The General People's Congress has 1000 delegates from the above organizations. It appoints its own General Secretariat and the General People's Committee whose members head the 20 government departments which execute national policy.

1. Elections suspended since 1976 as a result of civil war.
2. Since reorganization in 1979 Colonel Qadhafi has retained his position of leader of the Revolution. But neither he nor former RCC colleagues have any official posts.

Legal system: Civil, Commercial and Criminal Codes based mainly on Egyptian models. *Sharia* courts have jurisdiction over family matters. A commission was set up in 1971 to revise Libyan Law.
Date of independence: 1951.

Morocco

State religion: Islam.
Form of government: Constitutional Monarchy.
Power of head of state: King is supreme civil and religious authority. Appoints all ministers, has right to dissolve Parliament and to approve legislation. He is Commander in Chief of armed forces, can declare a state of emergency and initiate constitutional amendment.
Type of legislature: Single chamber with 226 deputies. 88 seats elected by indirect electoral college representing town councils, regions, commerce, industry, agriculture and trade unions. 176 seats elected in general election.
Distribution of seats: There are 8 parties represented in chamber of representatives. Government party is King's Party. Also a system of local elections.
Legal system: All judges appointed by the King, on advice of Supreme Council of Judiciary.
Date of independence: 1956.

Islamic Republic of Pakistan

State religion: Islam.
Form of government: Martial law (since 1977). (The 1973 Constitution provides for a constitutional democracy based on the principles of Islam. Equal rights, freedom of expression and the press, and the rule of law.)
Power of head of state: The Chief Martial Law Administrator has powers capable of being imposed by the military. (The constitution provides for a President who acts on the advice of the Prime Minister. He is elected for 5 years and must be a Muslim.)
Type of legislature: In July 1977, following martial law, all fundamental rights provided for in the constitution were suspended. In 1978 a provision was made for separate electoral registers for Muslims and others. The constitution provides for a Lower House consisting of 200 members elected directly for 5 years by universal suffrage. Senate has 63 members for 4 years. Senators elected by provinces and tribal areas.
Distribution of seats: The martial law administration provides for a

20 member cabinet, and a 4 member Military Council.
Legal system: In 1979 martial law established the supremacy of
military courts in trying all offences. The constitution provides for
an independent judiciary, and a system of higher and lower courts.
There is a *sharia* bench at High Court level which ensures that
Islamic law is enforced as the law of the state.
Date of independence: 1947.

Democratic Republic of Sudan

State religion: Islam (with freedom of religion guaranteed to large
Christian minority and others).
Form of government: One party socialist state.
Power of head of state: President nominated by Sudanese Socialist
Union. Responsible for upholding constitution. Appoints Vice-
President, Prime Minister and Ministers, Commander in Chief of
armed forces, and security forces, and Head of Public Service. Has
power to declare state of emergency which may suspend all civil
rights other than that of resort to courts.
Type of legislature: People's Assembly, 304 members: 274 elected by
universal suffrage for 4 years, 30 nominated by President.
Distribution of seats: All members must either belong to or be
approved by Sudanese Socialist Union.
Legal system: Judiciary independent from state, but appointed by
President. Civil Division of Judiciary headed by Chief Justice;
Sharia Division headed by Grand *Qadi.* System of civil courts,
criminal courts and local courts, with courts of appeal. *Sharia* courts
deal with personal and family matters.
Date of independence: 1956.

Syria

State religion: Islam.
Form of government: Constitution describes system as 'Socialist
Popular Democracy'.
Power of head of state: President (who must be a Muslim) has wide
powers. Nominated by People's Council and elected by referendum
for 7 year term. Appoints cabinet, military personnel and civil
servants. Commander in Chief of armed forces. Can amend
constitution.
Type of legislature: People's Council elected by direct universal
suffrage.
Distribution of seats: 195 members controlled by Ba'ath Socialist
Party via the Progressive Front of National Union.

Legal system: Civil judicial system introduced in 1974 with higher and lower courts and Courts of Appeal. Personal Status Courts based on *sharia* for Muslims.
Date of independence: 1946.

Tunisia

State Religion: Islam.
Form of government: One party state.
Power of head of state: President with wide powers; can legislate when Assembly not in session. Constitution provides that President is elected for a maximum of 3 consecutive terms of 5 years.[1]
Type of legislature: National Assembly. Single chamber system with limited authority.
Distribution of seats: In practice only members of Destourian Socialist Party elected.
Legal system: Integrated civil and religious courts.
Date of independence: 1956.

The People's Democratic Republic of Yemen

State religion: Islam.
Form of government: One party (Marxist-Leninist) state.
Power of head of state: President appointed by Presidium.
Distribution of seats: All seats in SPC held by Yemen Socialist Party.
Legal system: Justice administered by the Supreme Court and Magistrates' Courts. The judicial system is a mixture of civil, Islamic and local law.
Date of independence: 1967 (as People's Republic of Southern Yemen).

1. Bourgiba elected President for life in 1974.

Mohammed's Wives

Christianity has for its teacher, inspiration, and example a chaste and celibate bachelor who preached monogamy and set an example of sexual abstinence, which to this day is preached by the Christian church. As a consequence, the idea that a religion should actively promote sexual fulfilment and specifically discourage celibacy is difficult for many Westerners to accept. But not only does Islam preach this message, it also has it sanctified by its founder and Prophet[1]. Yet, as in all other matters in Islam, sexual relationships must be conducted within certain rules laid down by law.

There have been various interpretations placed on Mohammed's attitude towards women, and the motivations behind his marriages. His first wife apart, some Western scholars and many Muslims regard all his marriages as political in character, suggesting the need for him to secure the allegiance of a particular family or tribe in order to strengthen the position of the new faith. It is undoubtedly true that this is an important element in most of his choices, but some scholars believe that ordinary human instincts sometimes prevailed.

Whatever the precise truth of the nature and range of Mohammed's attraction to women, it is a fact that not only was he given divine authority to marry many women, but the relationships he had with them are referred to in the Koran itself, and have resulted in formulations in Islamic law which have affected permanently the status of Muslim women, and defined other important legal issues.

Probably because he was poor Mohammed remained a bachelor until he was 25. His first wife was Khadija bint Khuwaylid. She was a prosperous widow of Mecca who at 40 had already been married twice and had several children. Mohammed's marriage to Khadija was to have a security, warmth and affection that never wavered, and so long as she lived Mohammed did not take another wife. Mohammed used to say that she was the best of all the women of her time, and that he

---

1. Mohammed said: 'When a Muslim marries he perfects his religion'.

would live with her in Paradise in a house built of reeds, in peace and tranquillity.

Khadija gave Mohammed several children. Four daughters survived: Zaynad, Ruqayya, Fatima and Umm Kalthun, but all their sons died in infancy. During Khadija's lifetime Mohammed adopted his young cousin, Ali, and Khadija made him a present of a slave, called Zayd. Mohammed gave him his freedom and adopted him as a son.

It must have been an important matter to Mohammed that he had no male heir, bearing in mind that to Arabs and Semitic people in general this was a source of shame, (men who suffered it were called *ab-tar*, which means, roughly, mutilated), particularly in the circumstances of pre-Islamic Mecca, where polygamy was quite widespread and divorce was simple and frequent. It is possible that Mohammed did not take a second wife because his marriage contract with Khadija made that condition, but it is also possible that he chose to keep faith with Khadija.

Besides being Mohammed's first wife Khadija was also the first believer. She died in 619AD when Mohammed was nearly 50. She was the one who had believed and chosen him before anybody else, even before God. Initially she offered him social position and protection, and subsequently she had given him support and faith. Her position as Mohammed's employer, wife and follower is unique. After her death Mohammed was inconsolable, and Khawla, wife of Uthman, suggested he should marry A'isha bint Abn Bakr, or a widow, Sawda bint Zama. He married both.

Sawda was one of the first to embrace Islam. She was a charitable and good natured woman and as she was not young when the Prophet married her it is likely that his reasons were purely domestic, as there were children to look after. Certainly it is hard to find any kind of political motive.

As Sawda grew older Mohammed preferred to spend more of his time with A'isha, and in 8AH he divorced her. But Sawda asked to be taken back, offering to yield her day (the Prophet spent a day with each wife in turn) to A'isha, as her only desire was 'to rise on the Day of Judgement as his wife'. Mohammed agreed, and *sura* 4:128 was revealed allowing husband and wife to seek mutual agreements. Sawda died in Medina in 54AH.

A'isha was only six at the time of her betrothal but the marriage was not consummated until she was about ten. By all accounts A'isha was Mohammed's favourite wife and won a special place in his heart. She turned out to be a bright and vivacious young woman who not only inadvertently left an indelible mark on Islamic law, but had considerable political influence in her own right after the Prophet's death.

In the year 6/628 she was accompanying Mohammed back from an expedition when she was accidently left behind, the party believing she was inside the enclosed litter they were carrying. Finding herself alone at the overnight camp she happened to be found by a young man called Safwan. He set her on his camel and leading the animal by the rein caught up the main party. The sight of these two arriving alone gave rise to grave accusations and many influential Muslims were scandalized. The Prophet consulted Ali, who advised him to repudiate A'isha (hence her lifelong hostility towards Ali). The matter was resolved finally by a revelation (Koran 24:10) which lays down that no charge of illegal intercourse is valid unless it is supported by four witnesses, and that those who accuse but cannot bring witnesses shall be flogged.

The incident had other far reaching consequences. It was to result in the Prophet's wives being given more protection, and therefore seclusion from the mass of the followers. Revelations came to say that it was forbidden to enter any of their huts unannounced or to talk to the women except through a curtain. In addition they were to keep their faces covered.

A'isha was 18 when Mohammed, sick and dying, took to his sickbed in her hut, and she nursed him till the end. Subsequently she opposed the caliphate of Uthman, and when Ali, her mortal enemy, was elected Caliph she did her utmost to raise the Muslims against him. She fought on the side of Talha and al-Zubair in the battle against Ali in 36/656, being in the thick of the fighting. She opposed the plan to bury al-Hasan ibn Ali[1] at the side of the Prophet, arguing that the tomb was her property. In spite of extremely influential opposition, she had her way.

She died in 58/678 and was buried in Medina. A'isha occupies a prominent place among the most distinguished traditionalists: she reported no less than 1210[2] traditions directly from the mouth of the Prophet.

In about 2/624 Mohammed took a third wife. He wanted to secure the cooperation of Umar, so he married his daughter Hafsa, who at 20 was already a widow. For some reason still obscure she was repudiated almost at once, but restored to favour by divine command in consideration of her Muslim virtues. In Mohammed's *harem* she took the side of A'isha in endeavouring to secure the succession of Mohammed for Abn Bakr and Umar. Yet on the whole, in contrast to A'isha she played a modest political role, even during her father's caliphate.

Hafsa could read and write, and some authorities have it that the

1. Eldest son of Ali and Fatima, daughter of the Prophet.
2. Bukhari and Moslem, the two master-compilers of Islamic tradition, accepted 228 and 242 respectively.

suhuf (the separate leaves of the Koran, not yet set in order) came into her possession on the Prophet's death as a gift of honour. Hafsa had no children and died aged about 60.

Just over a year after his marriage to Hafsa the Prophet married Zaynab bint Khuzaima, who like Hafsa was widowed at the battle of Badr. She was known as the Mother of the Poor, but her presence was not to complicate life in the *harem* for long, as she died shortly afterwards.

Mohammed's fifth wife was the proud and beautiful Umm Salama, whose husband had died of wounds shortly after the battle of Uhud. She had several children by him, and her deep and abiding love for him explains her reluctance to remarry. She had offers from both Abu Bakr and Umar which she refused. Even the Prophet was not accepted without pressing his suit with some fervour and persistence. Finally she yielded and the marriage took place in 4/626. The introduction of the aristocratic Makhuzumite Umm Salama into the *harem* involved more than personal jealousies; she provided the nucleus of the political faction favouring Fatima and Ali as the heirs to power, rather than the fathers of A'isha and Hafsa.

But it is the story of Zaynab bint Jahsh, the Prophet's sixth wife, as normally told by Western scholars, that gives most offence to Muslims. These scholars, insisting that they are using the original collected texts, generally conclude that this is one case where Mohammed was ruled by nothing but physical desire. The Muslims reply that this treatment merely shows the extent to which Western racial and religious prejudice distorts the truth, and that the marriage was made to win the support of her powerful kinsman Abu Sufyan.

The essential facts seem to be that Zaynab, Mohammed's cousin, although a great beauty, was at 30 still unmarried until the Prophet (it is said with Zaynab's reluctance) arranged a marriage between her and Zayd, his freedman and adopted son. Some years later Mohammed, while calling to see Zayd at his home, chanced to see Zaynab in light disarray, and left in some confusion saying 'Praise be to Allah, who transforms men's hearts'. On hearing about this from his wife, Zayd went immediately to the Prophet and offered to divorce Zaynab if he wished to marry her. Although Mohammed sent him away urging him to keep his wife for himself, Zayd divorced her anyway.

After the usual period of waiting was over the Prophet married Zaynab, after specific permission from God, recorded in the Koran (33:36). Nevertheless he incurred the displeasure and criticism of the community, not because of any physical desire on Mohammed's part, but because custom regarded the marriage as incestuous, the position of an adopted son being the same as that of a natural son. A new revelation silenced the criticism by making the distinction, and by specifically permitting marriage with the divorced wife of an adopted son (36:38).

In the two years following his marriage to Zaynab, five new women joined the six wives. The first was the comely young Jewess Raihana bint Zaid of the Nadir tribe. She had married into the Qurayza tribe and had lost her husband and other male relatives in the massacre[1]. Tradition is undecided about her actual status in the *harem*. Some say she was a proper wife, others that she preferred to remain a slave concubine, which would enable her to retain her faith and escape from the limitations of seclusion.

Mohammed's next two marriages were certainly political in motivation. The first was to Ramla, daughter of Abu Sufyan, the leader of the Meccan opposition. She had embraced Islam in defiance of her father and had emigrated to Abyssinia with her husband, who died there. She was about 35 when she married the Prophet, who perhaps was signalling Islam's inevitable victory by uniting with his most able opponent's daughter, and the powerful Umayyads.

The next and last wife to join the household was Mayanna bint al-Harith whose wedding is thought to have taken place in 7/629. She was a young and attractive widow of 26. Her brother-in-law was the uncle of Mohammed, and the marriage, which took place in Mecca during his first visit for 7 years, can be seen as a wish on the Prophet's part for reconciliation with his own tribe.

Although the political nature of the Prophet's marriages is clear enough it is evident that feelings played their part both in the relationships Mohammed had with his wives, and between the wives themselves. In all material and mundane matters it was quite possible for Mohammed to treat them all with equality, but by common consent A'isha was his most beloved wife, although she never threatened the special place of Khadija, as Mohammed himself once told her.

For their part his wives during his lifetime were fertile ground for both political rivalries and personal jealousies, but they did not hesitate to speak their minds in answer to or in argument with Mohammed. Indeed in a domestic situation they were quite able to take on both Abu Bakr and Umar, when his friends seemed to be interfering in asking them to moderate their demands on the Prophet[2]. Yet it says a good deal for Mohammed's singular talents that in the thick of establishing a new religion, and transforming Arabian society, he could accommodate the affection and conflicts of the extraordinary women in his

1. See page 24.
2. Ibn Sa'd, Vol VIII, 129.

household. Yet one thing was missing. Apart from Khadija, none of his wives bore him any children. It was as if, once his mission was revealed, he was to have access to all except this.

After his death Mohammed's widows became known as the Mothers of the Believers. In 20/641 when he initiated state pensions from the tremendous revenues resulting from the conquests, the Caliph Umar placed them at the head of the list. At the same time he seems to have prohibited them from attending the mosque or going on the pilgrimage to Mecca.

It is difficult to be sure of the relationships between the widows at this period. No more stormy scenes are recorded, nor any challenge to A'isha's favoured position financially or otherwise. In public policy and conduct the Prophet's widows generally behaved and were treated as a unit and given a place of honour in the community. It seems that they continued to live most of the time in the mosque apartments and must have seen a good deal of each other. A few incidents connected with Zaynab's death indicate that they lived amicably, Mohammed's memory drawing them together as his presence sometimes pulled them apart.

A'isha was to live a widow for another 50 years, and although interesting anecdotes are recorded about some of the other widows the traditions give much attention to this remarkable and able woman. She played a full part in the politics and conflicts, ideological and physical, that marked the tumultuous and unprecedented changes brought about by the rise of Islam. Indeed, her involvement in the public affairs of the new Muslim state have provoked responses which have lasted to this day. To the Shi'ites she is a curse, while the orthodox Sunnis continue to sing her praises and honour her memory.

Chronological Table of Events in the Muslim and Non-Muslim World

		552 AD	Buddhism introduced into Japan
c 570 AD	Birth of Mohammed		
		597	St Augustine preaches Christianity in England
c 611	Mohammed begins to preach		
AH/AD			
1/622	*Hijra:* year 1 of the Islamic calendar		
2/624	Battle of Badr		
8/630	Mohammed enters Mecca		
10/632	Death of Mohammed Caliphate of Abu Bakr		
12/634	Death of Abu Bakr Caliphate of Omar		
17/638	Fall of Jerusalem		
20/641	Omar sets up fiscal system and initiates use of records		
22/643	Fustat (Cairo) founded		
23/644	Death of Omar Caliphate of Othman		
35/656	Death of Othman Caliphate of Ali First split in Muslim unity		
40/661	Death of Ali		
		685	Buddhism becomes official religion in Japan
92/711	Conquest of Spain Arabs reach the Indies		
98/716	Siege of Constantinople		
114/732	Battle of Poitiers: Muslim invasion of Europe halted		

133/751	Chinese defeated at R Tals	751	Pepin the Short elected King of the Franks
142/759	Narbonne falls		
150/767	Death of Abu Hanifa	800	Charlemagne becomes Emperor
204/820	Death of al-Shafi	820	Norman penetration of Gaul
210/825	Muslims conquer Crete		
217/832	House of Knowledge founded in Baghdad New world atlas Science flourishes		
		843	Partition of Verdun
231/846	Muslims raid Rome		
241/855	Death of Ibn Hanbal		
250/864	First attempt to make law unchangeable		
		885	Viking siege of Paris
c 300/912	Use of Indian system of numerals		
		921	Wenceslas: Birth of Czech state
c 312/922	Conversion of Bulgarians		
323/934	Muslims sack Genoa		
		936	Mongols take Peking
359/970	Al-Azhar university (Cairo) founded		
		973	Bishopric of Prague founded
		991	Danes invade England
390/1000	Expansion of Islam to India	c 1000	Beginning of Medieval church architecture
		1054	Break of Eastern church with Rome
		1066	Norman conquest of England
c 473/1080	Birth of Assassins sect	1088	Arab medicine taught at Salerno
		1094	Consecration of St Marks, Venice
		1095	First Crusade
492/1099	Crusaders take Jerusalem		
505/1111	Death of philosopher el-Ghazali		
520/1122	Death of Persian poet and mathematician Omar Khayyam		
		1147	Second Crusade
543/1149	End of Second Crusade		

		1154	Henry II crowned in England
		1158	Bologna University founded
554/1159	Greek and Byzantine Crusades unite against Muslims		
		1180	Philip Augustus becomes King of France
c 580/1184	Hospital and medical school at Damascus		
583/1187	Saladin retakes Jerusalem		
586/1190	Third crusade		
589/1193	Death of Saladin		
		1204	Crusaders take Constantinople
609/1212	Spanish Christians defeat Muslims		
		1215	Peking taken by Genghis Khan Magna Carta signed in England
615/1219	Genghis Khan attacks Islam		
626/1229	Jerusalem ceded to Frederick II		
628/1231	Persia conquered by Mongols		
641/1244	Turks finally win Jerusalem	1233	The Inquisition begins
		1266	Marco Polo's first journey to China
666/1268	Islam recovers Antioch	1274	Death of Thomas Aquinas
688/1285	Islam recovers Tripoli		
694/1295	Islam becomes state religion of Persia		
732/1332	Islam at its zenith	1321	Death of Dante
		1338	Start of Hundred Years War
		1348	Plague in Europe
756/1354	Ottomans conquer Gallipoli	1369	War between France and England
		1413	Henry V crowned in England
799/1397	Ottomans in Athens	1415	Battle of Agincourt
		1431	Joan of Arc martyred

		1434	Cosimo del Medici takes power in Florence
		1452	Leonardo da Vinci born
857/1453	Ottomans in Constantinople	1453	Printing works opened by Gutenberg
		1466	Birth of Erasmus
		1475	Birth of Michelangelo
		1483	Birth of Luther
		1488	Diaz rounds the Cape of Good Hope
897/1492	Fall of Granada: Islam loses Spain	1492	Columbus discovers the New World
		1497	da Gama rounds the Cape of Good Hope
923/1517	Ottomans occupy Cairo		
926/1520	Suleiman the Magnificent becomes Sultan		
935/1529	Ottomans conquer Hungary Moghul Empire founded in India		
936/1529	Siege of Vienna		
		1533	Accession of Ivan the Terrible
		1534	Henry VIII of England breaks with the Church of Rome
953/1546	Ottomans in Yemen		
c 957/1550	Islam in Cambodia		
		1564	Shakespeare born Galileo born
989/1580	Company of Isfahan established in England		
		1588	Spanish Armada defeated
11th/16th century	Islam in Borneo		
		1609	Kepler's Laws of planetary motion
		1618	Thirty Years War begins
		1620	Pilgrim Fathers land in America
		1623	Japan closed to foreigners
		1642	English Civil War begins

		1649	Execution of Charles I
		1658	Academy of Sciences founded in Paris
1076/1668	Turks conquer Crete		
		1675	Leibnitz discovers differential calculus
1094/1683	Turks besiege Vienna	1687	Newton's *Principia*
		1689	Bill of Rights in England
		1694	Bank of England founded
		1696	Savery builds first steam engine (England)
		1698	London Stock Exchange founded
1110/1699	Peace of Karlowitz: Ottomans relinquish territory (Hungary) for first time		
1134/1722	Afghans invade Persia	1713	Peace of Utrecht
1141/1728	Painting introduced into Turkey	1733	John Kay invents flying shuttle
1157/1744	Pact between Aba-al Wahhab and Mohammed ibn Saud		
1170/1757	British in India Afghans take Delhi		
		1763	Treaty of Paris
		1767	Watt builds steam engine
		1768	Cook circumnavigates New Zealand
1187/1773	Ibn Saud takes Riyadh	1776	American Declaration of Independence
		1788	*The Times* newspaper established in London
		1789	French Revolution
		1795	School of Oriental language founded in Paris
1212/1798	Bonaparte invades Egypt	1799	Coup d'état by Bonaparte
1805	Mohammed Ali in power in Egypt	1805	Battle of Trafalgar

1806	Wahhabis occupy Mecca		
		1814	First steam locomotive (England)
		1815	Congress of Vienna concluded
1820	Egypt conquers Sudan		
1830	French invade Algeria Greek independence		
		1833	Slavery abolished in British Empire
1835	Egyptians invade Arabia		
		1837	Victoria crowned in England
1839	England invades Aden and intervenes in Afghanistan		
1840	Bible translated into Arabic	1840	Opium War begins
		1841	British acquire Hong Kong
		1845	British subdue the Sikhs US annexes Texas
		1846	US invades Mexico
		1845-7	Famine in Ireland
		1848	The Communist Manifesto: Marx and Engels
1849	British conquer Punjab		
		1851	The Great Exhibition – London
1854	Crimean War		
1857	Indian Mutiny. Last Moghul Emperor deposed.		
		1859	Darwin's *Origin of Species* published
		1861	American Civil War begins Serfdom abolished in Russia
		1865	President Lincoln assassinated
		1866	Austro-Prussian war
		1867	Marx's *Das Kapital* published
1869	Suez Canal opened		
		1873	First international congress of orientalists
1877	Russo-Turkish War	1877	Victoria Empress of India

1878	War between Britain and Afghanistan Congress of Berlin
1885	Revolt of the Mahdi: Gordon killed at Khartoum
1893	French in Timbuktu
1897	War between Greece and Turkey over Crete
1899	Death of the Mahdi First strike in Egypt Quasim Amim writes *The Emancipation of Women*
1900	French destroy Rabah empire in Chad
c 1905	League of Arab Nations founded in Paris
1906	First Majlis (parliament) meets in Tehran
1909	Founding of Anglo-Persian oil company
1914	First World War begins Egypt becomes British protectorate
1917	Baghdad taken by British
1920	Turkish war of independence Muslim republics in USSR

1878	Edison invents electric light
1888	William I Emperor of Germany Internal combustion engine invented
1889	Second International Paris Exhibition
1897	Ader makes first aeroplane flight
1898	Spanish-American war
1899	The Boer War begins
1901	Death of Queen Victoria
1903	Wright brothers' first flight
1904	Russia and Japan at war
1912	Republic of China founded
1915	Einstein: Theory of Relativity
1917	Revolution in Russia
1918	Treaty of Brest-Litovsk

1921	Faisal king of Iraq Reza Shah Pahlevi takes power in Persia		
1923	Kamal begins reforms in Turkey	1923	Mussolini's march on Rome
1924	Saudis defeat king Husain of Hejaz First Egyptian parliament	1924	Death of Lenin
1927	Ibn Saud king of Hejaz		
1928	Disorders in Palestine Muslim Brotherhood founded		
		1929	Fleming discovers penicillin Economic crisis in USA spreads throughout world
1930	Iraq independent		
1932	Turkish women gain equal political rights		
		1933	Roosevelt US President Hitler elected Chancellor in Germany
		1934	Civil war in China
1936	British leave Egypt except Canal Zone	1936	Civil war in Spain Italians invade Ethiopia
		1938	Germany annexes Austria Munich agreement
		1939	World War II
1941	War between Britain and Iraq		
1942	Battle of El Alamein		
		1943	Battle of Stalingrad
1945	France evacuates Syria and Lebanon League of Arab States	1945	Death of Roosevelt Death of Hitler Germany surrenders USA uses A-bomb on Hiroshima and Nagasaki Japan surrenders UN founded
1947	Indian independence		
1948	State of Israel founded War between Israel and Arabs	1948	Gandhi assassinated Marshall Plan launched NATO formed
1949	Armistice between Israel and Arabs	1949	Communists win power in China
		1950	Korean War

1951	Persia nationalizes oil		
1952	Revolution in Egypt		
1953	Islamic Congress founded	1953	Death of Stalin
1954	Revolt in Algeria Nasser takes power in Egypt	1954	French defeated in Indo China
		1955	W Germany incorporated in NATO: Warsaw Pact formed
1956	British, French and Israeli occupation of Suez Canal Tunisia, Morocco and Sudan independence	1956	Russians invade Hungary Suez crisis
		1957	First sputnik (USSR)
1958	United Arab Republic – Syria/ Egypt	1958	de Gaulle President in France
1959	Cyprus independent	1959	Castro takes power in Cuba Lunik II lands on moon
1960	OPEC founded		
1961	Al-Azhar: women admitted into university	1961	Man's first space flight (USSR)
1962	Algeria independent Revolution in Yemen	1962	Cuban missile crisis
1963	Faisal king of Saudi Arabia	1963	President Kennedy assassinated Nuclear test ban treaty
		1965	Fall of Khruschev in USSR
1967	Arab-Israeli war		
1968	El Al airliner hijacked by PFLP Ba'ath party seize power in Baghdad	1968	Russians invade Czechoslovakia Nixon elected president in USA
1969	Qadhafi seizes power in Libya Arafat leader of PLO Marxist-Leninists seize power in S Yemen	1969	First man on moon (US)
1970	British and Americans leave Libya Death of Nasser	1970	First increase in oil prices by OPEC

1971	Treaty of Friendship between Egypt and USSR Independence for Bahrain and Qatar UAE formed Iran occupies straits of Hormuz Bangladesh independence Islam allows birth control Libya nationalizes BP Algeria nationalizes oil companies	1971	China joins UN
1972	Iraq Petroleum Co nationalized	1972	Denmark, Ireland and UK join Common Market
1973	Fourth Arab-Israeli war	1973	End of Vietnam war Death of General Franco Military coup in Chile
1974	First agreement between Israel and Egypt		
1975	King Faisal assassinated Khaled succeeds him Civil war in Lebanon Suez Canal opened		
1976	Creation of Arab monetary fund	1976	Death of Chou en-Lai and Mao 'tse-Tung
1977	Coup in Ethiopia Sadat and Begin meet in Israel		
1979	Islamic Revolution in Iran: Shah exiled, oil sales nationalized War between north and south Yemen Egypt leaves Arab League Israel officially annexes Jerusalem USSR enters Afghanistan		
1980	Iraq invades Iran	1980	Rhodesia becomes Zimbabwe

Bibliography

Abbott, Nabia *Aishah the Beloved of Mohammed* Univ of Chicago Press, 1942

Arberry, A J *The Koran Interpreted* Oxford Univ Press, 1964

Burton, Sir Richard *Personal Narrative of a Pilgrimage to Al Madinah and Meccah* Dover Publications, New York, 1887

Coulson, N J *A History of Islamic Law* Edinburgh Univ Press, 1964

Gibb, H A R *Islam* Oxford Univ Press, 1953

Gibb, H A R and Kramers, J H *Shorter Encyclopaedia of Islam* E J Brill, Leiden, 1974

Guillaume, Alfred *Islam* Pelican Books, 1967

Jaber, Kamel Abu *The Arab Ba'ath Socialist Party: History, Organization, Ideology* Syracuse Univ Press, 1966

Kiernan, Thomas *The Arabs* Abacus Books, 1978

Levy, R *Social Structure of Islam* Cambridge Univ Press, 1957

Quilici, Folco *Children of Allah* Chartwell Books Inc, 1978

Rodinson, Maxime *Islam and Capitalism* Allen Lane, 1974

Rodinson, Maxime *Mohammed* Allen Lane, 1974

Said, Abdel Moghny *Arab Socialism* Blandford Press, 1972

Schacht, J *An Introduction to Islamic Law* Oxford Univ Press, 1962

US Govt Printing Office *Area Handbook for the Republic of Turkey* 1973

Waddy, Charis *The Muslim Mind* Longman, 1976

Watt, W Montgomery *Bell's Introduction to the Qur'an* Edinburgh Univ Press, 1978

Watt, W Montgomery *Companion to the Qur'an* Geo Allen and Unwin, 1967

Watt, W Montgomery *Muhammed in Madina* Oxford Univ Press, 1956

Watt, W Montgomery *Muhammed, Prophet and Statesman* Oxford Univ Press, 1974

Watt, W Montgomery *What is Islam?* Longman, 1979

Background Reading

Arberry (transl) *Ring of the Dove* Luzac, London, 1953

Byron, Robert *The Road to Oxiana* Macmillan, 1937

Fernea and Bezirgan *Middle Eastern Women Speak* Univ of Texas Press, 1977

Saadawi, Nawal El *The Hidden Face of Eve* Zed Press, 1980

Thesiger, W *Arabian Sands* Allen Lane, 1977